GET OUT OF THE BOX AND DISCOVER YOUR LIFE

*Important Thoughts You Never Knew
You Were Allowed to Have*

DAVID L. PAYNE, D.O.

BALBOA.
PRESS

A DIVISION OF HAY HOUSE

Balboa Press books may be ordered through booksellers or by contacting:

Balboa Press
A Division of Hay House
1663 Liberty Drive
Bloomington, IN 47403
www.balboapress.com
1 (877) 407-4847

Because of the dynamic nature of the Internet, any web addresses or links contained in this book may have changed since publication and may no longer be valid. The views expressed in this work are solely those of the author and do not necessarily reflect the views of the publisher, and the publisher hereby disclaims any responsibility for them.

The author of this book does not dispense medical advice or prescribe the use of any technique as a form of treatment for physical, emotional, or medical problems without the advice of a physician, either directly or indirectly. The intent of the author is only to offer information of a general nature to help you in your quest for emotional and spiritual well-being. In the event you use any of the information in this book for yourself, which is your constitutional right, the author and the publisher assume no responsibility for your actions.

Any people depicted in stock imagery provided by Thinkstock are models, and such images are being used for illustrative purposes only. Certain stock imagery © Thinkstock.

Printed in the United States of America.

ISBN: 978-1-4525-9522-1 (sc)
ISBN: 978-1-4525-9524-5 (hc)
ISBN: 978-1-4525-9523-8 (e)

Library of Congress Control Number: 2014905786

Balboa Press rev. date: 06/10/2014

DEDICATION

I lovingly dedicate this book to my family –
my greatest source of Godly Love.

ACKNOWLEDGMENTS

Great thanks to Dr. Katrina Berne for her editing skills, my sister Wanda for allowing me to bounce things off her, and all those who helped by proofreading and commenting on my writing.

Thanks also to my niece, Shar Wilcox, of Lemontree Lane Photography for the mugshot, my nephew, Jared Payne, for the guy in the box drawing and Trent S. Walters for the cover art.

CONTENTS

PLEASE, READ THIS FIRST

The most common way people give up their
power is by thinking they don't have any.

Alice Walker

This is a book of permission slips. You may have had to have a parental permission slip to go on a scout hike or a school field trip. The permission slips in these chapters are different. These give you permission to think new thoughts, have new feelings about old topics, or behave in ways you once thought were forbidden. Many people are very sincerely dedicated to their "tribal rules" (the things we've been taught – spoken or unspoken – about what are acceptable thoughts and behaviors in one's culture). These tribal rules have usually developed over long periods of time and often for hard-to-imagine reasons. If you buck the rules, you will usually be made fun of at the minimum, and you may even suffer violent actions against you in an attempt to show more severe disapproval of your behavior. Bullies use tribal rules to inflict misery on young men who seem not to fit the image of manhood in one's society; nerdy, gentle or effeminate males are often their targets. And notice the looks you get if you don't stand up and put your hand over your heart when the National Anthem is being played. Tribal rules have a small role in keeping societies controlled, but mostly they keep individuals chained up in boxes and keep them from discovering who they really are.

The original name of this book was going to be *I Am Absolutely NOT an Absolutist*, with a subtitle of *Sorry Dude, You Missed Heaven by Three Points*. Then I realized that no one would know what that meant until they had finished reading the book. One of the things I have tried to emphasize in my writing is the wide variety of options we have in life, even though many of them seem forbidden to us. These options are not just the black and white choices that have been engrained in us, but there is a complete color spectrum of thoughts, feelings and behaviors that we may never have been aware of.

I started life in a culture where all that I was allowed to think, feel or do was well-defined and strongly enforced while, at the same time, I was encouraged to think for myself. The only caveat was that, after doing my own thinking, I had to come to those conclusions that my culture required. If not, I should start over and try other ways of thinking until I came to the "correct" thought processes. It took many years of battling the cognitive dissonance of what I *really* thought and what I was *supposed* to think before I decided to strike out on my own and rely on my own reasoning abilities to shape a worldview that is truly my own. Even after we realize that we have the option of disregarding certain tribal rules or modifying them to fit our newly modified worldview, it may take awhile to feel comfortable in leaving behind our old ways of thinking, feeling and doing.

Lest anyone should think that I have completed my research and am here to tell everyone the exact nature of God, the meaning of life and why babies die, I must tell you that none of these are revealed in these pages, but you will find some good ideas to help you when you are considering some difficult questions. I look at my life as an ongoing journey of discovery, lesson learning and spiritual evolution, and I allow my worldview to be sculpted and colored by new insights and information that I sometimes feel are mysteriously sent my way. What I believe today is somewhat different from what I believed a year ago, and very different from what I believed thirty years ago. But I'm okay with that because I enjoy the discovery process and love to find out how other people think about things. I have come to some conclusions that other people find hard to fathom at first, but they are the only ones that make sense to me. I have uncovered ideas that have helped me understand the people in my life and people on the other side of the world. I have unshackled myself from beliefs I would never have dreamed I could leave behind, and my life has soared to new and wonderful places. It is my hope that some of these concepts will be helpful to others as well.

It is my only intention to bring people out of fear, anger and distrust. There are ideas in these pages that may oppose the tribal rules to which some people are very loyal. If you read something that makes you angry or depressed, skip that chapter and go to the next one, and it may resonate with you more. Some ideas may seem taboo for you to even consider. Don't worry though – considering them can't harm you; these ideas are just options offered to people who are looking for new ways to look at their lives and better ways to relate to their fellow human beings living on this beautiful planet. When you consider any new concept, you have the options of accepting it and using it, rejecting it as not useful for you at this time, or putting the concept aside for possible consideration at a future time. Hopefully you will find a number of the concepts presented here helpful and uplifting.

Finally, I would like to promote one of the only absolute truths of which I am certain: You cannot defeat the dark emotions of fear, anger and hate that surround us with returned fear, anger and hate. These can only be eliminated by dissolving them in the light of peace, love and compassion. Man has spent his entire history building larger armies and more destructive weapons thinking that these would eventually bring us peace. That has never been the case, and it never will be. We have only a short time to understand this concept before we destroy our home and ourselves. It is time to try what has been tried only occasionally before – getting rid of the concepts of "enemy" and "different" and starting to love each other until fear can no longer survive among us.

May I wish each of you great joy in the lessons you learn here on Earth. I hope you will consider the possibility that there is a different way of feeling, thinking about, and living life – the possibility of love. Love has power that few understand and even fewer ever fully experience. It can create a healed planet with human beings that make each other's lives blissful instead of miserable. Sound too good to be achievable? We *must* begin to see the actual possibility of such a world, for if we cannot imagine it, we certainly cannot create it.

Chapter One

THE ROOM

*I'm good at thinking outside the box, so much
that you realize it's not a box to begin with.*

will.i.am

Dark… quiet… peaceful… but the awareness of an imminent transition gets stronger and stronger. There is in this darkness the knowledge and experience of a thousand lifetimes. Yet the longing for another chance to learn more about bottling the ego, controlling addictions, and getting closer to being a spirit of pure light helped make the decision to do another lifetime with a body. The importance of these physical existences for ones spiritual evolution cannot be overstated. How difficult, how frustrating and how painful these incarnations can be is clear, but the power of a mortal existence to indelibly imprint important spiritual attributes is even clearer.

Lucky, how really lucky to have been put at the front of the line to do an embodied existence on the beautiful planet called Earth. What will be experienced this time? Will the lessons that poverty has to teach be available, or will it be the even more challenging role of a wealthy person? What if bad choices are made? What if it's hard to even remember what lessons are to be learned? What if… oooohhh, the pressure is getting intense. Wave after wave keeps pushing toward an imminent transition. Noise... commotion... light... OWWW! A vicious slap on the butt and the transition is complete. Here at last – here at University Earth.

* * * * *

As a child is born into the world and comes into his mother's arms, it soon becomes evident that this sweet tiny creature has a definite personality that he seems to have brought with him. Those parents with more than one child know that children from the same genetic pool can have very definite differences in personality traits and attitudes. One child may be quiet and low maintenance except for his extreme stubbornness. Another may be the child that must always have her own way and later becomes someone who likes to be the boss of everything. Yet they all grew up in the same household with very similar upbringings. So there must be some sort of personality-defining energy, spirit or genetics that come with children on the day they are born. Some scientists believe that personality traits are passed genetically. With the huge amount of genetic material and all the possibilities for making proteins, we have discovered only a few over 25,000 peptides (small proteins) that appear to be encoded in our DNA. Perhaps some of these traits we seem to bring with us are passed in some way through this "unused" genetic material. Many religious beliefs and spiritual traditions include possibilities of pre-mortal existences or past lives (often referred to as incarnations). Some even believe that we have lived, or are living simultaneously, many lives and that we bring to each embodied existence all that we have learned from these earlier or concomitant periods of learning.

At the moment of birth the great forgetting begins, and all the knowledge and experience the new human being has brought with him begins to fade from memory. This great forgetting will make possible a much greater level of spiritual growth since only the strongest character traits will be likely to exert an influence on the new Earthling. If ego has been dealt with well in other existences, it will be an asset for the child as it starts on its path. If patience was never learned, it may cause problems in this existence and may even be the main reason for coming here this time. Any strengths achieved prior to this incarnation (a lifetime with a body) will be helpful during this one.

As the child grows, every experience, large or small, in some way affects what the child has brought with him to form a somewhat different child by the end of each day. What he experiences in his environment and his reactions to these experiences will create subtle changes from week to week. At any point in one's life, the totality of his experiences can be considered to be that person's "vector sum" (explained in the next paragraph). Thus a person can evolve in many different directions from any point in his life depending on what comes into his environment, what he experiences, and how he reacts to those experiences from that particular point on.

In physics we learn that a vector is a certain force acting in a particular direction. It was often explained using the horses and wagon image. If five horses are pulling a wagon directly north and three are pulling it directly east, the wagon will go approximately NNE at about a four-horse rate. In actuality, the wagon will probably break into many pieces and the horses will run off never to be seen again – but you learn that later in your physics class. There can be many vectors acting upon an object at any one time and the resulting course and force will be determined by mathematically finding the sum of all these vectors, i.e. – *the vector sum.*

Depending on our age, our lives have been acted upon by thousands to millions of forces pushing us in many directions. Our parents, families and societies create extremely strong vectors in directions mirroring our social environment. Religious organizations tend to create very powerful forces in our lives that can overpower many other forces. Our peers, especially our close friends, can often carry us further in the directions given to us by society and religion, or they can help create counter vectors in amazingly different directions. There are many points in our lives where a course of events will cause us to closely examine the place to which our own personal vector sum has brought us. Catastrophic events such as illness, significant loss, natural disasters or wars can change our evolutionary paths forever, but so can the accumulation of new insights, personal interactions, strong emotional experiences, and subtle chemical and energy influences.

Absolutism, as used in this book, is the existence of all-this-way-or-that-way thought processes that limit our range of experiences, insights or personal interactions by holding us within preconceived boundaries. These boundaries of thought and experience are usually created for us by other people in our environment: family members, friends, governing officials, religious leaders, schoolteachers and those who create our entertainment. Strangely enough, these people are usually only passing on that which was given to them. Rarely are these limiting ideas examined and even more rarely are they challenged before being handed down. These ideas are so deeply engrained that often we are not even sure it is an *option* to think otherwise, but we are very certain that we are very much *discouraged* from doing so. Many people are not even aware that they can control the influences that will shape their lives from the present moment onward. It is all fate or randomness. It is what we have been dealt by a God that doesn't always seem to care about our well-being.

But, instead of fate or randomness, it is most often the existence of these enslaving absolute thought processes that keeps us from changing our own lives and the direction the planet is going. It is clear that we can do nothing at this particular point in our lives to alter the vectors of the past that have created what we are at this moment. It is imperative, however, that we understand that we *do* have a part in choosing which vectors will be added to the sum to create what we are tomorrow at this time, a year from now, or a decade from now. Unfortunately, most people will continue to allow their lives to be formed by external controls, random events, and ideas and ways of thinking that are handed to them by people who may or may not have their best interests at heart. Ironically, it is often those who sincerely care about us the most who bind us with the mental shackles that are the most difficult to escape from.

Perhaps an easier explanation of what absolutism is would be to compare it to a room that has been built for us by other people. We are told that this room contains all that we need for a completely happy and fulfilling life. We sit in a large comfortable chair facing the door. There are windows to the right and to the left, but we are told not to look out of them as we may see something that could confuse us about why we need to stay in this room. There is a door in front of us, but we are told that we should not open that door and look out because there is an evil power (perhaps the boogeyman) waiting there to destroy us. There is a television in the corner with hundreds of channels, but we are admonished to watch only the videos left on top of the television for us – over and over again. On the wall is a framed poster with the title *Tribal Rules*. It enumerates what is allowed in this society and what is not acceptable. These rules contain phrases like "A real man does...", "A woman's role is...", "You will be laughed at and pointed at if you...", and "We require a monetary contribution of..."

The room is comfortable enough and, at first, we believe we can live happily in it forever. But occasionally boredom or curiosity overtakes us and we can't help looking out a window. What we see may be beautiful and fascinating or strange but irresistibly intriguing. We have been made to believe that we will be ridiculed if we let anyone know that we would like to explore that world. At first we get pangs of guilt and immediately turn our eyes back to the door. But each time we peer out the window and see the beauty and mystery outside, the guilt gets less and we linger at the view and turn back to face the door much more hesitantly.

As we mature and have more life experiences, we may begin to wonder what could be so scary outside that door, and we crack it open and take a quick look out. Although the boogeyman does not appear to be anywhere in sight, we begin to get nervous and fearful, saying to ourselves, "Oooooh, back to the chair, back to the chair." Eventually some of us will begin to doubt the boogeyman story altogether and will open the door and wander out a little bit. We may find the landscape in front of us to be beautiful and intriguing, but everyone knows that the monster we have been told about is lurking just out of sight and may grab us at any time. So we hurry back in and slam the door, imagining the monster nipping at our heels.

A rare few will eventually get fed up with watching the same videos, reading the same tribal rules, and not being allowed to ask any questions. They will throw open the door and exit the room with no intent to return.

In front of them lie many paths to strike out on, and it can be quite scary wondering where one will end up if one follows this path or that one. Fortunate are they that realize early on that all that is important is the journey. There is no path that will insure our happiness because, at the end of each day, the only place we *can* be is right where our day's journey has taken us. We think we must know a new path before embarking on it, but we actually create the path with each step we take. In other words, we need to pay attention to each moment in our lives and make the best choices we can and learn from every experience. By paying attention to each step, we gain control over where our paths take us. Even after we have left the room, absolutist thinking may take us on a journey right back into it. We must feel free to explore all directions and make course corrections at any point when we have gained new insights or experiences. Understanding this, it becomes very important to understand all the forces that can affect the direction of our journey.

* * * * *

The Buddha told a story called *The Lost Son.* A man who had lost his wife in childbirth lived in a village with his young son. The father had to go to another village on business, so he left his son with relatives. While he was gone, a band of thieves came and burned down the village and took the young boy with them. When the father returned he was horrified and heartbroken to find the burned out remains of his village. Upon finding the charred corpse of a young child, he assumed this was his son and began sobbing and yelling and blaming himself for leaving the boy behind. He arranged a cremation ceremony for the child and collected the ashes and kept them in a beautiful little bag that he always kept with him.

Sometime later the real son escaped from his captors and found his way home. He went to his father's new cottage late that night and knocked at the door. The father, who was still very distraught and sorrowful, answered, "Who is there?"

The young boy answered, "It's me, papa. It's your son. Open the door so I can come in." The father thought that this must be someone making fun of his constant grieving and he told the boy to go away because it wasn't funny. The boy tried several more times to get his father to let him in, but the man would not do it. Eventually the boy thought that this couldn't be his father, because his father would be very happy to see him and would let him in at once. He left and the father and his son never saw each other again.

The Buddha followed the story by telling his students, "There will be many times when you will take something to be the truth and feel that the evidence clearly supports you. But, if you hold on to it too tightly, when the truth shows up in person and knocks at your door, you will not open it." [1]

* * * * *

If we want to have lives that are continuously evolving in upward directions, we cannot limit the sources that could take us to that better state of being. Having unalterable thought processes binds our minds with strong bands that won't even let us look at information that could expand our consciousness to realms of greater knowledge and joy. Sometimes we are not aware that another way of thinking about something is even an option. If we believe that anyone or any organization we respect or love would only give us the most beneficial concepts, we might feel forbidden to challenge ideas coming from these respected sources, which may not be for our greatest good. When we believe only what we are *told* to believe and fail to critically evaluate information from *any* source, we allow ourselves to be manipulated for the benefit of people who might consciously or unconsciously desire to control us. The people who truly care about us did not intentionally give us ideas they thought might limit our evolution, but they probably just passed on ideas that were taught to them by loved and respected people in their lives. Thought processes that are passed from generation to generation eventually become entrenched as genetic memory in a society. Just as we observe that nearly every human being has arms and hands, we find beliefs in every society that seem to be just as immutable and impossible to imagine in any other way.

What I would like to do with this book is introduce new ways of looking at some things that could give us greater joy and fulfillment. Most societies on the planet teach that there is no need to learn anything outside that society's teachings and values or examine other ways of thinking about our roles on the planet. In fact, in any larger society, there are many sub-societies that want us to accept their values as a part of that larger culture. Religions, families, ethnic cultures, gangs, and circles of friends are only a few of the sub-societies trying to impose their rules and ideas on us. It can be very frightening to look in directions that have been forbidden to us all our lives. It is usually much easier to stay on a path that is familiar to us than to look for a new road to travel, even though the currently traveled path is taking us nowhere. But the most difficult path to leave is the one that seems to be working for us as long as we follow all the rules of the road. We can even be blissfully happy in our currently occurring life while there exist ideas outside our rooms that could expand that bliss even more – if we could allow ourselves to go there.

It's possible that some of the things you read in this book may make you angry. When they do, ask yourself why they bother you. Ask yourself first if you have ever really given serious consideration to the issue that is causing you to burn. Next, ask yourself if you have ever objectively and critically evaluated the issue at hand, or if your objection to the new concept is just the knee-jerk reaction that is expected from you. But, most importantly, ask yourself why getting exposed to new information and ideas of any kind should make anyone angry, even if the information stands opposed to one's currently-held beliefs. You should be able to simply evaluate the ideas as objectively as possible and either accept them, hold them for further consideration, or let them pass as ideas that are not useful to you right now. There is one thing to always keep in mind: *People who feel that their ideas are important for you to believe may try to attach strong feelings to those ideas.* You will be much less likely to evaluate anything objectively when strong emotions automatically explode when concepts which conflict with your present viewpoints are presented.

I hope that this book will be read as an opportunity to free oneself to be able to explore new avenues and find a few more useful ways to think about things. My intent is not to tell anyone that how he looks at certain aspects of his life is wrong, stupid or crazy. Instead, I would like to suggest that we all need to examine, explore and question what we have been taught. As we progress through life, many people and organizations will tell us to blindly follow their teachings without questioning or examining other possibilities. If we don't question anything, we can't become confused, frustrated or angry that we have stayed in a certain belief system for so long. But is it really better to become numb and indifferent just to avoid having to think for ourselves and possibly having to make the decision to make a momentarily uncomfortable shift? That is a question that each of us will eventually have to answer with very personal, and sometimes difficult, decisions.

If you wonder if you have allowed absolutist thought processes to inhibit your life, here are a few questions to ask yourself. Do you ever find yourself explaining your behavior to a real or imaginary person who might have witnessed it? ("I don't go to casinos very often, and when I do, I have a strict limit of $20.00.") If so, you are obviously very concerned about living up to other people's expectations and are very concerned about how people see you.

This concern can be very limiting, and living up to other people's expectations will keep you in a very small box all your life.

Do you ever find that you do not allow yourself to consider certain possibilities or options? Most people have a large number of things they do not feel are open for discussion. Are you OK with discussing the option of a national healthcare system in this country? Are you open to evaluating ideas from religious or spiritual traditions other than the one you are currently involved in? Does it make you uncomfortable to think about gay relationships and gay marriage? Do you let yourself realistically evaluate your government, thinking that it might possibly need fixing? If there are a lot of topics that you may not feel are open for debate, you may be unintentionally excluding many really good options that could open your mind, expand your understanding and make you more comfortable with the way you live.

Finally, you may ask yourself why you need to expand your thought processes if they are working very well for you just as they are. This is what I call the "Toast and Jam" concept. A person who has eaten dry toast every morning will find it quite suitable because it's what he's always done. If that person discovers butter, the texture and taste of his toast improves. But when someone presents him with his first jar of jam, that piece of toast can become a much more enjoyable experience than it ever was in its dry form. Earth life has far too much to discover and far too much to enjoy for us to allow ourselves to be confined to a room with doors and windows out of which we dare not peer because we have been taught that the room is quite satisfactory as it is.

Chapter Two

COMING TO TERMS

Convictions are more dangerous
enemies of the truth than lies.

Frederick Nietsche

In order to minimize confusion, I need to define some terms I use throughout this book. This chapter may seem a bit textbookish, but don't worry – there's no test at the end of the chapter. You can always come back to this chapter to review the terms, if needed.

Creative Energy of the Universe – Since there are many ways of visualizing the Creator and our relationship to that Creator (I call this the *God format*), many different titles have evolved for this Creative Energy. I will use terms like Source Spirit, the Universe, God, the Divine or even The Light Side of the Force. These terms will always be capitalized and I will try to never assign the Supreme Being a gender or number (he/she/it/they). This may sometimes create awkward sentences.

God Format – One's God Format is the way he visualizes God, what his relationship to God is, what he thinks God expects from him and what he expects of God. I work from a somewhat different God format than the one prevalent in America. I do not believe that an eternal spirit being (some call this the *soul*) can achieve the growth it desires in one lifetime. I believe that an existence with a body, on this planet or others, is one of the most powerful ways that exists for learning lessons and progressing spiritually as eternal souls. It seems unthinkable that we could be put here for one lifetime and then be judged and sent to heavenly bliss or eternal misery based on our behavior during this one physical existence. There are far too many variables for this to be the case – to whom and where one is born, what one's society teaches, and all the people and experiences a person encounters. The process of living sequential lives is often referred to as *reincarnation*. An *incarnation* (or an *embodied lifetime*) is simply a lifetime with a physical body, and I believe that we choose to do as many incarnations as we feel necessary to achieve the amount of spiritual evolution we wish to attain. That's why some people talk about old and young souls, referring to how spiritually evolved a person seems to be. This kind of belief is not a part of the *Abrahamic religions* (Judaism, Christianity, and Islam), but many people are now beginning to ask themselves how one lifetime could give us maximum opportunity to develop the traits of a highly spiritually-evolved person, one that lives an increasingly God-like life.

Spiritual Evolution – Spiritual evolution can be defined in many ways and these definitions can be interpreted even more diversely. The word "spiritual" can be connected to religion for some and used as a separator from religion by others. For some the word has a purely metaphysical meaning and for others it has great practical meaning in everyday activities. The word "evolution" has great emotional charge for many, but the fact is that we are all evolving every hour of every day whether we intend to or not. Every day's experiences leave us somewhat changed from what we were at the end of the day before – sometimes for better, sometimes for worse and sometimes simply different.

Spiritual evolution, for me, is all about energy. Whether you call it light energy vs. dark energy, high-vibration vs. low-vibration energy, or godly vs. satanic energy is irrelevant. Emotions and activities that are made up of high-vibration or godly energy include love, gratitude, compassion, nonjudgmentalism, peacefulness, joy, tolerance, humility and empathy. Low-vibration or dark energy feelings and behaviors include fear, hate, violence, intolerance, anger, revenge, arrogance, greed, power lust, judgment and lack of compassion. As with all energy, all of these fall along a continuous spectrum rather than on either side of an imaginary dividing wall. As we evolve spiritually, we move toward being in higher and higher vibration energy more of the time. Our life paths should *not* be reaching some goal, but learning from every moment as we climb the path. In other words, how we are feeling and what we are doing right now is all that we can have any control over. Seeing the present moment as an inconvenient obstacle in the way of getting to a more glorious future makes no sense. The future never really gets here because, when it arrives, it becomes the present. So, if we want to know what our future will be a year from now, we need to understand that it *can be nothing more than the sum total of all our present moments from now until then.* It is therefore vitally important to learn to live in the present.

As we spiritually evolve we should notice that our egos have much less control over our feelings and actions. We will also learn to overcome our addictions and to increase our self-control. We will begin to understand that the energy of love can be even more powerful in our lives when it emanates from us than when it comes to us. We will begin to have more joy in serving and helping others, and we will be less judgmental of the weaknesses and imperfections of others.

Ego – There are many different ways of understanding the term *ego*. Freud used the term along with "id" and "super-ego" to define the structure of the human psyche. The word *ego* comes from Latin and means "I". In English, it is often used to refer to the self or one's identity (how one sees oneself and all that makes up that picture). Ego is often equated with arrogance, but that is only a small part of it. In this book I will use "ego" as Dr. Wayne Dyer defines it: Your ego erroneously tells you that you are what you have, how you look, what you know, who you know, what you do for a living, and how much power you have. But, most importantly, your ego tells you that your value is based on what other people think of you (or at least what you perceive they think of you). Ego makes it important that you always be the winner in any discussion or circumstance. We do so many wrong things for bad reasons when our major concern is "what will others think?"

When our egos are running our lives, it is easier to let our behavior be ruled by greed, the lust for power and the seeking of popularity. Compassion for others runs low, and it is difficult to see others as our equals who are just living in different circumstances. Our egos take away the need to nurture the larger community as we focus our activities on ourselves. Ego is what makes it possible for us to be hurt by what others say or do to us. Without ego we are more likely to dismiss offensive behavior as immaturity on the offender's part, conduct resulting from a particularly stressful time in that person's life, or a complete lack of knowledge that such behavior might be hurtful to us. In other words, when our egos are not engaged, we see their hurtful behavior as something they need to work on – not something reflecting our own failings or weaknesses. ***The less our egos have control over us, the* easier *our lives become.***

Evaluative Thinking – Evaluative thinking, as used here, refers to the way one examines new or old information or ideas in as objective, unbiased and logic-based ways as possible. I originally planned to use the term *critical thinking*, but this term seems to connote criticizing – the judgment of flaws and faults – as in "She criticizes everything I do!" The phrase "evaluative thinking" replaces that judgmental overtone.

To truly achieve evaluative thinking, one must be able to take his ego out of the equation. If we lock out information provided by someone with no letters behind his name, someone who may have "sins" that we do not approve of, or someone who is less educated and sophisticated than we are, we take the chance of losing valuable insights and ideas. On the other hand, if we blindly accept information and ideas from people who have somehow gained a certain level of societal respect, we risk being led to completely erroneous and harmful thought processes. When we hear a so-called expert give his opinion on something, we need to ask upon what his opinion is based. Can he give us the science, data, facts and the calculations he used to reach his conclusions? If we check these out, will we come to the same conclusions ourselves?

Evaluative thinking is not easy and is something many of us are new at. "If it's on the television or the Internet, it must be true." "Our religious or political leaders would never intentionally lead us astray, would they?" "If he's a Ph.D. from Harvard, then how can I argue with what he says?" Evaluative thinking is a skill we can all develop if we put some effort into it. We must develop this skill by thinking for ourselves while taking into account and evaluating what others believe to be true. Our worldview will change radically when we do.

Sealed Premise – A *sealed premise*[1] is basically defined by the statement, "My mind is made up, so don't confuse me with facts!" A sealed premise is something we consider to be an absolute truth that is not open to examination or interpretation. For someone with a sealed premise, every bit of information will somehow be worked into support of that belief. E.g. – *"God blesses the righteous and punishes the sinners.* A person with AIDS is being punished while a person who gets cancer from years of smoking is only receiving a trial of his faith." OR *"All drugs are bad.* But the cigarettes I smoke, the alcohol I drink, the prescription medications I take and the fast foods I overeat are not really drugs because our government considers them legal. However, all pot smokers should spend time in jail, and I don't really believe that marijuana has medicinal benefits as the studies show."

Sealed premises are easy. They require no thinking, no changing your mind, no dealing with new and possibly uncomfortable ideas, and no confrontations with those who helped you develop your sealed premises. But where little is required, little benefit can be expected. Finding it inconvenient or threatening to examine the rigid beliefs they hold, people often hide behind the safety of what others have determined for them rather than taking the risk of determining their own beliefs. Those with lives full of unchallenged sealed premises will stay in their rooms with the shades down and doors locked, and they will miss a world full of new ideas, beauty and wonder.

Meme – A meme is a unit of information that invades the mind, and its existence influences our behavior to the extent that copies of it get created in other people's minds. In his book *Virus of the Mind*, Richard Brody looks at the cultural conditioning that is sometimes called memetic conditioning because it creates *memes* – a term usually attributed to Richard Dawkins. Memes are the psycho-emotional equivalent of the physical body's genes in that they have immense control over what we do and how we feel. A meme is a type of thought virus that infects us without our awareness. Viruses, whether in the body or on your computer, have three functions: invade, replicate and spread to others. As with viruses, memes may also mutate, lie dormant for a while and become less or more virulent (infective and harmful). Memes are ideas that usually have veiled beginnings – nobody knows where they originated. They are passed from generation to generation and laterally from person to person throughout a culture and are usually taken as absolute truths that dare not be questioned. Memes are ideas that are passed on with such an air of authenticity that everyone just keeps passing them on unchallenged until they have infected an entire culture.[2]

Some memes are beneficial and some are counterproductive, but each one should be evaluated separately. Memes include, but are not limited to, concepts that have to do with morality, normality, patriotism, manhood and womanhood, one's God format, right and wrong, good and bad, attire, political beliefs, and what is expected from one's tribe. We can think of memes as ideas that program us to think or feel a certain way – ideas that have great influence over us but are rarely evaluated because we don't even notice that influence.

There are three basic classes of memes: 1) Distinction memes – these are used to identify and distinguish the things in our lives. That building is a house; that animal is a dog; I live in a state identified as Arizona. 2) Strategy memes – these are beliefs about which things will cause certain results. Speeding will get you a ticket; not accepting Jesus will send you to hell. 3) Association memes – these link one meme to another and create our attitudes about things. We usually associate Christmas with good feelings and fun times, or we may associate an iPhone with being cool.

Part of any meme is the understanding that the meme is not open for discussion – it must simply be accepted as is. The stronger the questioning of a meme is forbidden, the more likely it is to become a sealed premise. Questioning memes like patriotism, religion, politics and what comprises manhood or womanhood is strongly forbidden, but fashion memes and what music one should listen to are more easily contested. Understanding that memes influence every aspect of our lives will help us recognize them and we will be more likely to evaluate them for their beneficial or detrimental effects.

Tribe and Tribal Rules – Your *tribe* is not an easy thing to describe, but it is certainly more than your family of origin. It is the culture, people and organizations that influence you most. Besides your blood ties, it includes your friends, religion, ethnicity, neighborhood, schools, workplace, peers and associates, politics, and the country and people with whom you hold common beliefs. Some of these have a stronger influence over you than others, and each adds its part to what becomes your *Tribal Rules*.

These rules can be thrown in your face over and over, or they can be subtly implied. These are the memes that are passed from generation to generation and person to person within your tribe. These rules range from when you will be praised or ridiculed to when you will be expelled from the tribe. If you are a sensitive person, you will try hard to obey every rule to the letter of the law. If you are less uptight, you will decide which rules can be broken with the least amount of consequences. As discussed in chapter one, Tribal Rules can deal with all imaginable issues, many of which are listed in the paragraph about memes above. Memes and Tribal Rules are closely related. They can help us understand how our society functions, but they can also keep us tightly stuck and fearful to look at options that could enhance our lives.

Morality is a word that is not as easily defined as most think. Most humans regard themselves as moral people and hope that others see them that way too. Morality, like normality, is a concept that must be defined by a person or group. Most often we have no choice in who is allowed to define morality for us. As our elders teach morality to us, it has already been defined for a long time. There are some things that seem to be fairly high up and universal on anyone's "Definition of Morality" list. Not killing or injuring another person or taking his stuff is usually at the top of the list. Sexual activity outside narrowly defined boundaries somehow sits high on most lists of immoral acts. But as we drop farther down the list, a consensus of what constitutes moral behavior is harder to achieve. In many societies, eating bacon or ham is considered quite normal and is certainly not thought to be sinful. But in Islamic culture and among Orthodox Jews, eating pork products is one of the most outwardly visible signs of immorality – so much so that every airline carrier flying in or out of Islamic countries has a card on every food tray in several languages stating, "This meal contains no pork products or byproducts." One can certainly see how religious traditions regarding food products such as shellfish and pork had their origins in the diseases they could transmit in Old Testament days. Shellfish could contain deadly parasites and pork could be infected with trichina worms. Today those diseases are not as great a problem, but the moral issue, because of scriptural traditions, has not changed at all. Most people accept people who they consider "moral" and reject people who they consider "immoral," but I hope your understanding of the concept of morality will metamorphose as you continue to read.

Rationalization must also be discussed in relationship to morality. Rationalizing can most easily be defined as making excuses for thoughts and behaviors that might be perceived as immoral. But it is much more complex than that. To tell a "little white lie" requires minimal rationalization. "It won't hurt anybody," or "Everyone does it," will usually suffice. But to kill one or many humans requires much more powerful rationalizations very often having to do with "For God and Country!" The most horrific slaughters and atrocities in history have been done "with God's blessing." These include the slaughter of millions of native Americans because they were viewed as heathens by the Catholic god, acts of terrorism perpetrated at the "command" of any number of gods, and genocides committed all over the world by people who often believe in the same god as those they slaughter, but think their group is favored over the other by that god.

However, some of the most difficult rationalizations are those that we make for behavior we somehow feel is not really wrong, but our society has pounded into our heads that it is. For example, a young person who realizes that he or she may be gay may try to mix church and same-sex orientation for a time. But, if he or she stays in the church, it will eventually be necessary to find a rationalization that is strong enough to allow the person to stay in the church that detests his/her existence, behavior or feelings. The very act of rationalization is based on our view of morality or sinfulness, which is often defined for us by someone else. Rationalization has very little real value on our path of spiritual evolution. It only serves to relieve us of the need to deal with conflicts that may exist in our lives.

Good vs. Bad – This may be the most difficult distinction of all. Humans seem to find it necessary, or at least easiest, to define people, events and ideas in six second sound bytes. This makes it much easier for all of us to decide how we feel about someone/ something in a few seconds.

"Do you know anything about the new girl that is starting next Monday?"

"I hear she's a black Republican lesbian Jew." (Okay, that's unlikely.)

"Oh… I can already tell I won't like her."

"How do you know that? You haven't even met her."

"Well, I don't want to sound prejudiced, but she just doesn't sound like my kind of people."

And so it is with "good" or "bad." These words make it all too easy to sum up our beliefs and feelings about any event, organization or person. But we all know deep inside that there is no such thing as a totally good or totally bad person. And we know this because we know ourselves so well. Everyone has participated in acts others would consider to be loving and beneficial or deeds that could be defined as dark and destructive. And every human being must be seen as the summation of many vectors that we cannot know or understand. For anyone to judge another person would be impossible without knowing all that person has brought with him, his entire genetic makeup, all that he has experienced in his life, and how he reacted to all those experiences. And what point is there in judgment, anyway? We must occasionally make judgment calls about another person's detrimental behavior and how it could adversely affect us if we stay in their presence. But to label a person all bad for his behavior is not useful in any way. Many spiritual constructs believe that we experience lives with bodies to learn certain lessons, have life-building experiences, and to begin to understand that we are all one and that we must have unconditional love and compassion for our fellow humans. Hate, prejudice, anger, and judgmentalism hurt most those who hold them.

The concept of good/bad is too simplistic and too absolutist to be of any benefit in our evolution. We need to seriously consider why we have the need to place a good/bad judgment on everything and everyone. Perhaps it is our ego saying, "Well I may not be as good as person A, but I am certainly better than person B." Has our ethnic or religious upbringing lead us to believe there must always be a good or bad evaluation (heaven vs. hell, sinner vs. saint)? Does a good/bad judgment make it easier for us to decide what we will think or do next? As we lose our egos and become filled with love, we will be more able to say, "He is who he is right now. I am who I am right now. It is what it is."

Vector Sum – In chapter one, the *vector sum* was defined in depth. It is simply the sum total of all we brought with us (nature) and all our earthly experiences to this point in time (nurture). It also includes our emotional reactions to the events and circumstances in our lives. Numerous forces in varying directions act upon us each day and we become slightly different people by the end of the day. The important thing to understand about the vector sum is this: *Most people let random events and pre-programmed emotional responses create their vector sums, thinking that this is just what life has dealt them.* They never become the creators of the forces that will shape their lives, and they never learn that they can change how they feel. Climbing out of the restrictive boxes that others have created for us will take us a long way in learning how to take over the directing of our own lives.

* * * * *

Bill Moyers tells the story of a young Native American man who asked his father what his secret to becoming a man of good character was. The father told the young man that he had two wolves inside him. The dark wolf thrived on greed, power, jealousy, intolerance, hate, violence, dishonesty and arrogance. The light wolf was nourished by compassion, modesty, generosity, honesty, love and simplicity.

The young man then asked, "Father, what determines which wolf is victorious?"

The father answered, "The one I feed."

Chapter Three

SEE THE SPECTRUM

*The sharing of joy... forms a bridge between the
sharers, which can be the basis for understanding
much of what is not shared between them,
and lessens the threat of their difference.*

Audre Lorde

When white light is projected through a prism, it separates into a continuous spectrum of color beginning with red and progressing through orange, yellow, green, blue, and purple. In a spectrometer one can heat an element such as sodium and put the light emitted from that element through a prism and it will project as bands of color of very specific wavelengths. These spectral patterns are well known for each element and can be used to identify elements in compounds, on distant stars and wherever they are found. Human thought processes tend to limit us to seeing only certain bands of the entire spectrum in most aspects of our lives. What would our planet be like if we had only a few elements to build such a complex and beautiful place as Earth. Even the elements that are only found in trace amounts can be vital to the biology of life. Seeing a greater part of the spectrum opens up new possibilities in all areas of our lives.

A person seeking ways to improve his health and well-being can be stuck in many different wavelengths. He can see FDA approved medicines and surgery as the only possibilities for treating health related issues. Or he may reject standard medicine altogether and rely only on herbs and supplements for dealing with illness and health maintenance. He may think that preventative practices like meditation, yoga, exercise and good eating are all that anyone will ever need. Or he can look at the entire spectrum and choose those things that are useful to his health at any particular place in his life. A little extra vitamin C will not fix acute appendicitis, but surgery is certainly not the most beneficial treatment for the common cold. "Whatever works" has been my motto in treating patients and planning my own healthcare. And there are more healthcare options that really work than one might imagine.

In political discussions we hear words like conservative, liberal and socialist. But there are so many ways of defining these terms that it is difficult to use them without first explaining our own understanding of each term. Our political discussions tend to be more emotionally based than rationally based because we read into each term our own biases without knowing what the other person is thinking of. By adding terms such as "right wing" or "left wing," we only increase the emotional heat of the discussion. It is far more productive to talk about what a government should be and what it should do for its people across the whole spectrum. In the United States we have programs that are socialist in nature – fire and police protection, Medicare and VA medical benefits, public education and infrastructure (highways, water and sewage systems, bridges, etc.). We also have social programs like Social Security that would be considered liberal. And we have fiscal conservatives in our legislatures who are opposed to new programs that would cost more money and raise our deficit. In our political discussions we should allow ourselves to look at the whole spectrum of ideas and see what parts would be most beneficial for the entire population of our country. Most likely we would find that a combination of concepts from all these areas would make the best possible government. But, if we continue to put all possibilities into exclusionary pigeonholes, we will limit the benefit to all that our government could have.

Religions, by their very nature, tend to be highly limited in the amount of the spiritual spectrum they recognize. If you are a part of an Abrahamic religion (Judaism, Christianity, or Islam), you are not likely to ever be encouraged to study Buddhism or Taoism. Religions have their own dogma and rituals that are given to their members as all that they could ever possibly need for maximum spiritual growth. As individuals in any particular religion discover that their inherited beliefs are unfulfilling or even harmful, they tend to look for another religious tradition. Their belief is that there must be ONE TRUE RELIGION out there. But my own personal experience has shown me that there are great truths and benefits all along the spiritual spectrum. Many people become atheists, or at least agnostics, when their religious affiliation begins to look superstitious or antiquated. I have heard people say, "If the Bible isn't the absolute literal word of God, then THERE IS NO GOD!" But there are so many ways to look at our relationship with the Universe, the Creator, Source, Spirit, God, or whatever one's designation might be, that to look at one small sliver of orange in the entire spectrum and try to make that color work for us in every way is absurd.

The spectrum permeates every aspect of our lives. We like to think there are absolute truths, but the truth seems to change as more knowledge and insights are gained. We look for absolute definitions of right and wrong, but the longer we live, the more uncertain these definitions become. We expect to be able to judge everyone as either good or bad, but we know the reality is far more complex.

We seek a perfect solution to every problem we encounter when actually there could be any number of solutions that might work out well if we approached the problem reasonably. It feels very destabilizing at first to give up the need for just one or two bands of color in the different aspects of our lives. It seems there must be a right way and a wrong way to think about everything, one correct way of doing our lives, a way to distinguish between good people and bad people or a way to determine absolute truth. But, if life is that easy for us, we are surely excluding options that could make our lives more interesting. Imagine seeing just the green band of a rainbow. It might still be a pretty sight, but when all the colors appear it becomes much more beautiful. If we are so close to the rainbow that we see only one color, maybe we should back away and enjoy the whole spectrum.

Human beings are very complex and each one has a unique combination of spectral bands. When we come to understand that no one can be described in a six-second sound byte, and when we truly recognize that all human beings are the summations of millions of very complex vectors, we will begin to see humanity in a different light. But most people can understand their own complexity and humanity much better than they can see this intricacy in others. And just as importantly, if we cannot see the complexity in ourselves, it will be impossible to see it in others. Our species will not survive or prosper much longer if we cannot see the connective energy that binds each one of us to every other person on the planet.

* * * * *

I grew up in a very conservative home but did not perceive my parents as terribly prejudiced. My entire culture and the whole of my society had very subtly instructed me about all those other very different people who just happened to live on the same planet as I did. During my childhood we were in a cold war with the Russians, and Communists only existed to do only one thing – take away my freedom! I knew they really wanted to kill me with all the nuclear warheads aimed at my country, and the only reason the Russians didn't send them our way was that we had the wisdom to aim even more warheads at them. It was called deterrence. At school we learned to "duck and cover" which was supposed to protect us from a nuclear blast. Even at that young age I knew that ducking under a wooden desk was a futile act of survival. At the State Fair I saw all kinds of bomb shelters, air filtration devices and emergency supplies being sold. And I wondered what kind of horrific people all these Russians must be and what would make them so different from us. Was it their culture, their government, their genetics? Or had God just created people in other countries to be strangely different from people in our country? Oddly, I rarely considered what their thoughts about Americans might be, but I was quite sure they knew we were the good guys on the side of right. We were all that was keeping their evil plans from prevailing.

This was also the time when the civil rights movement was just beginning, and I saw all the racism that existed in other parts of the country. In my school class, we had only one black person, and he was one of the coolest and most popular people in the school. I could not imagine why other parts of the country had such difficulties getting along with black people. But we had a lot of Latinos in our school and there was definitely antagonism toward them. I didn't understand that either since I liked all the Latinos I knew personally. But I figured there must be some stuff I didn't know about them since so many people complained about them. And, having been raised in a staunch Mormon family, I just did not understand the depravity of the beer drinkers and was amazed that some of my favorite teachers drank coffee (Mormons are forbidden from drinking alcohol, coffee and tea and from smoking cigarettes).

In short, I was one giant bundle of prejudices. It seemed that anyone who was different was painted as bad. But, even at that young age, I thought a lot about stereotypes and how so few people I knew fit the stereotypes that had been painted for me. At first I thought that this might just be a fluke of where I lived or whom I knew. But as I began to know more people, stereotypes only confused me more. I even met a student who had come to the Phoenix area as a baby with his family because his father was recruited to work at an aerospace plant just before the U.S.S.R. was closed to emigration. His family, including his parents, had no horns and seemed very nice and compassionate, which just did not compute. The parents loved their children and the children loved their parents and grandparents. His parents did not seem like they wanted to kill Americans and seemed to be very happy here. I just figured they were one of those exceptional families who had been born in a dark land and had just managed to escape, but it seemed strange that his parents talked about their homeland with happy memories and longing. As my spiritual understanding evolved, I understood that foolish prejudices had been programmed into me without my awareness, and I began to look at all human beings as people just like me who happened to be born in a place with different tribal rules.

* * * * *

The word *stereotype* comes from early printers. They used to have to pick each letter out of a box and set it in a holder with other letters to form words, then lines, then pages. They would then print a page by lining up all the lines in the printing press and inking up the letters and pressing the ink onto a piece of paper. If they had a lot of pages to print, they might not want to tie up all the individual letters, so they would take some kind of matrix, usually clay based, and press it onto the typeset lines. The clay would then be peeled off, allowed to harden a bit and then they would pour molten lead over the clay impression of the type and the lead would harden as a copy of the typeset page. It was called the stereotype because the newly formed plate made impressions that looked just like the typeset page. This plate could then be kept for long periods and subsequent printings, and the individual letters could go back in the box for other printing jobs.

Webster's dictionary defines *stereotype* as "something conforming to a fixed or general pattern; especially a standardized mental picture held in common by members of a group and representing an oversimplification, affective attitude, or uncritical judgment (as of a person, a race, an issue, or an event)." Stereotypes are not totally useless. If we say that people with blond or red hair burn more easily in the sun and need to take precautions, it can be a short and easy way of enlightening people. But usually stereotyping is a very restrictive practice. It sculpts an image that is too easily accepted as a quick and easy way of judging all people in a particular group. It denies the uniqueness of individuals and makes them seem much less than the complex sums of vectors that they are. It brands them with only a few characteristics (usually negative) that keep us from looking at their real souls and recognizing their worth as integral parts of the planet. Stereotyping erects an instant wall that keeps us from connecting with other human beings, creating animosity and mistrust.

When I first lived in Germany, it took me awhile to realize that Germans not liking ice in a beverage or not drinking tap water were not matters of right or wrong. They were simply cultural preferences that had evolved from earlier circumstances. At one time, water that had not been processed into beer or soda could contain dangerous bacteria and was not generally drunk. But the fact that tap water in

Germany is now pure and safe does not get rid of those earlier cultural traditions. As I traveled around Europe, and later the world, there were many other things that could have seemed "wrong" because they were different from our American customs. The way things were built, the way traffic moved, the food and the customs – all these things were different from home. But, as my attitude changed, I found them to be delightful as well as different. New tastes, new traditions and new people all became wonderful discoveries for me. Although I did not take delight in every new taste or tradition, I realized that this was only because I had been raised in a culture where other tastes and traditions prevailed. And when my German friends came to visit and found that pancakes with that "disgustingly sweet maple syrup poured all over them" were yucky, it didn't bother me because I knew that it was just a taste they were not used to.

Mark Twain said, "Travel is fatal to prejudice, bigotry, and narrow-mindedness, and many of our people need sorely on these accounts. Broad, wholesome, charitable views of men cannot be acquired by vegetating in one little corner of the earth all one's lifetime." Through travel we learn that other humans in other places are really just like us except for their customs, food, and languages. Parents love their children and work hard to put food on the table. These "different" people suffer joy and grief for the same reasons we do. When we have an opportunity to see other cultures and actually interact with them, we begin to see the entire spectrum of the planet instead of just one band.

There are so many moments in life where we think we must choose box a, b, or c when very often "d) all of the above" or "e) parts of all of the above" may be a better answer. Maybe we think we can tell what a person is like by whether he is in jail, a CEO of a large bank, a prominent religious leader or a politician. We judge our fellow human beings as if only black or white existed with no other shades to choose from. But then come the scandals where big evangelists turn out to have dirty little secrets, and there is rarely a time when one or more of our politicians isn't involved in something that is hypocritical and/or illegal. Many people are noticing the ever-increasing redistribution of money toward the wealthiest people going on in our type of capitalism and are wondering if our economic system might not need some major rethinking. As we begin to see the broader spectrum, we begin to understand that our prejudices against other people have been planted in us and that prejudices other people have against us were ingrained in them at a young and impressionable age. As the song in the musical "South Pacific" goes… "We learn to hate all the people our relatives hate by the time we are eight." If we continue to limit our view of the spectrum to the few narrow bands that have been projected for us by our tribe, the dark energy in our world will continue to grow. If we can open our eyes wider to see the whole rainbow, the darkness will begin to be replaced with beautiful light and richness.

Chapter Four

HOUSES OF CARDS

*A deck of cards is built like the purest of
hierarchies, with every card a master to those
below it, a lackey to those above it.*

Ely Culbertson

Many of us have seen a house of cards being built. First, a number of cards are laid out edge to edge along their longer sides. Then, over each card, two cards are leaned together creating a triangle with the first card. This is repeated for each card on the table. Next, a card is laid flat from one peak to another peak until the floor of the second story is finished. Then cards are carefully leaned against each other to form a new layer of peaks. Each layer is completed on top of the other layers until the final peak is in place.

Building a house of cards requires a steady hand, an undisturbed area, and patience. The final product is an admirable accomplishment. One can make it larger by adding another row on either side, and another and another. But the larger the house gets, the less stable it becomes. The more rows one adds, the less tolerance there is for sloppiness in earlier rows. Larger houses are more easily destabilized by air movement. One thing is for sure – trying to remove a card from any layer and replace it with another will cause a total collapse of the house.

Many people construct their lives as they would a house of cards. Most often the architectural plans and building materials are given to us by our families, societies, religions – i.e., our tribes. Our tribal members lay our foundations for us while we are yet too young to be thinking about how we want our life's "house" to look or how it should serve us later on. Eventually we are carefully taught all the memes and sealed premises that were used to build our house to this point. We know that we are expected to use the plans and materials we have been given to build the rest of our home. We continue to build, one card at a time, in a way that does not disturb the part of the house that has already been constructed. The political system we live in can affect large parts of our house. The religion we inherit from our family of origin may easily entangle itself into almost everything we think or do. Our friends, our families and our societies are all anxious to add a card or two of their own to our house in progress. The problem is that, if we later see a window in the attic or a fireplace in the garage, it is very difficult to change anything at this point without disrupting the entire structure. So we rationalize, ignore, or somehow try to make these dysfunctional parts work for us. (In case you haven't noticed, this chapter is a giant metaphor.)

The more we live absolutist lives, the more our lives become dysfunctional houses of cards. When we allow our lives to be filled with memes, sealed premises and tribal rules, it becomes more difficult to change anything about our homes without starting all over again. But, at some point in time, a person may feel that his house in its current state is unstable and not serving him well. He may feel uncomfortable there and will start to look for ways to remodel that uneasiness.

The idea of starting from the foundation and rebuilding everything is simply too frightening or daunting for most people. So they try to add some sort of glue to the edges of the cards with hopes that their houses will be stable enough to withstand all disruptive forces. Unfortunately, the more glue they add, the more difficult it becomes to change any aspect of their houses that might become problematic. Their lives become convoluted and difficult as they try to integrate into their structures pieces that don't jibe with the rest of the house. They have to find stronger glue and more inventive ways to add on rooms, perhaps hanging off the sides, which make their houses even more unstable.

* * * * *

Chana had grown up in an Orthodox Jewish home in a modest size village. Like most families who live within a religious structure, almost everything that went on in her home or community was tightly bound to her inherited faith. Most holidays and other family gatherings had to do with Judaism. Most of her daily thoughts and activities were based in her religious traditions. Her family was important and dear to her, although they often drove her a bit crazy. All of her closest friends were Orthodox Jews. Her parents let her know on a continuous basis what the expectations of her faith were and therefore what their expectations of her were. Her mother, Esther, was particularly concerned that she hadn't found someone to marry yet and was always looking to introduce her to nice eligible Jewish boys in the area. But Chana was not interested in any of these eligible bachelors. She was already in love with someone she had met at the bakery where she worked. Her name was Naomi.

Naomi also came from an Orthodox Jewish family. The two had kept their relationship hidden from their families for over a year now, but things were beginning to become more difficult. They wanted to celebrate Shabbat (the Sabbath) together as well as the Jewish holidays that are usually spent with the ones you love. But they had to celebrate apart, and this had become increasingly painful. The girls were considering coming out to their families, but had to consider all the consequences of this action. Both realized the possibility that their families would disown them, regarding them as dead. They knew that their friends would be expected to shun them, whether they really felt that way or not. Everything in their lives would change if they tried to slide this one card out of the structure and replace it with another.

Their coming out did not go well. They were not completely disowned, but excluded as a couple and were never included in family functions. They eventually decided to move to a large city and find jobs, even though it would mean leaving behind all that was near and dear to them. At least they could begin a life of their own. But, even as they began this new life, they found themselves incorporating most of the traditions that had been celebrated in their families, even though these religious traditions were responsible for separating them from their families. They celebrated Shabbat in their own improvised way. They performed all the rituals of the various holidays that had brought them so much joy as children. They talked often about how they could reconcile who they were with what they understood G_d expected from them. They often talked about whether the joy of their relationship and being themselves was worth the pain of separation from G_d and family. It was an issue they would struggle with for a long time.[1]

* * * * *

When people finally realize that they are living in a very dysfunctional house and want to move out and build something better, absolutist thought processes may again keep them from

36

building a new and improved home. Many people just try to replace the dysfunctional cards, or color over the suit of the card with a marking pen. It just creates too much fear of loss to tear down the whole house and start all over again. These are the gay people who enter a regular marriage so they can pursue politics or continue in their current religious traditions. Or they may become priests or nuns so they don't have to deal with that issue at all. These are the preachers or politicians who have facades of piety with dirty little secrets behind those facades. Some may continue to live in these dysfunctional houses their entire lives, shimming up here or bracing there, hoping that everything doesn't collapse around them. But they always live lives that are more stressful and less joyful and meaningful than they could be.

Others may decide to take a wrecking ball to the house and start rebuilding from the ground up. Most of them believe that they can use none of the building materials from the old house and that they must start with totally new architectural plans. This can leave them fearful and lost in the wilderness until they have looked at an overwhelming array of new plan ideas and all types of building materials.

Indeed, in some cases, the old house may be too wobbly and decrepit to allow any of the old plans or materials to be salvaged. But in most cases, the old house had a lot of good stuff and ideas that can be used in the new construction if we don't throw everything out simply because some parts of the old house didn't work. People who hate their jobs may have to completely retrain for a new job, but often they can use the skills and knowledge they gained from their current job as the new foundation for better employment in the same or a related field. If they are extremely bitter about what happened at their last place of work, they may not even consider this possibility. Many people become so disillusioned about their past religious affiliation that they conclude that there is no God rather than look at other ideas of what God could be.

Give yourself permission to discard anything you want to when you find it doesn't work for you. But, more importantly, give yourself permission to keep all that is beautiful, joyful, interesting and useful from any aspect of your life. Some people will tell you that you can't keep any part of what you had unless you keep all of it. Don't believe them! Search for new insights, information, people, organizations and concepts that you find interesting to add to your vector sum. They don't all have to fit together perfectly initially. Maybe someday they will, or maybe we will never figure out how all the wonderful things in our lives correlate. It's okay for life to have a bit of mystery and eclecticism about it. Don't discard really good things solely on the basis that they were associated with something that caused you pain or chaos. Look in as many places as you can for all the useful beautiful things you can find and each day you will find you have evolved into a happier and more fulfilled person.

If you abandon your old domicile, be sure to consider carefully what you will build for yourself in the future. You do not want to abandon one dysfunctional structure just to create another built on the same principles. Keep your structure flexible and easy to remodel because every day will bring new ideas about what you want your home to be like. Look at lots of floor plans and consider new and different building materials when building your new structure. Try to escape the restrictive bonds of old thought processes that no longer work for you.

If you are particularly adventurous, the new structure may not resemble a house at all. It may be something more like a tent, allowing for movement and the continuous reshaping of your world views as you have new experiences and gain new insights, often in unexpected ways. The journey is the essence of life; we cannot allow the perceived need for structure to bind or restrict us. We cling to the past for a sense of security it cannot really provide. As scary as it is to leave old ways behind, growth is essential. The shedding of old skin must occur to allow for new growth.

Flexibility and change, broadening and expansion are parts of personal transformation that move beyond traditional structures and rules. Our perceived need for order and predictability can keep us stuck in fixed traditional ways that do not allow for exploration of alternatives, mind expansion or personal growth. Rather than be constricted by fear, we can adopt what works for us right now, knowing that this too will continue to change over time. We should build our living spaces in a way that will allow for easy remodeling, the incorporation of new ideas, and lots of windows so we can always get a good look at what else is out there.

Chapter Five

GREAT EXPECTATIONS

To free us from the expectations of others,
to give us back to ourselves – there lies the
great, singular power of self-respect.

Joan Didion

I remember the turning point clearly, even the intersection I was in when the epiphany occurred. I was Chief of Staff at the hospital where I practiced and was headed for a staff meeting. As usual, the surgeons and internists were jockeying for power, and I had received several calls to put a number of really petty items on the agenda. For some reason, on this particular day, I was being assaulted with guilt-laden feelings from every side: "I am not a good Chief of Staff because I can't keep everybody happy. I'm not a good doctor because I can't heal everyone who comes to me. I'm not living up to all the expectations of family and friends. And I can never live up to the expectations that God has of me. I'm not a good son because..." Then I just exploded, and the words came flying out of my mouth: "THERE IS NO ONE ON THIS PLANET WHO KNOWS MORE ABOUT WHAT I SHOULD BE DOING THAN ME! Why have I spent my whole damn life trying to please people who can never be pleased? They aren't living in my shoes, and they don't have any more intelligence or savvy than I do. I know they think that what has worked for them will work for everyone, but that is just stupid! They are just putting themselves up as authorities on all these subjects, but they are no better authorities than I am. They're just arrogant idiots..." And the soliloquy went on. How I had let myself come to this surprising thought process amazed and somewhat frightened me, since I had been the ultimate pleaser all my life. I'd had it. This was my tantrum, my response to irrational thinking and trying to live up to everyone's expectations but my own.

That day changed the direction of my life. My initial reaction to my own outrage was terrible guilt since my religious upbringing had taught me that God, and God-like authority figures, wanted only obedience without question. But after the guilt came unbelievable freedom – the freedom of not having to live up to other people's expectations, the freedom of being able to evolve on my own path, not someone else's. And then the guilt rushed back in. Why was I being so rebellious? It took several years of bouncing back and forth before I felt more freedom than guilt, but the process of cutting through my chains had begun.

When we analyze the pain, inner conflict, self-hate, familial stress, and anguish that occur in our lives, we come up with many reasons for these negative feelings. "My kids just won't do what I tell them to." "My parents don't understand me." "I don't want to be in the military like my father was." "If I leave my church, my family will disown me." "My wife just does not understand what she needs to be doing in this relationship." These are, of course, only a tiny fraction of the situations that can cause great grief and stress in our lives. But seldom do we ever really come to the core issue of our misery.

What is it that causes any society to be so full of unchallenged ideas? What is it that creates so many sealed premises on so many topics for members of that society? Where do the memes that surround us come from? Why do we become disappointed with people so frequently, and why are they continuously disappointed with us? Why do so many people live their lives unfulfilled and frustrated?

Please consider this as one of the major causes of the societal dysfunction and personal anguish that exist around the world: ***Most people on the planet spend most of their time, energy and passion trying to live up to the expectations of others!*** These expectations are passed on unquestioned from generation to generation and person to person. Those who question these expectations become the outcasts, the troublemakers, the rebellious and the sinners. But those who do not question the need to live up to the expectations of others become the conflicted, the unfulfilled, the shamefully guilty and the frustrated.

When I first saw the bumper sticker *QUESTION AUTHORITY*, I was young and still filled with the indoctrination of my upbringing. I thought, "Now there's a rebellious hippie type in that car." Later in my life that same bumper sticker evoked a cheer of "Right on!"

* * * * *

In 1961 psychologist Stanley Milgram created an experiment to see just how far people would go in inflicting pain and injury on others when instructed to do so by a perceived authority figure. He designed a machine with switches and voltage labels that he called a *shock generator*. Nearly a thousand people (the study subjects) took part in his experiment. The study subjects were going to play the role of a teacher and they were told that they were going to test the effect of punishment on a person's ability to learn. Each study subject was to ask a learner (in a separate room) to answer questions. Whenever the learner got the question wrong, the study subject was to shock the learner with ever-increasing voltages. At some point the learner would scream in pain and beg the study subject (the teacher) to stop. But the study supervisor would say in a neutral tone, "Please continue." Before the test, it had been mentioned that the learner could have some minor heart problems. Even when it appeared that the learner might be suffering some heart-related symptoms or might even have been knocked out, many of the study subjects continued at the insistence of the supervisor. Two out of three study subjects administered 150 volts or more to their learners – more than comes out of your wall plugs!

It turned out that the shock generator did not actually deliver any shocks, and that the "learners" were just actors who could scream really loudly. But the results of his experiments led Dr. Milgram to conclude, "I would say, on the basis of having observed a thousand people in the experiment, and having my own intuition shaped and informed by these experiments, that, if a system of death camps were set up in the United States of the sort we had seen in Nazi Germany, one would be able to find sufficient personnel for those camps in any medium sized American town."

Fifty years later, psychologist Jerry Burger repeated the Milgram experiment, wondering if people had become more compassionate. In 1961, 65% of study subjects (teachers) were willing to go up to and past the 150-volt shock. In 2011, 77% administered shocks exceeding 150 volts. But Dr. Burger took the experiment one step further. He added a second "teacher" who, like the learner, was also in on the experiment. As the two teachers reached higher voltages, the study subject (teacher #1) would begin to be hesitant about continuing. When the supervisor said, "It's imperative that you continue," teacher #2 (who was in on the experiment) would say to teacher #1, "You're right, it wouldn't be right to continue the shocks." In *every case* where this was done, teacher #1 said, "That's it. I'm not continuing."[1] Understanding the power of one person standing up and decrying the madness is vital if we are to dam the stream of cruelty before it becomes a raging river.

One interesting side note is that, when the test subjects were asked who would have been responsible for damaging a learner's heart, some said that they would have personally carried a lot of the blame. But most pointed at the test supervisor and said, "He would be. He was in charge of things. I trusted him to know what was right." One of the most horrific and absurd rationalizations that people give for carrying out inhumane behaviors is that they are "just doing their jobs" – i.e., just following orders. We often erroneously assume that people who are considered authority figures must know what they are doing or telling us to do, or they wouldn't have been given that position. This is an unacceptable excuse for our bad behavior and a complete rejection of personal responsibility. Each of us *is* responsible for our own behavior, whether it is our job, a responsibility we've been assigned, what we are told is a commandment from God, or a direct order from someone in authority over us.

* * * * *

The desire to please or avoid disappointing someone is so strong that it can lead people who consider themselves ethical to do things that they would find horrific if someone were to predict their behavior in advance. We hesitate to confront inappropriate behavior in others because we don't want to be rude or interfere, it could cause us to lose our jobs, or our religious leaders advise us to "forgive and forget" – but don't report it! But children are abused, sexual harassment continues and crooks get away with crime when we look the other way. Very often, a person learns that he can get his needs or wants met by imposing expectations on certain sensitive individuals because those individuals are always anxious to please or at least not disappoint. There *is* such a thing as being *too nice*. The great plight of society, in general, is that only a few of us are willing to take our personal responsibility seriously and stand up for the right thing even if it interferes with our own status quo. If we want society to change for the better, we must be willing to occasionally move out of our comfort zones.

Very often it is difficult to identify the authoritarian sources from which certain expectations come – but we *know* they are there. Religious upbringing, the prevalent images of manhood or womanhood and national patriotism create deeply embedded expectations that are adhered to on a very large scale. When we go against these expectations, the cost is severe disapproval and even violence. Parents let us know from an early age, either implicitly or explicitly, what they desire and expect from us. Our peers, especially in our teenage years, have a very strong influence over us since their non-acceptance can leave us isolated and miserable. Then there are those things that are more subtly but firmly embedded in our psyches such as prejudice and bigotry, familial or societal traditions, and the violence, stereotypes and misbehavior portrayed in the popular media.

Even children who hate going to church and inwardly reject its teachings have difficulty pulling away from a religion in which they are entrenched – a religion that could eventually hinder them from understanding how connected we all are with our Creator. People who have long since left the Catholic Church and might be horrified by the misdeeds and criminal acts of its priests and other leaders may still feel compelled to genuflect and cross themselves when entering a church. Old habits and beliefs are powerful and live within us long after we wish them gone. Gay men and women who are expelled from a religion or leave because they feel excluded may join organizations such as Dignity (for Catholics) or Affirmation (for

Mormons) to keep somewhat tethered to the organizations that have been such a strong, though painful, part of their lives.

As people move from childhood into the teen years, peer pressure becomes increasingly strong. If a person has the wrong kind of shoes or wears an inexpensive shirt with no designer label, he may begin to feel less accepted by his peers. This is the time when the perception of popularity hits maximum intensity. And popularity truly *is* an issue of perception. Who is popular and who is not is often based more on the self-confidence of certain individuals, and the lack thereof in others, than any other personality trait. While it can't hurt your popularity rating to be athletic, smart or exceptionally attractive, it is the person who, for whatever reason, has developed a sense of cool self-esteem who attracts followers. Some teens catch on early and learn to fake high levels of self-esteem and confidence regardless of their inner feelings. It is the unfortunate child who thinks of himself as a nerd or a sissy that gets bullied because he is always radiating what he feels inside. The saddest thing about the popularity scam is that the popular students are only popular because they have convinced other students to see them that way. We feel bad that we are not popular because we believe their insinuations that we are less then they are – less trendy, less important and less cool. They have somehow convinced us to allow them to create expectations in this sub-culture that they can live up to, but we cannot. Unfortunately, we often do not outgrow the roles we learn at this early age.

Popular, normal, moral, attractive, fashionable, part of the in-crowd, cool and so many other yardsticks of how we judge ourselves and others have to be created by someone. We rarely have any say about who is allowed to do this. The definitions have already been put in place by invisible committees and widely distributed by those who will benefit from these selective and exclusionary definitions. Oddly enough, these definitions include all the things that the definers see themselves as and exclude people who are not like them. These definitions become the memes of society – the unquestioned rules that are passed from generation to generation without critical evaluation or consideration of their origins. Very often they have no basis in reason or logic, but their stranglehold on us is powerful nevertheless. Fashion changes from year to year to the great benefit of fashion designers while other concepts such as normality and morality remain relatively fixed over time. But eventually even these concepts can metamorphose as we have seen with race and slavery, the role of women in society, and attitudes toward certain religious doctrines such as birth control and divorce.

For many people the most important expectations are those of their parents, and these are consequently some of the most difficult chains to break free from. "If I don't become a lawyer, it will shatter my parents' dreams." "If I come out of the closet and tell everyone I'm gay, it will break my mother's heart and humiliate her." "My father is determined that I will follow in his footsteps and become an officer in the army, but I have no interest in that." Many parents truly believe that it is the duty of their children to make them proud, happy and fulfilled, and children often feel the need to fulfill these expectations. Parents say they just want a better life for their children and want them to be happy and lead fulfilling lives. They sincerely view their expectations as what would be best for their children. Any child that really loves his parents can begin to feel very guilty when these expectations are brought up over and over, but the child simply wants something else for his life. However, it is *not* a child's responsibility to fulfill parental expectations. A child needs to seek his own path with his parents' guidance and help, but without expectations. Very often it is more a matter of the parents wanting to relive their mundane lives vicariously through their children, and their children's accomplishments become a great source for bragging. Or it could be that it will bring great embarrassment to the parents if a child chooses to travel an unconventional road. But again, *it is no child's responsibility to fulfill his parents' expectations!* And it is certainly a destructive thing for the child who has spent his life trying to live up to his parents' expectations to pass on this need to please to the next generation.

And what about God? It is amazing to me that people can attribute to the Creator of the Universe all the petty emotions of a relatively unevolved human. We flatter ourselves to think that God is watching our every action and adding or subtracting points from our heaven/hell tally. We say God has created us in His image, but the reverse is true; we have invented a god in our own image – in human physical form (male, of course), petty and judgmental, micromanaging our every move. But God has no ego. God has no need to judge. God is not jealous and is not waiting anxiously to send us to hell for not living up to godly expectations. God, or whatever your name for Source Spirit is, wants only that each eternal spirit evolves into an egoless, compassionate, nonjudgmental, loving and joyful being. God does not need to punish us because each dark thought we have or harmful act we commit is a punishment in and of itself because it adds a negative vector to our vector sum and inhibits our spiritual evolution. God's only desire is that we do those things that will bring us real light and joy.

To many people it is unthinkable not to have expectations of others. In his book "The Path to Love"[2], Deepak Chopra wrote about the destructive power of expectations. At first reading, I didn't comprehend this part of the book at all. How could I live my life without having expectations of others? Certainly everyone needs an idea of what would be expected from an ideal partner; and who could possibly raise children without having expectations of them?

How could God not have expectations of his creations? It was certainly a concept that did not compute. But the more I thought about it, the more this concept began to gel within me. I began to understand that most people get stuck trying to live up to the expectations of others or become frustrated when other people are not living up to theirs. I began to see it as a huge waste of time, energy and emotion. I became aware of people, including myself, that were miserable because they didn't want to disappoint anyone who had preconceived ideas about how they should live their lives.

I thought long and hard about the topic of expectations, and gradually I began to understand that expectations had no real benefit and that, most of the time, they just keep us stuck and hinder our personal evolution. This doesn't mean that we can't teach our children what we think are helpful ideas about getting through life, especially by example. It also doesn't mean that spouses can't talk to each other about what they would like to see more or less of in a relationship. And it certainly doesn't mean that we will have no reason to do good if God, our parents, and other authority figures don't lay their expectations on us. But it *does* mean that a mother whose heart can be broken because her children do not take the path she wants for them needs to understand that this is her problem to deal with, not her children's. A father's dreams that can be shattered because his children want to be something other than what he has imagined for them needs to start having more useful dreams. It also means that a person who expects his or her spouse to fill a gap in his or her life needs to develop a life of his or her own. *Our happiness is not the responsibility of our spouses, children or anyone else – it is only our own.*

Some of the most powerful forces in any society are gender-based expectations. Those who do not fit the image of manhood or womanhood are penalized and may be dealt with very harshly,

49

even violently. Usually the rules for being a man include the vilest of human behaviors: crude language, physicality (might makes right), not ever showing "soft" emotions, dominating others, destroying things, exercising power and the conquest of women (and never eating quiche, of course). In primitive times, some of these traits might have seemed necessary. But, in our day, they lead to gang violence, spousal abuse and lots of psychologically messed up men.

In more advanced cultures women have made significant progress in defying their former passive roles. But in less advanced cultures, women continue to be expected to play a subservient role to men. In addition to taking care of the home and children, women are often required to work in the fields and walk long distances to get water. Their roles in relationship to men can be very restrictive and most of us would view these roles to be unfair. Some cultures require women to walk behind the men, stay at home while men go out to restaurants and clubs, and do everything their husbands command them to do and never express their own opinions. Some cultures expect women to look beautiful and wear colorful clothing whereas other cultures cover their women from head to toe in ugly clothing in an attempt to avoid sexually arousing the males. In many of these cultures women are not supposed to enjoy sex at all and thousands of women have had their genitalia mutilated to prevent sexual pleasure and leave this pleasure only for the men. Women have been beaten and even killed because they displeased their husbands or other men. Guess who created these tribal rules.

Long held gender-based expectations are extremely difficult to change. No male wants to be a sissy-boy, especially when he could easily be bullied or worse for not being a "real man." Women are often afraid to be anything other than what religious traditions (mostly created by men) have told them they can be and risk being abused when they step outside their traditional roles. After being raised in highly religious communities, some women become very compliant with their given roles. In the 1970's an amendment to the U.S. Constitution was proposed which would give women a more equal standing with men. I remember being astounded at the number of Christian women (mostly in the Bible belt) who were interviewed and said something like, "My pastor says the Bible tells us that a woman should be subjugated to her man. And if the Bible says so, then God says so. And who am I to argue with God?" With women comprising more that 50% of the population of the U.S., the Equal Rights Amendment was soundly defeated.

The teachings of the Abrahamic religions are full of expectations. The Law of Moses in the Old Testament is full of commandments concerning diet, sexual relations, Sabbath day restrictions and almost every detail of daily life. Those who practice these religions may have particular difficulty grasping these new ideas about expectations. It is interesting to note, however, that the teachings of Jesus focus more on what will bring us greater joy and fulfillment rather than obsessively warning us of the punishment that will be incurred with the breaking of each law. The idea that expectations are detrimental is a relatively new concept for most people. The greatest problem with expectations is that they keep us from understanding the very important principle that *we each have the responsibility to learn for ourselves what will bring us the greatest amount of joy and spiritual evolution.* The day we rid ourselves of the often arbitrary and irrational expectations of others will be the day we feel like caged birds that have been set free to fly to the heights. It might be uncomfortable at first, but after a little flying time, it will be one of the most exhilarating of all the joyful events we can ever experience.

Chapter Six

EVOLVING ISN'T BETRAYAL

The whole point of being alive is to evolve into the
complete person you were intended to be.

Oprah Winfrey

Why is it so difficult to evaluate new information critically and replace old thought processes and attitudes with those that are more accurate and useful? Sometimes the problem is that we don't know how to evaluate new information from a truly unbiased standpoint based on reason and logic. Often, however, the bigger problem is that we don't want to consider new ideas or attitudes because they would conflict with those we were given early on in our lives with the expectation that we would keep and honor these forever.

From our earliest days we view some people as people we should revere, look up to, respect or honor. Sometimes these are people we truly love and admire – parents, family members, spiritual leaders, good friends and mentors. Sometimes they are people in positions of authority whose respect we would like to earn and whom we believe we should love and admire, whether we truly do or not. The power they have to create feelings of loyalty is great, and their ability to engender feelings of betrayal if we should abandon the things they have taught us is often even greater.

When respected people in our lives teach us values and give us information, most often what they do is well intended. Our parents teach us what they believe to be good and useful concepts, but most often these concepts are the same ones their parents and other teachers gave them with best intentions. These teachings usually are not critically evaluated before being passed on to us. Usually our parents just accepted these beliefs and information as being true because they did not want to betray the respected people in their lives. So religious, political, ethnic, social and worldview ideas are passed from generation to generation with little thought as to their validity or usefulness. Unfortunately, it is ideas that we get in this way that usually have the most power to bind us with thin threads that should be easy to break – but we dare not even struggle to free ourselves from them.

* * * * *

In some countries elephants have been used to do much heavy and difficult work and can accomplish things that humans alone cannot do. When fully grown they are massive and can perform great feats of strength. It therefore puzzled a man who was passing some work elephants that they were being held by only a small rope tied to one front leg on one end and a small wooden stake on the other end. The elephants obviously could have broken away easily, but they didn't.

Seeing a boy training a small elephant a short distance away, the man walked over to ask him why the elephants did not break loose.

"Well," said the young man, "we use the same size rope to tie them up with when they are very young and much smaller. At that time the rope is sufficient to hold them. They grow up believing that the rope will always hold them, and they never try to break free when they are fully grown unless something scares them or they need food or water."

* * * * *

Perhaps the strangest loyalty we have is loyalty to ourselves. If we accept a new thought process, are we not betraying what we have thought and believed for so many years? How could we have been so wrong for so long? The reality is that being "wrong" doesn't matter. We simply arrive at a point in our evolutionary process at which we have a choice. We can continue to believe in what has not served us well or we can embrace new ideas and a better and more useful worldview. We don't have to feel stupid, ashamed or guilty about abandoning the ideas that previously shaped our lives. We should feel joyful and enlightened to have a new and better way of looking at things. If we decide in the future that the new ideas we embrace today need to be updated, we should just consider that a part of evolving and growing. The joy of discovering new information and putting old information together in new ways should never create guilt or feelings of self-betrayal.

Unfortunately many of us spend most of our lives trying to satisfy the expectations that were kneaded into us when we were young and most vulnerable. Most often we see it as an unquestioned truth that the authority figures in our lives have given us all that we need and all that is correct for living the rest of our lives; we need not look outside the box they told us contains everything necessary. Since we had great love and respect for these people while we were growing up, the need for an absolute all-good or all-bad judgment call creates great difficulties. It is rare that anyone with an absolutist mindset will judge parents and friends to be entirely bad, so they are left only with the all-good option. When we deem people as all-good, we feel we have to accept the entirety of what these loved and respected people gave us in order to avoid defining them in a non-revering way.

When we cast off old learnings, how do we deal with feelings that we are betraying important people in our lives? What about parents who taught us the religious concepts that may now be holding us back? What do we tell those who taught us that patriotism must be absolute and unquestioned? How about our friends who helped us form racist or sexist attitudes? What about religious leaders who created the beliefs that non-Christians, gay people, or people who have sex outside a sanctified relationship are going to burn for eternity in hell? Perhaps we could say something like this. "Thank you for giving me the best ideas you could about what I should think about life and how I should live it. I have listened to it and taken all of it into consideration. Much of it I find wonderful and useful to this very day, but some of it no longer works for me and I have replaced it with concepts that I find more helpful. I am not criticizing your beliefs. Please do not feel angry or guilty about giving me what you sincerely believed, because you meant it well and I love you for it. And do not feel disappointed because I have chosen to go my own route. Perhaps you would like to know why I have come to a different way of thinking. If not, that's okay too. But please realize that I will no longer feel guilty about not living up to your expectations of me."

Regardless of what we know or feel on a conscious level, the actuality of telling someone, even ourselves, that we no longer can live by the principles we earlier lived by is far more difficult than it should be. When we spend most of our lives trying to live up to others' expectations, we usually end up disappointing them as well as limiting our own lives. It can be a very difficult process to decide that we ourselves are the ones who, in the end, have to decide what will bring us the most joy and progression in life. Sometimes we make mistakes and have to re-evaluate our choices. When we are concerned with what works for us rather than whether others will react with disappointment or feelings of betrayal, we will make far better choices.

Here we need to remember that nothing is absolute. If we reject some of the things our parents, religions or peers have given us, it does not mean that *all* they have given us is wrong. It is very common for humans to become disillusioned and even bitter when they realize that someone or some institution has created unnecessary roadblocks in their personal evolution. This bitterness is not useful and may keep us from benefiting from any wonderful concepts they gave us.

Most of us have heard the phrase "Recovering Catholic" or "Recovering Mormon," meaning those who have left the religions they grew up in may still have flashbacks of guilt or of longing for past beliefs and practices. Abandoning a former church or being abandoned by it may create bitterness and resentment for anything connected with it. This might include family, friends, feelings of closeness to God, prayer, spiritual music or scriptures. But why throw the baby out with the bathwater? The church might try to teach us that it is our only connection with our Higher Power. That is nonsense! We are all a part of God and God is part of us. One spiritual energy flows through all things in the Universe. What our relationship to God is after separating from a religious organization is all in our minds. If we think that our connection to God is gone, it will be – but only because we have severed that connection. If we think we're not allowed to pray anymore, we won't be able to. If we think that God will not bless us with abundance if we don't give money to the church, we may create that lack of abundance.

If we think we are damned to hell, we will certainly create that hell within ourselves.

Why can we not keep the joyful things we got from religion and discard that which is not useful to us? The church doesn't want us to be able to do that, but it cannot control what we believe unless we allow it to. Excommunication or disfellowship from a religious society is a traumatic process, even when we are told it is all done in love. But it is only a process of men, not of God, and it should not separate us from God. On the contrary, deciding that we can look outside of a closed religionist box can open up a whole new world of possibilities for spiritual growth. We may develop a better understanding of the God that lives within us and the Source that we can connect with outside of a religious setting. We are certainly allowed to keep all that is good and beautiful about our religious heritage and add to it. We may enrich our lives by adding meditation (mindfulness), yoga, reiki, intentional thinking and other practices to our religious traditions. These practices do not detract from our religious lives unless we are convinced that they do, but they do give us greater depths of spiritual understanding.

There are times when it is necessary to completely disassociate ourselves from that which has caused us so much pain and has inhibited our spiritual progression so intensely. That is okay, too. If a job causes so much stress that it affects physical or mental health, then we need to look for another place to work, as difficult as that may be. After years of feeling guilt and oppression from a particular religion, we may need to get completely away from it in order to heal. If any of our relationships become so toxic that they are doing more harm than good, then a time of complete separation may become necessary, at least for a while.

Relationships are some of the most difficult situations in which we may need to let go of the old. All societies place high value on the longevity of relationships. When children are involved, the reason for this is clear. But it is a simple fact that individuals do not always evolve in the same direction. At the beginning of a relationship we experience infatuation, sex and new discovery, but these fade over time. When physical intimacy fades, the basis for the relationship will wane if other common interests and activities are not in place. Sometimes religion will provide a common bond, but religion without spirituality is usually not enough. Sometimes relationships stay together for the children, but when the children leave, the reason for the relationship often leaves too. There are numerous other reasons for relationships to continue even when its members have evolved in divergent directions. Business, social, financial, and familial considerations often keep people together when their lives would actually be better if they separated.

What's important here is that people should not remain in a relationship strictly for the sake of longevity. When two people have evolved in different directions, there is not necessarily a good direction or a bad one. They are just different directions. But good/ bad judgments will almost always enter into the dysfunctional behavior during this time of stress, and one or both parties may feel betrayed. How can one leave a relationship that, at one time, was so positive and significant? Removing judgment from these situations leaves us free to make decisions based on current conditions. Starting over can be frightening, and many people choose to remain stuck in the current miserable conditions that are familiar rather than face a scary, but possibly better, unknown. Being stuck in a place of fear is one of the biggest inhibitors of people moving into new realms. It can affect both parties or just one.

Where do we turn at such a time? Sometimes an outside observer such as a counselor can offer insights that will help us see what we have been blind to because of emotional shadings. Sometimes a state of peaceful coexistence can be reached allowing each person to pursue individual interests while sharing a common living place and enjoying those things they continue to have in common. But no one should think that the way they have lived in the past is how things must continue. We all have stereotyped ideas of how couples should live together. The "happily ever after" couple that agrees on everything and lives in wedded bliss exists only rarely, and usually because one or the other keeps quiet a lot or is a doormat. There are many ways to live as a couple, and sometimes a new, less intense perspective will help. The little irritating things that go on in a relationship do not have to have the charge they have had – perspective is so important here. The things that irritate us do so because we have assigned them a value of being irritating. Leaving the toilet seat up or forgetting an anniversary can cause a tiny or huge annoyance – we get to choose. After all has been considered, as scary as it may be to jump off the cliff, sometimes a relationship may have to be dissolved.

Another very difficult situation to deal with is a miserable job. Not all of us can have jobs that keep us fulfilled and happy all week long. However, the moving of wealth toward the top has created a situation that makes the workplace in corporate America more and more difficult to live with. The top one percent of Americans now owns 42% of the wealth. Since the mid 1970's wages in America have flattened out while productivity and corporate profits have skyrocketed. We are being required to work longer and harder for less. As long as we continue to believe that this is just how capitalism has to work, we will never demand the changes that so badly need to be made in the workplace. For, just as we have done with concepts like patriotism, we have allowed ourselves to be convinced that our current form of capitalism is the best way to structure a society's economy. We dare not even speak criticism of this system. However, capitalism, like any other economic structure, can be redefined to benefit all people. Capitalism is like fire – a good servant, but a terrible master.

That being said, we need to consider the adverse effects versus the benefits of remaining in our jobs. Sometimes the way we see our jobs is more a matter of perception than actual circumstances. A person may think that his coworkers are ridiculing him when, in reality, they feel just as insecure as he does. Or he may think that more is expected of him than others in his workplace while others are thinking that he gets away with doing too little. Most of the time better communications will help resolve any perceived stressful areas. There is, unfortunately, a good chance that someone with a bad perception of his current workplace will carry that perception to the next workplace. If we expect every moment of every day to be joyful and stress free, we will have a hard time finding any job that will suit us. Very often we have the same fanciful expectations of a job as we do of the perfect spouse. However, neither a spouse nor a job needs to be perfect for us to be able to enjoy our relationship with it. We should, however, not feel that we are betraying the company we have been with for a long time if we find there is something out there we would enjoy doing more.

The places in life where we can get stuck are far too numerous to mention here. There will be many times when we won't think we are stuck because we have been taught, "that's just the way life is." Seeing life as an evolutionary process helps us understand that what we loved and benefited from yesterday may be causing problems for us today. The concepts that made sense to us at one time may need to be replaced or modified as we gain new information and insights. The jobs, relationships, religious and social organizations, or the friendships that were once so meaningful to us may change in their value as our vector sum gradually changes. The things that brought us warm and fuzzy feelings so strongly at one time may eventually lose most of their warmth and fuzziness. It's acceptable, and important, to evolve. The transition to new thoughts or circumstances may be awkward and uncomfortable at first. We may lose our source of connection with familiar people, leaving us lonely and disoriented, but new connections can be found. We should be careful, though, that we don't become disillusioned with our early life teachings and become angry, mean-spirited and self-destructive as we rebel against those teachings by making ourselves into the exact opposite of what we were taught. In the Mormon religion, children who want to rebel against their parents and/or religion will often show that rebellion by beginning to drink and smoke – things that can ruin their health and even destroy their lives. Rebellion doesn't always work in one's favor.

Change is inevitable, and it can be powerful or nominal. Change can be created by random outside influences or by choices made within. The more we control the changes in our lives, the more likely those changes will bring us to a better place. We must not allow feelings of guilt or betrayal to keep good changes from occurring. Even though we may be aware of this, breaking through these deeply implanted feelings and moving on in a better direction remains one of the most difficult things anyone can do. Just as it took others years to implant these feelings in us, it can take us a long time to break free from them. Rather than feel frustrated, we can marvel at, and find joy in, the learning experiences that are taking place each day. Feelings of self-betrayal or the betrayal of others should never keep us crouching in our boxes.

Chapter Seven

GOOD VS. BAD

*There is nothing either good or bad
but thinking makes it so.*

William Shakespeare

Throughout the ages, the concepts of good versus bad, sin versus righteousness, and heaven versus hell have permeated all cultures in some form or another. For these concepts to exist, at some point in time, a consensus on what makes something "good" or "bad" must be reached. There are things that are generally seen as harmful to the society such as doing harm to others or depriving others of things that make their lives happy and peaceful. These concepts of bad or evil acts generally result in societal rules (laws). Those individuals that act counter to these laws are usually punished or excluded from the society (imprisoned or exiled) for at least a time with the hope that they will learn that their disruptive behavior will not be tolerated.

As a society becomes more complex and more diverse groups struggle for power, the delineation between good and bad becomes less clear. Slavery may be considered acceptable in a society where the wealthy and powerful can benefit from this practice. Killing may become "necessary" if a leader can convince the society that it has something to fear or that there is something important to gain from war. In a capitalistic society, doing anything to accumulate wealth can in some way be rationalized as being acceptable and even lauded, even if it adversely affects a large number of people.

What is considered good and bad can also be a part of the memes that infect any given society. As mentioned before, eating bacon, ham or other pork products is completely moral in a large part of the world. But in Islamic societies it is one of the most visible sins that a person can commit. A friend of mine who was stationed in Turkey for several years often had Turkish friends over for dinner. Even though they had all been there before and discussed the pork issue with him, each time they arrived, their first inquiry was whether there were any pork products in the meal – just to be sure. In Hindu cultures it is just as much of a sin to eat beef because cattle have somehow become sacred in that religion. In my Mormon upbringing, coffee, tea, tobacco and alcohol were forbidden and the great debate was whether one could drink colas because they contain caffeine. As a child it was strange indeed to see teachers and other people I respected drinking coffee or beer. Somehow I had to rationalize how they could still be good people and do this. "Don't judge them. They just don't have the higher law," I was told.

Memes, or mind viruses, can affect many aspects of a society, thereby causing people to see all sorts of things as good or bad. When I travel, I always try to learn the customs of a certain area. Should one take his shoes off when entering a household? If it is acceptable to leave them on, is it acceptable to show the bottoms of one's shoes when crossing one's legs? In America it is considered effeminate for a man to sit with his legs crossed with knees touching and the soles of both feet facing the floor. But in older societies, including Europe and Middle Eastern countries, it is extremely poor manners to sit with one ankle on the other knee with the bottom of one shoe showing. This obviously comes from the days when there were no paved roads or sidewalks and one could have mud or even manure on the bottoms of ones shoes. But origins are usually not considered as reasons for whether or not traditions should persist.

Our families, religions, ethnicities, schools, media, entertainment and daily interactions also indoctrinate us on what we should regard as good or bad. We are all very much influenced by the environments we grew up in. So, you may ask, what is the problem with making good/bad judgments as you journey through life? When you judge something or someone as being bad, it automatically inhibits you from looking at anything beneficial that might come from that person, organization or idea. There may be enlightening books you won't let yourself read or television programming you won't let yourself watch. There may be people you never allow yourself to get to know and concepts they might bring you that you will never hear. There may be useful ideas that never get considered and inspirations you may never enjoy if you have already judged their source, for whatever reason, to be bad. In short, you cannot see the full spectrum of anything or anyone if you make good/bad judgment calls right from the beginning.

To judge something or someone as being good can also be problematic unless certain things are understood. Again, if we consider someone to be a good person, we find it difficult to understand how he or she could possibly have given us information and traditions that might inhibit our lives. We may feel an obligation to live up to their expectations, even when we want and need something very different. We may have difficulty understanding the flaws and weaknesses of those we consider such good people. In the Harry Potter series, Harry tries to comprehend how his father could have been anything less than perfect when he was a young man. He also tries to deal with the flaws he hears about in Professor

Dumbledore. It simply does not compute that people he thinks are so extraordinary could ever have been less than the admirable characters they later evolved into. Everyone is in the process of evolution. We have strengths in some areas and challenges in others. We are all learning. Seeing people as generally good is a great way to think, and we don't have to let occasional flaws interfere with the good we see in them, nor do we have to believe that everything they want to pass on to us is perfect and right for us.

We come to realize that ideas, organizations, cultures, governments and belief systems can be good without being absolutely perfect, or flawed without being absolutely bad or evil. This means that we can consider our government and country to be great while still understanding that corrupt people and bad laws need to be replaced by people of integrity and laws that benefit all. It means that the religion we grew up with may have given us some moments of warm acceptance, but it can still contain dogma and behaviors that can hurt and hinder our full development. One's metropolitan, small-town, religious, Hispanic, Asian, African-American or other ethnic culture may be the best ever, but there can still be memes and traditions in any culture that would be better abandoned if one wants to be free to explore all of life's possibilities.

Since things have only the value we assign to them, putting good/ bad judgments on everything can create the need for rationalization. As discussed in chapter two, the need for rationalization is based on what we think is immoral or sinful. If we have come to the belief that eating junk food is a terrible thing, it can create almost as much guilt as stealing that junk food from the grocery store. But neither of these will bother people who are good rationalizers. Rationalization is our attempt to get rid of the pangs of guilt. Some people will say that guilt is a good thing because it will keep us from doing bad things. Why then do we try to get rid of the guilt in any way possible? Why don't we just get rid of the behavior that causes the guilt? Therein lies the fundamental problem with rationalization. We feel the initial discomfort from the guilt, but our behavior never really changes because rationalization gets rid of that discomfort. In fact, guilt very often increases the detrimental behavior. The guilt smokers have from lighting up one cigarette when they are trying to quit often causes them to crave the comfort of their best friend – another cigarette. A dieter who blows his rigid diet will often eat what he shouldn't to console the guilt resulting from eating what he shouldn't have.

Guilt, as emotions go, is far more destructive than it is useful. How then do we change undesirable behavior if not through guilt? While many religious traditions try to control our behavior through guilt, some spiritual ideologies believe that becoming conscious and aware is the answer to changing without guilt. The concept of being conscious and aware is largely unknown and somewhat difficult to define in western cultures. Here we think that everything we do, think or desire is either good or sinful. It is nearly impossible to view ourselves without self-judgment and negative emotional charge. Becoming conscious and aware allows us to simply pay attention to what is happening presently in our lives and to determine whether our current thoughts and actions will help or hinder our development. We try to observe our actions and those of others without the knee-jerk feelings that we usually attach to the events in our lives. We take a moment to reflect on things as they happen, detrimental or useful, and try to determine what we might do to avoid a recurrence of the detrimental and promote the useful. We may need to apologize and make restitution if our actions have harmed others, but endless shameful guilt will seldom help us change our behavior for the better. Guilt may even take us to adapt the victim's stance where one must try to find someone or something to blame for all that is amiss in his or her life, whereas consciousness helps us realize that we have within us the strongest force for positive self-change.

When you're conscious and aware, your life becomes like a movie starring you that you are watching from the audience. Being able to watch your life more objectively as an observer removes the emotional charge and judgment from how you deal with the drama in your life. You are more able to stay emotionally detached and to make decisions based on reason and logic rather than on anger, hurt feelings or a desire for revenge. You consider the long-term consequences of your emotions and actions rather than responding with pre-programmed impulses such as anger or depression. As you practice paying attention to your life rather than merely reacting to it, you will find that your ego plays a smaller role in your decision making. You will find that being "right" becomes less important than being effective or kind. Winning becomes less important than cooperating for the benefit of all. If you can keep your ego out of your interpersonal relationships, you will create an energy between yourself and others that is healing rather than divisive. If you can refrain from judging yourself as bad, you will not have the need to blame other people for your weak areas. When you watch your own life-movie, you can more clearly see the triggers and the circumstances that cause you to revert to old addictions or participate in self-defeating behavior.

Most people have not developed the ability to focus on the things going on in the present moment. They are always worrying about and planning what they will do if this or that happens in the future or looking back and fretting over the past. They see the present only as an inconvenience that must be tolerated until a more desirable future arrives. What they do not realize is that the future never gets here. When the future arrives, it suddenly becomes the present. What one's life is in the present is only a summation of all the vectors created in the "now" moments of the past. (This may all sound tangled and twisted, but after a few moments of thought, it should become clearer.) We can plan for the future, but we cannot live there. The past is only a history of all the moments that were once "nows." The sum of all those past nows is what we are at this moment in time. Most importantly, what we will be a week from now, a year from now, or ten years from now *can only be the sum of all our present moments between now and that future time.* Therefore, we cannot ignore what we are feeling, thinking or doing right now hoping for something better in the future, because the future depends totally on what we are feeling, thinking or doing right now. Eckhart Tolle has some great discussions of the power of living in the present in his writings.

Many of us find it uncomfortable or even miserable to live in our current condition – or at least parts of it. We would much rather live in a more glorious future. However, if we cannot see the good or find something to learn in this current moment, our future cannot be any better. It is all a matter of perspective. One person can have pretty much the same material goods and circumstances as his neighbor, but one will be miserable and the other will be blissfully happy. If we get stuck in a less-than-lovely "now" that keeps repeating itself, it can be difficult to escape to a more positive future. The more we allow ourselves to be trapped by other people's expectations, the less we will be able to move forward with hope. Escaping rigid definitions of good or bad that have kept us confined allows us to discover other perspectives that will help our spiritual evolution. The more we live in the past or the future, the less attention we will pay to the nows, and the nows are, after all, the building blocks of our entire existence.

* * * * *

There is a Taoist story of an old farmer who had worked his crops for many years. One day his horse ran away. Upon hearing the news, his neighbors came to visit. "Such bad luck," they said sympathetically.

"May be," the farmer replied. The next morning the horse returned, bringing with it three other wild horses.

"How wonderful," the neighbors exclaimed.

"May be," replied the old man. The following day, his son tried to ride one of the untamed horses, was thrown, and broke his leg. The neighbors again came to offer their sympathy on his misfortune.

"May be," answered the farmer. The day after, military officials came to the village to draft young men into the army. Seeing that the son's leg was broken, they passed him by. The neighbors congratulated the farmer on how well things had turned out.

"May be," said the farmer.[1]

* * * * *

If we buy into the mentality that people or events have to be all good or all bad, we are much more likely to be pliable clay for the people who desire to have control over us. We will play into the hands of the fear mongers who come up with endless strings of things to be afraid of. They shout from our radios and televisions that the terrorism danger level is orange and about to turn red. When we become numb to that, they tell us that gay marriage will destroy our society. When that topic becomes blasé, they talk about the threat of socialism, then illegal immigrants, and then the Muslims. If they can paint any group or concept as something to be feared, we will let them take us into insane wars, strip us of our civil rights, take our money and turn it to dust, and lead us in any direction they want to. Of course, the things that we are supposed to be afraid of rarely turn out to be as dangerous as they have been painted. Gay marriage, in the states that allow it, has not brought commerce to a halt or caused the disintegration of anyone's family.

Fortunately, younger generations are breaking away from the typecasting that others are trying to convince them is necessary. They tend to see people everywhere as human beings with complex spectra like their own, only with cultures, traditions and governments that have created different circumstances and thought processes. We need to get rid of the simplicity of labeling everything good or bad, and instead, we need to look for solutions to problems. Poverty, greed, intolerance, poor education, the deterioration of our environment, and constant conflict and violence are problems that can be solved, but not by saying, "Those are the bad guys over there." In our own lives, we should first question why we have been told that some things are good and others are bad. Being conscious and aware allows us the ability to reasonably determine which things are of benefit to us and which things will hold us back. If we decide that something in our lives is hindering us from moving in the best direction, it is far better to look for effective ways to tackle the problem than to wallow in the depressive energy of guilt.

In a time when people need to come together to solve some serious problems, it is critical that we understand that divisive forces will prohibit solutions. We need to drop the walls that separate us from other people, discard the stereotypes and get rid of the anger so that we can work cooperatively for the benefit of all. Seeing everything and everyone as good or bad only divides us when we need to be dropping our swords and embracing our sameness.

Chapter Eight

THE SINNER MUST
BE PUNISHED!

*Power is of two kinds. One is obtained by the fear of
punishment and the other by acts of love. Power based
on love is a thousand times more effective and permanent
than the one derived from fear of punishment.*

Mahatma Gandhi

In the Sermon on the Mount, Jesus said, "Ye hath heard that it hath
been said, An eye for an eye, and a tooth for a tooth: But I say unto
you, That ye resist not evil: but whosoever shall smite thee on thy
right cheek, turn to him thy other also. And if any man will sue thee
at the law, and take away thy coat, let him have thy cloak also. And
whosoever shall compel thee to go a mile, go with him twain. Give
to him that asketh of thee, and from him that would borrow of thee
turn not thou away. Ye hath heard that it hath been said, Thou shalt
love thy neighbour, and hate thine enemy. But I say unto you, Love
your enemies, bless them that curse you, do good to them that hate
you, and pray for them which despitefully use you and persecute
you." (Matt. 5:38-44, King James Version)

Most Christians would tell you that they truly believe in these words and even that they live by them, but the United States has the largest number per capita of incarcerated people in the world. We continue to execute men and women, and we jail non-violent people with drug addiction and mental problems and offer them little help in conquering their demons. It's as if people who don't conform to established moral standards somehow become non-humans. Our primary concern is that, above all – before any other consideration of compassion, humanity, nonjudgmentalism or giving our fellow man a helping hand – first and foremost, *the sinner must be punished!*

The concept of sin varies widely from culture to culture. In many non-Abrahamic religions the concept of sin is quite different from that in Judaism, Christianity and Islam. Many people have a very different view of man's relationship with God. The Abrahamic belief is that God has given man a large number of rituals, commandments and rules that must be adhered to in order for man to *please* God. The better one adheres to these rules and rituals, the more one wins God's favor and the greater is his reward in the hereafter. Man has only one existence to reach his maximum evolution and to win his place in Heaven. Any unrepented screw-ups will send him to hell for eternity. According to some Protestant versions of Christianity, all you really have to do is accept Jesus Christ as your personal savior. Others, such as Catholicism and Mormonism, require adherence to a large number of rules and rituals. But there are other God formats to consider.

Other religions and traditions see the human being as an eternal spiritual entity that continues to incarnate (I'll call it "suiting up") in order to learn more life lessons, overcome spiritual weaknesses, experience new circumstances in order to gain depth, or help others in their evolution. We get to choose which things we want to work on in this lifetime and also what we want to experience to help us become as spiritually evolved as we want to become. This God format believes that God exists in all humans and all humans are part of God. That is, God and man are not separate. In this case, the concept of sin is much less cut and dried. There is Yin and Yang, the light and dark side of the force, the beneficial and the detrimental in all of us. *Sin is simply something we do that inhibits our spiritual evolution.* They can be sins of commission or omission (bad things you do or good things you don't do). As we progress we will choose to learn more difficult lessons until we become self-controlled, compassionate beings. If we get caught up in ego and do a lot of damaging things, we will accumulate a large amount of dark energy that will need to be compensated for as part of our spiritual progression. This payback is sometimes called karma. But this karma will not necessarily hold us back if we deeply and truly learn the necessary lessons from our mistakes. Each lifetime is a chance to evolve in ways that may not have been available to us in earlier lives. We may have mentors that help us learn our lessons more effectively, or we may need to figure things out by ourselves. "Sin" becomes a part of our course work and has a very beneficial role to play if we understand its true nature.

When we talk about the concepts of sin and punishment we are really talking about ego, judgment and revenge. All people are at different places in their evolutionary journey. To require that every sin be met with its punishment is totally based in ego. It is our way of saying, "I am a better person than you because I did not make the particular mistake you made. Therefore I should get a prize and you should get a punishment." That is pure ego talking.

But what about justice? Is it fair that a person who is only a vicious gossip should be treated no differently than someone who holds up a bank? Surprisingly, justice is also purely a requirement of the ego. In societies where people are rewarded with heaven or punished with hell, justice has great importance and it becomes very intricate and complicated. Someone must figure out how severe every transgression is and what the appropriate punishment will be. Religion almost always plays a part in the making of the laws and meting out punishments (Jesus drank wine, but we never hear of him smoking a joint – therefore we celebrate alcohol and punish weed). At one time speaking out against the church was punishable by death. So justice is always connected to the tribal rules, and there is always conflict regarding the determination of who gets to make the rules. Does abortion become a crime? Do corporate robbers get any punishment at all? Why are acts that harm the planet minimally punished, but we feel we must continue an incredibly expensive war on illegal drugs?

In the 20th chapter of Matthew in the New Testament, Jesus tells the parable of the laborers hired to work in the vineyard. Throughout the day the lord of the vineyard went out and hired laborers to work in his vineyard. At the end of the day, he paid them each a penny, regardless of when they started working. (That was in the days when a penny would buy a burger and a shake – lots of inflation since then). The ones who had worked all day grumbled that it was not fair that they should get the same pay as those who started much later in the day. The vineyard's owner told them that they had all received fair pay since they were getting what they were promised, so why were they concerned about what the others received? Jesus told other parables about justice vs. forgiveness and, from the cross, he said, "Father, forgive them, for they know not what they do." He did *not* say, "Father, I'm glad you have some nasty punishments lined up for these sinners, because this really hurts!"

Generally revenge is what people want when they say they want justice. When people say they have closure after someone has been punished for a crime against them or someone they love, they really mean that vengeance has now been meted out. People who understand and have fully developed the attribute of compassion will be thrilled when someone with problems finally learns an important life lesson, whether at the beginning of the day in the vineyard or at the end. Justice and revenge are not as important to these evolved people as healing. They have chosen to put out a higher-vibration energy rather than a lower one. In doing so, they have not only benefited their own physical and spiritual health, but they have radiated the energy of Love out into the world, and it will be felt.

The other reason that people seem to love punishment is because it is supposed to be a deterrent to crime or breaking the tribal rules. From the many studies that have been done on this over the years, some interesting things have been found. In Cincinnati, gang members were brought in to meet with police, clergy and social workers. They were asked to stop the violence and were given a clear message that violence was wrong and that it killed innocent people and damaged their community. Surprisingly, the gang members were dissuaded more from violence with a moral plea than with the fear of punishment alone.[1] In a number of studies it was shown that prison time has very little deterrent effect until around the age of 18. After that point it seems to increase deterrence somewhat for a time and then decrease with age. It also depended on the length of the prison sentence. One's first introduction into prison is a deep psychic and social shock. The first few days have the greatest deterrent impact and that increases for up to two years. After that it diminishes very rapidly. A sentence of five years means the prisoner is twice as likely to commit future crimes than if he had not been imprisoned at all. For ten-year sentences, it is four times more likely they will commit crimes. Crimes committed after a prisoner is released from jail become more destructive and serious the longer he has spent in jail. This is understandable since prison is a college for crime. It hardens criminals making them more antisocial, vicious and dangerous, and it creates the desire for revenge on the society that required "justice" for them. By the time they come out of longer prison stays, all they know is the criminal mentality, and they have very few skills for living in a non-prison environment.[2]

Then there is the problem of non-violent drug addiction. We have over two million people in America's prisons, and about one-fourth of them were convicted for drug offenses. In one typical state (Minnesota) it costs taxpayers approximately $32,700 per year for each inmate. Providing drug addiction treatment outside of jail costs about $2,000 to $7,000 per person. The addiction patients are also *not* imbued with the prison/crime culture and, in many cases, can continue to take care of their families and earn a living. After a patient has been treated and has a relapse, jail time is actually harmful to the users' sobriety since they no longer have their normal support system, which is an important part of recovery. Participants in Brooklyn's Drug Treatment Alternative to Prison (DTAP) program were 67% less likely to return to prison than a group leaving prison without completing any similar program. When drug addiction is actually treated appropriately rather than just punished, it cuts down on the crime associated with it, and addicts become functional tax-paying citizens. Such treatment shows them that we see them as human beings with treatable problems instead of monsters with no value at all.[3]

Judging other people makes no sense when we fully understand what a complex sum of vectors each person is. Many powerful influences have contributed to create what each person is at a given moment. A person's genetics not only determine how he or she looks but also how he or she thinks or feels. Genetic coding, along with environmental factors, determines the levels of important neurotransmitters in a person's mind and body. Many scientific studies have shown that these neurotransmitters play a large role in pathologic criminal behavior. Some people have such severely deranged brain chemistry that they must be removed from society to prevent harm they might cause until we can come up with a better way to deal with them. For these people incarceration is an unfortunate necessity.

Neurotransmitter levels can also have a large influence on whether a person has an addictive susceptibility and tends to use alcohol, tobacco, prescription or illicit drugs or other things to self-medicate deficits in these important brain molecules. Such molecules may help determine whether a person overeats, reacts poorly to stress, has large amounts of anxiety and/or depression, or is constantly angry and aggressive. It is easy to believe that people simply choose good behavior or bad behavior when, in reality, our lives are much more complex than that.

The circumstances under which a person is raised also contribute greatly to his behavior. The memes and sealed premises a person inherits from his tribe will play an important role throughout his life. How he interacts with society, what his ambitions and goals are, and what opportunities he has are very much dependent on the circumstances of his younger years. We've seen many times how young people with the right teacher, mentor, friends or family members have pulled themselves out of their less-than-optimal circumstances to become bright and inspired contributors to society. This does not happen, however, unless someone in that society sees these people as more than what their early life circumstances have created. To see a person's hidden potential, one must bring love, compassion, patience and hope where very little of these things have been present before. We must, as a nation and planet, determine the kind of future we will create for ourselves by changing how we treat each other. In these trying days we have the option of living in a dog-eat-dog, every-man-for-himself society or living in a cooperative, compassionate and caring way so that we can all survive and thrive together.

* * * * *

Clinton Truman Duffy had worked at San Quentin State Prison for several years as a secretary to the warden. In 1940, the Governor fired the prison board and Duffy was asked to be a temporary warden while another was sought. As he began his 30-day stint as warden, he remembered the words of his father concerning prisoners, "These men are human. They are much the same as the rest of us. They are unfortunates who have been imprisoned. If these men were given a chance, they might redeem themselves, and we should try to help them."

Up to this point, prisoners at San Quentin had been treated like filthy animals. Duffy wanted to change this dynamic and began by doing away with corporal punishment and started dismantling the dungeon. Where prisoners once ate out of buckets, he established a cafeteria complete with dietician, and he desegregated the dining hall. He fired the Yard Captain who encouraged brutality and eliminated whips and other brutal devices. The board of prison directors sensed the change in the atmosphere among the inmates and the employees and hired Duffy on permanently.

During his eleven and one-half year administration Clinton Duffy built a better educational system, introduced a job-training program and started a guidance center. He instituted a prison newspaper for which he wrote a regular column and later instituted the first inmate-developed radio programs. He put inmates to work on reclaiming materials from the Pearl Harbor wreckage and manufacturing supplies for the Navy. He used "honor camps" where carefully selected inmates worked on state roads, assisted in farm labor and even fought forest fires in the mountains. Many men distinguished themselves with bravery and great loyalty.

Eventually Duffy gained so much respect that he could walk through the prison and interact with the inmates with no armed guards. During his time as warden there was little violence in the prison. Why did he treat inmates with so much dignity? Because he firmly believed in the potential for good in every person, even those who had made bad choices and terrible mistakes. One of his critics said to him, "Don't you know that a leopard can't change his spots?"

His answer was, "I don't work with leopards; I work with men. And men change every day." [4]

* * * * *

We treat criminals in this country as if they were no longer humans like us. As is the case with war and any other type of cruelty we inflict on each other, the process of dehumanization is extremely important if we are to avoid guilt stemming from our lack of compassion. It is much more difficult to treat other human beings inhumanely as long as we see them as being just like us. We must realize that all humans *are* just like us in the most basic ways, but their vector sums may have taken them in a socially unacceptable direction. Their cultural upbringing and the circumstances of their lives may be somewhat different than ours. However, parents in all cultures love their children and feel pain when their children suffer. All men and women need connection with other people and need to feel that their work in life is useful. All human beings have addictions to deal with and things for which they feel shame and things for which they feel pride. We may try to dehumanize other races, alternate sexual orientations, people who commit crimes, people who are not of our religious beliefs, or people of different social or economic statuses. However, we are all alike in all the most important ways.

It seems that, any time there is a problem to deal with, we think we have to declare a war on it. We have the "War on Drugs," the "War on Terror," the "War on Poverty," and the "War on Illegal Immigrants." We are so tuned in to the war mentality that this is the only way we can think. Declaring war requires that we dehumanize those against whom the war is fought. They become the enemy and must therefore be demonized and eliminated. Wouldn't it be a much better option to educate and offer to help and lift people up rather than declare a war on them? Wouldn't it be more useful to teach our kids the consequences of drug use and give them opportunities to work through their issues when they have abuse problems than to spend billions of dollars and lots of bad PR trying to keep drugs from coming into our country? Going to countries like Colombia to spray their farmlands with herbicides in the hope of protecting our children from drugs is the height of insanity. This isn't working, it is costing us billions of dollars, and it doesn't deal with the huge amount of drugs such as meth that are created right here in this country. Nor does it deal with the real issue of drug abuse – the fact that young people are trying to self-medicate increasing feelings of not belonging, not being cared about, being depressed, and lacking a meaningful purpose in life.

We are raised to believe that retribution is the most satisfying way to deal with people who do not live up to our expectations. At a gut level, getting even and punishing people for their "moral transgressions" seems to give people great satisfaction. But those who have helped someone overcome their issues to become happier and more successful know the real joy that comes with compassionate service and non-vengeful thinking. Helping others to conquer their demons can give us great strength for facing and conquering our own problems. This is why Jesus emphasized the importance of forgiveness, being nonjudgmental and serving others. He knew of the importance of these things to the survival and well-being of any society as well as the spiritual strength of the individual.

The greatest dissolver of the need for retribution on a national or personal basis is *forgiveness*. When we forgive someone and let go of the blame, animosity and resentment, we rid ourselves of a festering cancer that will devour our immune system, our soul and our joy. "But," you may say, "there are some things that I just *can't* let go of." Yes, you can. *One of the most important lessons I have ever learned is this:* EVERYTHING – every occurrence, every event, everything anyone says to us or does to us, every circumstance and every thought we have – has only the value we assign to it. These things have no intrinsic value that is not assigned by us. The value we assign to something also determines the *emotional charge* that it will get. Every word and every picture that offends you does so only because you have assigned an offensive value to it. (Actually, your tribe probably assigned the value and you just went along with their decision.) Anything hurtful someone does to you or says to you is only hurtful because you have imputed hurtfulness to such behavior and given it a negative emotional charge of resentment, hate or psychological pain. Every gain or loss, every change in your life, and every new situation can be assigned any value you choose to give it. And you will feel joy or sadness, excitement or disappointment, anger and resentment or nothing at all because of the value you assigned it. Since this is such a difficult concept to grasp, a few examples might be helpful.

You are at your high school class reunion and someone you used to be friends with says to you, "My goodness, it's a good thing we each have a name tag. I wouldn't have recognized you without yours." You can certainly give this statement a negative value and emotional charge if you want ("Well, I know I've gained weight and gotten wrinkles and gray hair, but that was still cruel to say.") Or you can give it a positive value and charge ("Oh, thank you. I was kind of plain and dumpy in high school, but I feel great about myself now.") Or it can be a completely neutral statement that causes no emotional charge at all ("I don't know what that meant, but I too am glad we have name tags since my memory is not what it used to be.")

Perhaps a colleague at work gets a position you were hoping for because he did and said some vicious and underhanded things. Then he says to you, "Too bad, but you weren't the man for the job anyway. Better luck next time, loser." There is no ambiguity here, but you still have the option of assigning any value and emotional charge to this situation that you choose. You can become angry and bitter and boil inside anytime you see this person or think about him, but that will only eat away *your* joy and disturb *your* immune system. Or you can say to yourself, "This person seems quite immature and is very much caught up in his ego. He is not learning the lessons he needs, and I hope he will eventually see that his behavior is only hurting him. I wish him well." Though very difficult to do, putting a neutral emotional charge on this situation is possible, and it will benefit you much more than holding angry and bitter feelings toward this person. Understanding that only we are responsible for assigning the value and emotional charge to the events in our lives will help us reduce our anxiety, our depression and our blood pressure as well as increase our joy and well-being.

Perhaps our most important forgiving capacity is the true inner ability to forgive ourselves. There will always be moments when we realize that something we have just done or have done in the past will create pangs of guilt and pain. Guilt will most often detract from the beneficial role sin could play in our lives – that of giving us learning moments. Guilt causes us to continuously mourn our sins and can keep us seriously stuck. It is better to simply learn from these less-than-optimal moments and then move on to living our next moment. To avoid paying for our sins over and over, we must learn to completely let go of the emotional energy associated with them. We must do this for ourselves and for any sins we feel may have been committed against us. Being able to let go of this dark energy is absolutely vital to our physical and spiritual health.

In order to maximize our spiritual evolution, we must learn not to be judgmental and punishing. The need for retribution and punishment is ego-based and does not have the benefit to society that helpful compassion has. What kind of society is willing to spend trillions of dollars on wars where the lives on both sides are destroyed or made miserable, yet is unwilling to spend a significant part of its budget on making the lives of its own citizens less miserable and more productive? Why do so many feel that the less fortunate have created their own conditions and say to themselves, "If they would only shape up their lives and get down to work, they would be out of that situation." This kind of attitude discounts the tremendous complexity of a person's circumstances and keeps us from giving our love to him as well as our help.

To the absolutist, the concept of sin and sinners is very limiting. Anyone who has "sinned" must be a "sinner," and sinners are unacceptable people to the absolutist. Yet absolutely everyone could be labeled a "sinner." Even the absolutist cannot reject and disassociate himself from all other human beings. He must, therefore, rationalize some of the behavior of the people he likes so that he can keep them as friends. This can become a very bizarre game that has no winner. How much easier it is to simply understand that all people, ourselves included, have struggles and problems as well as strengths and good aspects in their lives. It would be so nice if we could be open and honest with each other and say, "I've got some struggles in areas where you seem to be strong, and vice versa. How about I help you with your issues from my experiences and you help me with mine?"

But this lofty goal would require the destruction of walls of intolerance that we have constructed out of bricks labeled, "You are so different from me." Anyone who has had the opportunity to get outside their village, their country, or their culture can come to know how mislabeled these bricks are. When we really get to know other people and cultures, we begin to understand how much other people are like us. They just happened to have been raised with different traditions and thought processes that might be somewhat irritating to us, just as ours are to them. But each of us is just where we are on our learning paths, stumbling at times, taking occasional ego-influenced side trips and getting stuck in the deep thick mud of tribal rules. We will really begin to understand what joyful living is about when we become the ones that can help people get up when they stumble, help them find their way back to the path when ego has misguided them, and gently pull a fellow sojourner out of the mud that keeps him or her stuck.

Chapter Nine

PAID PROGRAMMING

*Too often we hold fast to the clichés of our
forebears. We subject all facts to a prefabricated
set of interpretations. We enjoy the comfort of
opinion without the discomfort of thought.*
John F. Kennedy, Yale University
Commencement, June 11, 1962.

My brother was unhappy with the way his life was going. My sister
and I had often discussed with him the *law of attraction*. We pointed
out that he had created his life and could create a happier life with
the things he wanted in it if he so desired. For a long time he couldn't
really grasp this concept and continued to view himself as a victim
of past and present circumstances. Then, one day he borrowed his
wife's car to run errands and she had left a CD from the audio book
The Secret in the CD player. He must have been in just the right
frame of mind at just the right time. Something that was said while
he was listening to that CD helped him understand that his thoughts
and perceptions really do create his life. In the days that followed
he began to enjoy this new thought process and the difference it
made in his life. He began to use the law of attraction to bring those

"meaningful coincidences" into his life and he began evolving into a much happier person.

One day he was trying to explain to a co-worker that he had discovered a whole new way of doing his life by controlling his thoughts and creating vectors that were beneficial and omitting those that were not. His co-worker said, "Yes, but aren't you just brainwashing yourself by telling yourself that your life is good when it's really not that great?"

"Perhaps," said my brother, "but everything in our lives is a form of brainwashing. That being the case, wouldn't you really rather choose your own programming?"

And indeed he was right. Almost everything that happens to us during a typical day is a type of brainwashing. The television we watch while getting ready for work and the radio we listen to on the way to work, discussions with our co-workers, interactions with the people we encounter at the store or anywhere else, the television shows we watch at night and the interactions we have with friends and family – all these affect the remolding of our psyches by the end of that day. On the weekends our religious activities, the movies we watch, online social media, any books or magazines we read and any interactions with other people will shape the way we perceive our life whether or not we are conscious of it. Even our emotional reactions to all of these things stimulate within us a slightly different way of looking at our world from moment to moment.

Most of the time we let our programming occur randomly, allowing all information and occurrences to come in and be stored unfiltered and unevaluated. Our emotional reactions to these events also bury themselves in our souls without our noticing they have been imprinted. We thus allow a random world to determine what our new vector sum will be at any point in time. Most of us allow our early life programming to color the events of our days, and this limits what we can experience and become as we mature. Even when we do come to realize that our early programming could have been better, it is often very difficult to disconnect ourselves from the emotional background noise that persists long after we cognitively understand that there is a better way of thinking about and reacting to the events in our lives.

People who want to sell us something, politicians who want our vote, corporations who want to distract us from what they are perpetrating, religious organizations and anyone who has expectations of us will try to persuade us to come to their way of thinking. Advertising and public relations companies know from a vast body of research that there are ways to program our thinking that work very well. Of the many techniques used to program us, we will consider only a few.

In chapter 2, the concept of *memes* was introduced. A meme is a thought, belief or attitude that can spread from us to other people's minds or vice versa. Memes program us into thinking, feeling, and behaving in certain ways without our being aware where these thoughts, feelings and behaviors came from. To refresh your minds, the three types of memes are: 1) distinction – used to identify and distinguish the things in our lives; 2) association – used to create our attitudes about things by linking one meme to another; 3) strategy memes – certain behaviors will cause certain effects.

Conditioning – is programming by repetition. Some conditioning is beneficial. Learning multiplication tables or vocabulary words by rote creates skills we will use. Conditioning by repetition occurs in almost every aspect of our lives, but we are never told that we are being programmed or what the purpose of that programming is. From our earliest days we repeat the Pledge of Allegiance without knowing why. We know only that everyone else in the class is doing it. We are given distinction memes defining country (we are superior because we live within the arbitrary borders that we call our country). If we grow up in a religious culture, we are given God-format memes that tell us what God is and what is expected of us, and they are repeated often! Rituals strengthen these memes by adding a physical aspect – incense to smell, wafers and wine for the tongue, music and chanting, gestures and special clothing. As a young Mormon boy, I had three hours of indoctrination on Sunday, a lesson taught during Family Home Evening on Monday, more lessons at youth group meetings during the week, and a message was always left by the Home Teachers (people who come to see how you're doing each month). There was rarely an event just for the sake of getting together and having a good time. There was always conditioning going on.

Conditioning by repetition can be based on lies rather than useful information. Even if we know we're being fed lies or propaganda (like advertising), if it is repeated enough and with enough authority, we may begin to ask ourselves, "Am I the only one who doesn't believe this? Could I be wrong and these people on the television be right?" This is how political propagandists work. In the election of 2012, *HUGE* amounts of money were spent in an attempt to sway the electorate to vote for candidates of a party that supported American corporations, wanted to deny gay people equal rights, thought that old men knew more about women's bodies than women did, and wanted to dissolve all the safety nets for the American working class so that rich people could get richer. Very often people can be persuaded through conditioning to support and vote for people who do not have their best interests at heart. But in the 2012 election, the American people resisted intense media programming and voted, at least partly, not to support that particular party.

Association memes are used in the advertising that surrounds us 24/7. Certain beverages are associated repeatedly with the beautiful people of the "in crowd" (and who doesn't want to be part of the "in crowd?"). Certain medications are associated with a new and better life walking on the beach, being able to do all the things you never could before, or having intimate moments with sexual partners. Marketing research companies test these associated images on focus groups to see what appeals to them most. These association memes appeal mostly to egos and try to make people believe they need products they could easily do without.

The term for using repetition to create strategy memes is *operant conditioning*. Operant conditioning occurs when a particular behavior is rewarded or punished, leading to increased or decreased repetition of that behavior. Praising children for good grades, giving gold stars for good behavior and providing a treat after chores are done reinforce good behavior. However, operant conditioning can also reinforce the worst behaviors. The greed of wealth accumulators starts with the reward of profit from an investment that goes well. They now have money to invest again and they are again rewarded with new wealth. Many of them learn to manipulate the monetary system until they are rewarded again and again to the point that they have far more money than they need to live comfortably, but they have become addicted to the rush of watching their bank accounts in the Cayman Islands grow. Power, which usually accompanies wealth, becomes a person's passion in much the same way. Getting a promotion by sabotaging a coworker reinforces that behavior. Cheating on tests, or in any number of circumstances, has its benefits and builds the desire to cheat again and, as always, the need to rationalize it.

Much of conditioning's ability to mold our lives is based in our egos and our need to be regarded highly in the eyes of others. We go along with obvious lies because we don't want to be taunted as one of the few non-believers (as in "The Emperor's New Clothes"). We think we absolutely *must* have the latest cool gadget because all our friends have it. Conditioning isn't necessarily a bad thing as long as we are aware we are being conditioned, we understand who is doing the conditioning, and we know what they are trying to accomplish with it. Using conditioning to promote a cleaner atmosphere will improve the human condition, but using it to encourage young people to sign up for the war machine can bring disastrous results. Conditioning by repetition is around us all the time, and we can be sure that we will be negatively influenced by it if we are not cautious.

Cognitive Dissonance – *Cognitive dissonance* occurs when people try to hold two or more conflicting beliefs, ideas, values or emotional states. Since people seek consistency in their beliefs and perceptions, this conflict creates a great discomfort that needs to be eliminated. We achieve *dissonance reduction* by decreasing the importance of one of the conflicting beliefs, creating greater agreement between the two, or by changing one of the dissonant factors. This happens in religion all the time. A person may have been taught that he should never work on the Sabbath, but the great job he has requires him to do so. He has three options: 1) Decrease the importance of his religious teachings; 2) Get a different job; or 3) Try to rationalize well enough to make religious teachings and keeping one's job work well together. When Jesus was criticized for healing on the Sabbath, he said: "Thou hypocrite, doth not each one of you on the Sabbath loose his ox or his ass from the stall, and lead him away to watering?" (Luke 13:15, King James Version) Many people rationalize working on the Sabbath using this scripture saying that sometimes the letter of the law is not as important as the spirit of the law. Needing to lead the ox to water becomes the rationalization, "…my kid needs braces."

Cognitive dissonance is usually caused by absolutism. Avoiding cognitive dissonance would require that all new ideas mesh perfectly with all our currently held beliefs. If we are to avoid the discomfort of clashing beliefs, we will not be likely to consider new concepts. The discomfort of trying to hold two clashing beliefs is felt as guilt. The greater the guilt a group can inflict on a person, the less likely that person will entertain ideas not endorsed by the group. Loyalty and submission are the desired effects of creating this guilt. In fact, fraternities have hazings, the military has boot camp and some religions or spiritual disciplines require that people give monetary offerings and participate in rituals before they will be fully accepted into the organization. This, in turn, cements a person's loyalty to the organization. The more you sacrifice for an organization, the more you show yourself and others that you are dedicated to it. The more loyalty you have, the greater your guilt is if you disregard their rules. Cults depend on this type of brainwashing. Cognitive dissonance programming depends on creating guilt with the goal of keeping us tied to a certain belief system. The more absolutist we are, the easier we are to program.

A fascinating aspect of operant conditioning is that it has a stronger effect if the rewards are intermittent rather than given each time the desired behavior occurs. This creates cognitive dissonance ("I get rewarded when I perform a certain way" vs. "I *don't* get rewarded when I perform a certain way.") We may feel we need to work harder and longer at performing in a manner that gets rewarded so that we can resolve this cognitive dissonance. This is exactly what the programmer wants. People become addicted to gambling in this way. A daughter may work harder to gain her mother's approval if it is seldom given. A person may spend more hours at his workplace in order to get a "Good job!" from his boss. One may stay in a bad relationship hoping that there will be just one more moment of joy and praise from the partner.

Trojan Horse – The Trojan horse strategy is based on bundling less believable ideas with those that we already feel strongly about. The "horse" meme is always the strongest belief and it can be positive or negative. Other memes are easily smuggled in with the horse meme.

This is the best country in the world and God loves it most.
(This is a very strong meme, and the
following can be added to it easily.)
We have more freedom than any other people.
People hate us for our freedom.
Those who hate us want to take our freedoms away from us.
If our government wants to wage war to
"protect our freedoms," I must go!
If this *is* the best country in the world, our government
would never do anything that is detrimental for its citizens.
Therefore, there is very little that needs fixing here.

Many people employ the strategy meme that says, "I will believe things consistent with what I know and be skeptical of all else." These people will be easily programmed with new information that jibes with their current beliefs, and they will be very resistant to ideas that do not fit in. If you are programmed that X is the voice of God (be it a person, a book, or a spiritual practice) you will easily be programmed to believe that *anything* associated with X must also come from God.[1]

A somewhat related programming concept is the "if this, then that" logic. The programmers give you something that you likely already believe (or at least can be easily convinced of). Then they add something that they want you to believe and act as if this belief *must* follow the first one.

"You believe that all good things are made by God, don't you?"

"Well, yeah… I guess."

"Then you must believe that anything not made strictly by God is bad for you. This means you should never take any medications or eat processed foods. Only raw fruits and vegetables are just like God made them. That's why you want to go on this macrobiotic diet, isn't it?"

"I do? Well, I suppose so."

There are so many ways that people lead us into what they call logical conclusions, but the logic is based on false premises, false equivalencies, false "if this, then that" sequencing, and reasoning based on lack of complete knowledge of the real circumstances and issues. A good salesman is aware of these word-play tricks. But these same tricks can be used, consciously or unconsciously, by anyone who would like to sell you on an idea or behavior ("you should do this because…"). Here are a final few to consider.

Asking questions – Asking questions that seem to be impartial, but are really very pointed, is a very good way to slyly sneak in the information you want somebody to know. I was very disgusted with people who would call me during the recent campaign and say something like this:

"If you knew that Candidate X said that women who don't work outside the home are blah-blah-blah, would you be more likely, less likely or about the same likely to vote for her?"
If you knew that Candidate X voted against blah-blah-blah, would it change your likelihood to vote for her?
If you knew that Candidate X was seen clipping her toenails in public, would that affect the way you vote?
(Notice that it's not said that she ever actually did this.)

Fortunately, some Candidate X's were elected despite the huge amount of nonsense that was disseminated in the media.

Appealing to vanity – Almost every ad you see on television is based on making you want the product so you will be sexier, more attractive (how many ab-working machines do we need?), have more fun or a be a real pleaser (who wants more cookies?). It is certainly our egos that keep the economy growing.

Trust and confidence – We are more likely to believe someone and go along with him if we feel he can be trusted and if he makes us feel like his buddy. Political candidates do this all the time. They try to be seen doing things that other "real Americans" do – going to ball games, drinking beer, and attending church. More important than a politician's platform is building voters' trust. Invariably, people who want to borrow money from us start off with something like, "...old pal, old buddy, dear chum..." Con men (from the word confidence) seek first to gain our trust by showing us that they trust us first, and then adding the part we didn't see coming ("could I borrow a hundred dollars until payday?"). It's certainly not bad to trust someone or have confidence in an acquaintance, but this trust develops over time and with experience.

Sounds right to me – This is an especially powerful programming method based on people having too little information to come to correct conclusions. Someone might say, "We've had one of the coldest and snowiest winters in years. Global warming can't possibly be happening. If it were occurring, every day would be warmer than the last." Well, that sounds right – unless you know that global warming is actually called *global climate change* (some scientists are calling it *global weirding*). This includes changes in weather patterns, droughts, large storms, floods, and bad winters.

Or someone might tell you that taxing very wealthy people at a low rate will create more jobs since the wealthy people will have more money to invest in job creation. This seems believable... unless you know that the Congressional Research Service – the non-partisan research office for Congress – says, "...there is little evidence over the past 65 years that tax cuts for the highest earners are associated with savings, investment or productivity growth."

Things we hear or read may seem true and accurate based on the knowledge and biases we now have, but if we look into things a little deeper, we will find that what once made sense does not anymore.

* * * * *

I went to dinner with a good friend and his wife, and I could see his wife's eyes roll as my friend began to take us into the realm of politic discussion. He was a Tea Party Conservative and thought that socialism was our greatest threat. We needed to get government out of everything and then we would be *really* free. My friend had just moved back to Arizona from Texas and was convinced that our current president was taking us down the road to pure socialism or worse. He thought all public benefit programs like Social Security and Medicare should go. He believed people were just slackers if they couldn't provide for themselves.

I looked at him incredulously and said, "You were a doctor before you became disabled, and yet you had no private disability insurance or retirement plan because you didn't think you would need such things. Now all you have for your survival is Social Security Disability payments and your Medicare. You have been in the hospital twice since you have been back in Arizona. Without these two "socialist" programs, you would have nothing! You'd have been on the street or dead by now. Have you lost your mind?"

"My kids would take care of me if it came to that," he said.

"Oh, I'm sure they'd love to hear that!" I replied. "Would they also pay for two very expensive hospital stays you recently had?"

"Well, I've treated patients a large part of my life, and some of them didn't pay me in full or at all. I deserve free medical care."

"The hospital collections department wouldn't quite see it that way," I repliedl. I was getting a bit irritated, but had one last thing to say, "How can you be so easily brainwashed into supporting people and ideas that do not have your best interests at heart? How does that happen?"

By that time the food had come and his wife was very glad to see this conversation come to an end.

* * * * *

So, as we go through each day, how do we stay in charge of our own programming? How do we keep each day from being just a series of random events followed by preprogrammed emotions and predictable reactions and behaviors? How do we make each present moment into a building block that will create a better vector sum by this time tomorrow? The answer is PAY ATTENTION!

In chapter seven, consciousness and awareness was discussed. This is a state in which we simply pay attention to our lives without the emotional charge that is usually present, allowing us to respond to life events more objectively. As we practice paying attention to our lives rather than reacting to them, we will find that our egos play less of a role in our decision making. Let's take some common situations and see how paying attention and evaluating the occurences in our lives makes a difference. Most people have experienced such things as traffic rage, irritation or anger with a coworker, and dysfunctional family moments. Hopefully most of us have experienced the difference between reacting emotionally and just paying attention to the situation and coming up with actions that will defuse it instead of heating it up. When we make purposeful choices in every situation, we begin to do our own programming that will lead us to having self-created lives instead of lives programmed by others. We begin to examine what gets our attention and what things we filter out, and we begin to ask ourselves why we place so much importance on some things and so little on others. We may choose to turn off the news and go outside for a walk. We may return a smile and say something pleasant to someone who has been rude and arrogant. Most importantly, we will be consciously making the choices that will lead us to more fulfilling and happy lives.

"But that just ain't right," you might say. "The other person was definitely in the wrong when he cut me off." The need to be right or to always win is just your ego exerting its control over you. The need to be effective and healing comes from a much higher consciousness. The reality is that you always do yourself the greatest disservice when you react from your lower emotions such as anger. The other person often doesn't even know that he has caused your adrenal glands to release adrenalin, your blood pressure to go up, and the rest of your day to be ruined. And, if he does have malicious intent, why do you want him to have the satisfaction of playing such an important role in the happiness in your day or the lack thereof.

As mentioned before, memes are thoughts, ideas or beliefs that spread in a way that is similar to microbial infection. To maximize our creative control, we must decide first which memes we will let ourselves be infected with. In order to do this, each of us must first decide what the purpose of our life is. If we want a life full of discovery, happiness and ascending spiritual evolution, we must disinfect ourselves of any memes that disallow that discovery. If there are thoughts we think or things we do automatically, we must ask ourselves where these came from and whether they have beneficial, detrimental or neutral effects on our lives. When our tribe tells us there is only one possible way to think about something, do we have enough courage to say, "Thanks for your input, but I like to do my own thinking."? When we receive new information from any source, do we have the ability to check it for accuracy, put it to use if it is beneficial information or set it aside if it will lead us into dark, angry or useless places? Are we willing to evaluate new ideas that disturb our current worldview with the possibility that these new ideas could actually be great new discoveries? Do we have the personal willpower to reject lies and stupidities no matter how often they are repeated or how many people believe them?

We must choose which memes we will pass on to others. Will we mindlessly pass on those that we have been given so that those who gave them to us will feel honored? Do we really want to pass on guilt and fear to our children simply because someone taught us that this is the correct way to raise children? Or can we make a conscious effort to keep things positive and hopeful and pass on memes that will increase the joy and compassion around us?

We are bombarded every day with attempts to program us for other peoples' purposes. Paying attention to the information that is thrown at us will give us the opportunity to consciously evaluate this information and disinfect ourselves of beliefs and ideas that will not benefit us. Being aware of all that we pass on to other people will help our societies work for the good of all individuals. What we think and believe eventually leads to what we do. As Norman Cousins said, "Time given to thought is the greatest time saver of all."

Chapter Ten

THE POWER OF
EVALUATIVE THINKING

Your perspective is always limited by how much you know.
Expand your knowledge and you will transform your mind.

Bruce H. Lipton

In our search for useful information and positive vectors, the ability to think critically is one of the most important skills we can develop. Critical thinking refers to evaluating information and ideas honestly and accurately. It does not mean being critical in the judgmental sense, but most people still feel a judgmental charge associated with the word *critical*. For this reason I have chosen to use the phrase "evaluative thinking" in talking about the ways we deal with new information.

Evaluative thinking requires that we somehow detach ourselves from preconceived attitudes and thought processes and look at everything with a mind based in reason and logic and the most accurate information. This does not mean that we cannot include our past experiences and emotions in our evaluations, but we should be cautious that past experiences and resulting emotions do not distort that which we want to see clearly. Sealed premises, memes and tribal rules will hinder any objective viewing of new ideas and therefore keep us from adding new and beneficial concepts and experiences to our vector sum.

Each day we are bombarded with a great deal of information from many sources. Advertisers, politicians, religious leaders, teachers, co-workers and friends will try to influence the way we think and do things. To expand our current vector sum for maximum benefit, we must evaluate this multitude of input or we risk naively accepting it and forming erroneous conclusions and faulty beliefs. As mentioned previously, we often reach erroneous beliefs and conclusions because we are given information from respected people and authority figures who we believe would not purposely lead us astray, but that may not be the case. We expect certain people to be experts on certain topics because we've been told they are. Unless we have evidence to the contrary, we tend to believe what such so-called experts tell us. We want to believe their intentions and their information are good.

In the media and in our communications with others, we hear *statistics* quoted that we just believe without ever questioning how the statistics were generated or interpreted. In trying to support one's point, a person may quote statistics that we are expected to take as being factual, but often they are inaccurate. When someone makes his case using skewed statistics and dubious "facts," most people are influenced by these regardless of their authenticity – especially if it supports their current way of thinking. We usually quickly dismiss them as rubbish if they do not fit one of our sealed premises. Information from *any source* must be evaluated properly before we incorporate it into our beliefs and behaviors. Statistics and facts can be checked out, and it is also important to pay attention to how the statistics were generated. Regarding a politician in his time,

Andrew Lang said, "He uses statistics like a drunk uses a streetlight, more for support than enlightenment."

An *expert* is someone who has sufficient education, knowledge and experience in a certain area to give us information that we *should* be able to rely on. However, such information should be looked at with skepticism since experts often disagree with each other on any particular issue. How is it possible that experts on the same topic will so often disagree on facts and conclusions? We should always remember that an "expert" can always be found to tell us *anything* at all if he or she has the proper incentive to do so. Let us remember that experts have told us that cigarettes have no health risks, that there is no global climate change and that there were weapons of mass destruction in Iraq.

In fact, expertise is difficult to ascertain in an absolute way. Opinions are often biased. Education and training may vary considerably. Experiences in the field of expertise and information accumulated can be widely divergent, but there are other less pure reasons for bias in an expert's opinion. Be cautious about what you believe, since the expert's job may be dependent on his stated opinion. People who work for Fox News certainly have differing incentives than those working for Public Television or Free Speech TV. A so-called climate scientist whose opinion is being paid for by large oil, coal and gas companies may have quite differing opinions from 97% or other climate scientists who are not associated with big energy companies. We expect our experts to be of high honesty and character, but their opinions may be motivated by financial benefit, political gains or esteem among colleagues. Always check out who paid for any study to be done.

And so it is with expert advice. We must assess those who portray themselves as experts. We should consider their credentials, try to find any reasons for bias, and look at who is telling us that they are experts. But most of all, we need to see if they have good rationale behind their opinions and check out for ourselves the information, science, evidence and logic upon which their conclusions are based. In the end, the most important thing to keep in mind is that it is our OWN expert opinions that are the most important. Thousands of people during our lives will try to convince us, even bully us, into accepting their ideas as the only feasible and valid ways of thinking. Our evaluative thinking skills need to be developed so that we may gather accurate information from reputable sources and come to our own conclusions that will truly benefit our lives.

Absolutist all-or-nothing thinking is a dangerous trap when considering expert opinions. An "expert" may present, all in the same breath, information that is accurate and useful and information that is erroneous and misleading. We may come to admire the writings or spoken words of individuals that seem to have accurate information and a good understanding on most issues, but each issue requires its own scrutiny and evaluation. Giving such people blind and total carte blanche to influence our vector sums is not a good idea.

Statistics that are spouted often have a much more powerful influence on our thinking than we realize. In America our access to unbiased news reporting is becoming more and more limited. We hear reporters, politicians and talk show hosts spewing out statistics that are seldom accurate and rarely unbiased. We have all received surveys in the mail or participated in other surveys that come from organizations that have a slant on the topic. For instance, anyone receiving a survey on gay marriage from the Family Values Coalition will probably have been carefully selected to receive the survey based on his or her religious and political affiliations. Political parties send out surveys to their members and then quote their responses as "some percentage of Americans think..." How much credence can we give to statistics that are skewed in this way?

It is also becoming increasingly popular to make it look like a lot of people have strong feelings on certain topics by deceitful methods. During the discussion on healthcare reform, town hall meetings were seeded with "grassroots people" ranting and raving about "death-care" and socialism. The media recorded people calling the president a racist and a Nazi, and guns started appearing at these town hall meetings. When one dug deep to find out who was behind these passionate shouters, much of it came back to surreptitiously named organizations that were largely funded by large healthcare companies. Similar shenanigans have occurred in other industries. Letters on fake letterheads were sent to congressmen supporting the coal industry and its right to continue to pillage and plunder. Turns out this nonsense was created by Americans for Prosperity, which is underwritten by Koch industries, one of the largest coal and natural gas corporations in the world. They have removed hundreds of mountaintops in the Appalachians and destroyed many streams, lakes and communities with their activities and would love not to have to provide their workers with healthcare to treat the maladies created by their greed. We always need to remember that the people with the most money have the greatest ability to put out information that benefits them. Always take note of who sponsors a political ad, and try to look up the organization if you don't recognize it.

It is very important that we do not simply accept information as it is given to us but ask for people's sources and check them out when possible. Often we do not know where politicians or news people get their information, but someone who wants to be believable will usually give their sources, and these can be checked out on the Internet. Others just hope you will unflinchingly believe them and be influenced by what they say. We should ask ourselves why the opinions of others should influence our opinions so strongly. If 95% of people thought it was a good idea to set themselves on fire, would we think, "Well, they must know what they're talking about."? Or would that be a survey we might tend to be less influenced by?

We often hear statistical information quoted from *studies*. "Studies show..." is one of the most often-used phrases in arguments that mean to sway our opinions. As a physician who has done numerous medical studies as a part of his practice, I can attest that creating an unbiased and meaningful study is not so easy. In scientific studies there are many variables that have to be considered and isolated from what is being studied. For instance, if you are doing a study about the effects of diet on heart disease, you also have to consider factors such as smoking, stress, exercise and hereditary influences to get an accurate picture. Protocols must be designed very cautiously to avoid bias. As rigid as the FDA's protocols are in determining the efficacy and safety of a new drug, they still occasionally approve medications that eventually do a great deal of harm to humans as evidenced by all the commercials from legal firms that start with, "Have you or any of your loved ones ever taken the medication...?" Medical "truths" change on a regular basis. Peptic ulcers were once thought to be caused by stress and bad diets, but it is now known that particular bacteria are most often implicated in this disease. The same principles hold true in all areas of science. One day there is global warming, then there isn't, then the polar ice caps start melting.

In designing psychological or sociologic studies, the number of variables becomes almost overwhelming. Concepts and parameters must be set before the study is designed. For instance, to decide whether a particular group of people makes better parents, you must first define the characteristics of a good parent. This may be open to considerable debate and bias and may open up a discussion of morality or normality, which are controversial and subjective. You may want to look at endpoints, i.e. how children turn out. You must then determine whether a child who gets a college education is a better endpoint than one who ends up in a rock band. So to decide whether gay parents or single parents are as good as two heterosexual parents, you have to wrangle with a lot of issues in designing the study, and even then you cannot guarantee that you have eliminated all sources of bias.

So the next time you hear the phrase, "Studies have shown...", be somewhat skeptical. Studies can show whatever you want them to show if they are designed right. I am not saying that studies have no value. They can certainly give us useful information to help us make life decisions, often appropriate and positive ones. Many people change their lives for the better after learning the results of health related studies. Many people learn better ways to interact with their families, coworkers and life partners from information learned from sociologic studies. Studies can provide us with useful accurate information or skewed useless data – and often somewhere in between. As long as we keep in mind that studies are subject to bias and distortion, we will be more likely to critique statistics generated by them before accepting them as absolutely factual.

"It's a fact that..." is another phrase that is too often used to try to manipulate our thinking and our decisions on all sorts of issues. Stating something as being factual tries to make an issue absolute and not open to further discussion. Often people go on to build incorrect or illogical arguments if they can get you to swallow the "fact." It's likely that non-facts get propagated at least as often as evidence-based facts. It was a fact for a long time that the earth was flat and that the sun rotated around it. Facts are only provable with the investigative means that are available to us at the time. As new ways of observing and measuring are developed, what was once considered factual may prove incorrect. Facts can also be observed from a number of different angles making them accurate from one perspective but inaccurate from another. You often hear that exercise is good for everyone. If you are a couch potato with a history of diabetes in the family, some good interval training will most likely be helpful. But if you have certain illnesses such as myalgic encephalomyelitis or cardiomyopathy, intense exercise could aggravate your condition. Some "facts" are actually nothing more than commonly held ideas (those pesky memes) that may or may not be reality-based. So, if someone starts a statement with, "It's a well-known fact that…", you can be certain that the statement is meant to sway you to agree with his opinion – and the fact may not be accurate at all.

Finally, it is important to understand what people who want to deliberately influence your thoughts or behavior know. If you can present your message with strong emotions, your influence will be multiplied many times. Using just the right emotionally charged images or phrases can sway the most stubborn non-believers to one's point of view. Hitler's speeches were full of hate and garbage, but he could work his audiences into a frenzy. There is nothing wrong with feeling strong beneficial emotions, but anger and hate can be destructive. Always be aware that people around you may be unknowingly or deliberately trying to manipulate your feelings and boost their message by attaching a strong emotional charge to it.

* * * * *

The arena of politics is perhaps the best place to test our abilities of evaluative thinking. The Citizens United decision from the United States Supreme Court said that corporations are the same as people. It made the 2012 elections the most expensive elections ever. Huge amounts of money from corporations with vested interests were poured into ads and other propaganda that were heretofore not allowed. We were bombarded from every side with statistics, surveys, polls, opinions, studies and emotionally charged rhetoric. Many politicians admitted outright that what they were saying was not factual, but they said it anyway. Why would they do this?

Joseph Goebbels, Hitler's chief propaganda officer and master of "the big lie" for the Nazi State, said it most blatantly:

> *If you tell a big lie enough and keep repeating it, people will eventually come to believe it. The lie can be maintained only for such time as the State can shield the people from the political, economic and/or military consequences of the lie. It thus becomes vitally important for the State to use all its powers to repress dissent, for the truth is the mortal enemy of the lie, and thus by extension, the truth is the greatest enemy of the State.[1]*

The masters of deceit in any country, including ours, know that Goebbels was right. Even when people know that they are being told a lie, the more the lie is repeated, the more people will begin to believe it. The more people that appear to believe the lie, the easier it becomes to convince others to believe it. This continues until the number of people who believe the lie reaches critical mass. They can now be convinced to support and vote for people who do not have their best interests at heart. Eventually, those who continue to call the lie a lie will become the outcasts or even the enemies of the State. If one uses words or terms that have been focus group tested to cause the greatest emotional fire in people, the lie will be even easier to promote.

The designers of campaign ads depend on what they call low information voters (people who have little desire or ability to evaluate information rationally) to react viscerally with great anger and passion to the information they spread through news media, churches and Internet social sites. This anger and passion infects others until large numbers of people begin to think, "All these people are very passionate about their views – perhaps there is something I don't understand about what seems to me to be a lie." Even people who are generally rational thinkers can sometimes be moved from their positions to also believe the lie. Violent actions (such as pepper spray and bullets) taken against dissenters can discourage them or galvanize them even more in their beliefs.

It is during these election cycles that we have the opportunity to resist programming by these individuals and practice evaluative thinking. In this age of digital information there are dozens of fact-checking sites such as PolitiFact.com, FactCheck.org and Snopes.com, but not all fact-checking sites are accurate since many are supported by biased organizations. Your tribe has rules about how you should think and act on political issues. Try to detach yourself from your tribe's influence and determine what makes sense for you, your society and the world. Investigate and think about the facts, statistics, surveys, polls and other propaganda that bombard you. Does it *really* make sense for you personally that we allow our politicians to destroy our social safety nets in order to increase the profits of the few and have lower taxes for the rich? Are corporations *really* the same as people and should they have the influence they have in the governmental process? Do we *really* need more guns than we have people?

We no longer have the luxury to believe that each of us needs more, more, more because we are destroying the source of that "more." If the entire societal organism does not thrive, can its individual members have a good life? Our elections can be the platform for the wealth-accumulating puppet masters to manipulate our thinking, or they can be the way we take back our society and make it a compassionate, Earth-conscious and love-filled place.

* * * * *

I find that there is often a more important consideration in evaluating information that is meant to influence my thinking. I gauge the information in statistics, facts, expert opinions and studies by what kind of energy it creates. Hateful rhetoric cannot bring love energy to our country or planet. Studies that try to create an image that one group of people is superior to another are usually biased, and they are meaningless to me – all people are just trying to get through their University Earth courses. An expert opinion that tells me there is nothing wrong with polluting our air, water and land for economic growth gets no consideration. I have learned to not get into discussions with people who believe that Armageddon must occur before there can be lasting peace. What an insane concept that such a horrendous war could lead to peace, but their sealed premises will not even let them hear what I have to say anyway. Sometimes we don't need to fact check if the statement we are checking does not lead to a higher state of peace and cooperation. If a "fact" leads to fear and intolerance, it gets rejected.

Thomas Jefferson said, "If a nation expects to be ignorant and free, in a state of civilization, it expects what never was and never will be." Thinking evaluatively is using all of these concepts plus some good old common sense to limit the influence that biased information has on our lives. Completely unbiased evaluative thinking is impossible to achieve. Our experiences and feelings influence what we believe to be true, and there is often no easy and immediate way to fact check what we hear. It is difficult to find an absolutely objective way to evaluate anything. Although I'm sure Science Officer Mr. Spock would disagree, I doubt pure logic is achievable, much less a good thing. However, the more we are able to avoid being programmed by someone else's skewed information, the freer we become. When ego and prejudice are not part of our assessment of life's events, we make decisions and do things that are more in accordance with our own best interests. Only when we reach higher levels of consciousness will our relationship to our planet and the people on it become clear. Developing good skills for thinking evaluatively will help us shape our worldview more beneficially. We will then come much closer to being the programmers of our own lives.

Chapter Eleven

MONEY MAKES THE WORLD GO 'ROUND

*We must make our choice. We may have democracy,
or we may have wealth concentrated in the
hands of a few, but we cannot have both.*

Louis Brandeis,
Supreme Court Justice – 1916-1939

"My grandmother was a wonderful person. She taught me
how to play the game of Monopoly. She understood that
the aim of the game was to acquire. She would accumulate
everything she could, and eventually she would become
the master of the board. And then she would always say the
same thing to me. She'd look at me and say, 'One day you'll
learn to play the game.' One summer I played monopoly
almost every day all day long, and that summer I learned
to play the game. I came to understand that the only way
to win is to make a total commitment to acquisition. I came
to understand that money and possessions – that's the way
that you keep score. And by the end of that summer I was
more ruthless than my grandmother. I was ready to bend the

rules if I had to in order to win the game. And I sat down to play with her that fall. I took everything she had. I watched her give her last dollar and quit in utter defeat. And then she had one more thing to teach me. Then she said, 'Now it all goes back in the box. All those houses and hotels, all the railroads and utility companies, all that property and all that wonderful money – now it all goes back in the box. None of it was really yours. You got all heated up about it for awhile, but it was around a long time before you sat down at the board, and it will be here long after you're gone.' Players come and players go, houses and cars, titles and clothes, even your body. Because the fact is that everything you clutch and consume and hoard is going to go back in the box and you're going to lose it all. You have to ask yourself, when you finally get the ultimate promotion, when you've made the ultimate purchase, when you buy the ultimate home, when you've stored up financial security and climbed the ladder of success to the highest rung you can possibly climb it, and the thrill wears off – and it will wear off – then what? How far do you have to walk down that road before you see where it leads? Surely you understand, it will never be enough. So you have to ask yourself the question, 'What matters?'"

John Ortberg in the movie
Zeitgeist: Moving Forward [1]

Every society has to have some sort of economic system. Barter and trade, trinkets and baubles, paper money and coinage, or balance sheets on some computer – we have to be able to trade our skills and our stuff for other people's skills and stuff. This means we have to assign values to different skills and different stuff. Are five artichokes worth eight zucchinis, one cow worth one horse, one doctor's visit worth two chickens, or seven million mortgage guarantees worth twenty million oil futures? It is very difficult to assign the right value to every skill, service, and product in comparison to all others.

In most cases the economic system in a country is tied to the system of governance. In the feudal system the king owned everything and allowed the serfs to work on his ground and keep a small portion of what they produced for themselves. The greedier the king was or the more a war was costing, the more would be required of the peasants until it became very oppressive (sound familiar?). A dictatorship or military-run government was/is pretty much the same. Marxism, Leninism and communism all claim the goals of stateless and classless societies where all things are owned in common and the proletariat (common workers) runs the society while these goals are being achieved. But, as we've seen, a small group of powerful, greedy and ruthless men with the police and military behind them inevitably seems to appear and say, "We'll take over for now until these lofty goals are reached." A plutocracy is a government in which the wealthy rule, and the economic system is whatever they say it is because they make all the rules. Socialism is defined as collective or governmental ownership and administration of the production and distribution of goods and services. Capitalism is a system in which the money or goods needed to produce more goods is owned by or provided by private or corporate entities and is often put up by investors who expect to make a profit from providing the money needed to make production possible. Some people are now referring to a corporatocracy, where large corporations control the government and its laws.

These are all just dictionary-like definitions. The reality is that governments and economic systems in any country are far more complex than any one word can describe. Yet there is such an intense emotional charge attached to these words. When we hear the words *communism* or *socialism*, outrage and anger may swell up inside some people. When we hear the word *capitalism*, we want to stand up and cheer. And yet most of us could not even give a dictionary definition for these words that describe economic systems. As with patriotism we only know the knee-jerk reactions we are supposed to have, and we know for sure that we will be pointed at and laughed at if we react in any other way. This was stated clearly in the tribal rules. And the McCarthy era of communist witch hunting showed us that there could be even more dire consequences for the appearance of being associated with one of the demonized systems. This kind of tyranny happens often when a tribal rule is taken to the extreme.

We look to our elected officials to insure that our monetary system works well for all members of our society. Unfortunately, they are only puppets. As with any puppet show, all attention is focused on the puppets and we seldom see the puppet masters pulling the strings with their great wealth and power. As long as our governing officials are in the spotlight they love, the puppet masters will operate in anonymity, which is exactly what they desire. They would prefer we don't know their names or the locations of their many mansions or yachts. A few wealthy puppet masters have boasted that they could start wars whenever they desired or build and destroy governments at their whims. This is what happens when an economic system allows people or corporations to accumulate great wealth. Even elected governments cannot fight their power.

Like a flowering dogwood tree whose roots, trunk, bark, branches, leaves and blossoms all work together in synchronized wonder to create its splendor, any society that is going to thrive needs a plethora of skills and passions working together for the good of the entire organism. A society needs people who love to teach and know how to do it well. It needs men and women with a passion for healing and the education to make that passion work. It needs strong people who can build roads and buildings, and it needs people who are good at keeping track of all the goods and money that are produced and where everything goes. A society with only a few skills and talents working for it will stagnate and eventually fall apart. Again, it is quite difficult to put a value on each service and product. The degree of dedication, education and financial output that is required to provide a certain service or product will certainly need to be factored in. In a capitalistic society the law of supply and demand will help determine what monetary value something will have. Entertainers such as athletes, musicians and actors may earn a disproportionate amount of money because we place such a high value on being entertained. Teachers and laborers usually earn much less because their contributions are often taken for granted, and our roads and schools are just things that have always been there and we expect they always will be.

Money was invented as an easier way to barter. Originally there were coins and later paper money – which could be redeemed for gold or silver in the past. These were used to ensure that the trading of goods and services was as equitable as possible. Now 97% of money in this country exists only as bank account money on computers in the banking system. Money is nowadays based on debt more than anything else. Banks do not need to have actual money. If they loan out a bunch of money, they can say that they have that much money in their system since people owe it to them and they expect to get it back with interest. In the computer they then appear to have a lot more money than they do, and they can then loan out a lot more money or use that computerized money to create more wealth in a large number of ways. Since money is now almost entirely manipulated from within a mainframe computer rather than based on goods and services, it is easy for the wealth accumulators to draw more and more wealth to themselves. But, as we have seen in recent years, this manipulation can be disastrous for the entire planet's economy. *Currently, the 85 richest people on the planet have as much wealth as the poorest half of all the people who live here; i.e. 3.5 billion people – the populations of China, India, the African continent and Australia.* [2]

One thing is certain, especially in a capitalistic society – money makes money! Those who are fortunate enough to have money to invest in businesses or money they can manipulate in the banking computer system will make money that they can reinvest and continue the cycle. "It's not simply good fortune," some may say. "I worked long and hard to get where I am now." But, if we look at their vector sums, we will see some measure of hard work and a large measure of good fortune. Many people who have worked just as hard will end up with much less. Perhaps it is the result of where they were born or to whom, or it might have more to do with what their experiences taught them about their role in society. It's hard to say what all the factors may be, and it doesn't really matter because we are all here to learn the lessons of living together for the benefit of all. We seriously need to learn that the whole society cannot flourish if the individuals in the society do not flourish. Just as a beautiful car you just purchased will need fuel before it will take you anywhere, a gorgeous new factory will produce nothing without the fuel of its laborers.

One of the most important and powerful documentary productions of our time is Peter Joseph's Zeitgeist series: *Zeitgeist: The Movie, Zeitgeist: Addendum* and *Zeitgeist: Moving Forward*. I highly recommend *Zeitgeist: Moving Forward* for all people who seek to understand how money works. The evolution of the monetary system throughout history is discussed, especially that of our free-market capitalistic system. At first this system dealt in real tangible life-supporting goods and services. It was never imagined that the most profitable economic sector on the planet would be financial trading or so-called investing, where money itself is gained simply by the movement of other money in an arbitrary game that has zero productive benefit.

Money itself has become a commodity – as if money itself could be eaten, used for energy or to create shelter. It is believed by some that creating more money, regardless of where it goes, will create more happiness and well-being in society. If the stock market, consumer price index and gross domestic product are doing better, shouldn't the people of that society be doing better? Peter Joseph asks, "Is the condition we have created in our modern world actually supporting our health? Is the bedrock of our socioeconomic system acting as a positive force for human and social development and progress? Or is the foundational gravitation of our society actually going against the core evolutionary requirements needed to create and maintain our personal and social well-being?"

I recently watched a travel documentary with Michael Palin in the Himalayas. He was in the small country of Bhutan (about the size of Switzerland with only a little over a million people). The King of Bhutan's maxim is, "Gross National Happiness is far more important than Gross National Product." The goal of economic and governance systems should be that the members of their countries, kingdoms, tribes or clans are all able to contribute and are all free from hunger, fear, insecurity or suffering. But this has not been the case for most of man's history. Inevitably power mongers who scheme and use fear to gather support for their need to control will appear. They are sufficiently cunning to convince people that the sky is falling and that those in control will protect them if they will give them their money, goods and services – much of which goes to establish a corps of enforcers. Once these power mongers have the control and resources and they have used the money to pay for police and military who become loyal to them (because of the paychecks), it is not easy for the rest of society to say, "Hey, wait a minute! This isn't what we were thinking of when we gave you our support." The enforcers, whose salaries are being paid by the power freaks, will show up and squelch any dissent. The more ruthless and brutal the enforcers are, the less the peasants are likely to rise up – up to a point.

We are now in the twenty-first century, and it is time for this kind of social structure to go! But we keep thinking that the alpha males will somehow be different this time if we put them in charge of our societies. We are led to believe that electing this one or that one will somehow bring a change from what has always been. We are trained to become outraged at our politicians when things go wrong economically, but they are only the puppets. It is the bankers and corporate giants that we need to hold accountable. Women play a minimal role in our society, and those who do often emulate the alpha males. We need a new paradigm.

* * * * *

In "Stress: Portrait of a Killer", a National Geographic Documentary seen on PBS, we are introduced to Robert Sapolsky, a neurobiologist at Stanford University, who has studied extensively how stress and stress hormones affect humans and animals. He spends a few weeks each year on the plains of the Massai Mara Reserve in Kenya, Africa studying colonies of baboons. Here he has drawn blood to study the stress hormone levels of different members of this society. These primates are not stressed much of the time by needing to escape from lions, so they spend a good part of their time stressing each other, making them the perfect human corollary. There is a direct relationship between stress and one's place in the hierarchy. Every male knows who can torture whom and whom, in turn, the tortured can torture. Therefore, a baboon's stress hormones are determined by his rank. If you're a dominant male, your stress hormones will be low. If you're a submissive, they will be much higher. Females get the brunt of all the males' bad moods. The have-nots have increased heart rates and blood pressure, decreased immune response, and increased plaque in their arteries. In addition it was found that stress killed brain cells in the hippocampus (the brain's center for learning and memory) and increased a dangerous type of fat that accumulates in and around the abdomen and trunk.

One year a tragic event occurred for the first troop of baboons that Robert ever studied. They started feeding at the garbage dump of a popular resort and ended up eating meat contaminated with tuberculosis. Nearly half the males died, and Robert was devastated. But then he began to notice that it was only the alpha males that had died. If you were aggressive and not socially connected, no one took care of you and brought you food when you were sick, and you died. Every alpha male was gone. Now the troop consisted of twice as many females as males, and the remaining males were the "good guys" – the less aggressive and more connected males.

The whole mood and demeanor of the troop changed overnight. And it appears that it was a change they liked. As baboon males become adolescents, they leave their home troops and search for a place in another troop. When new males entered the troop that was devastated by TB, it took about six months for them to be taught that this troop was different; aggressive behavior was not tolerated and bullying males were booted from the troop. When Robert again measured the stress hormones of this troop's members, he found them to be decreased all around. But the most startling observation of all is that this particular troop has maintained its increased sociality and decreased aggressiveness twenty years later. [3]

* * * * *

This would be a very good time to look at governing and economic systems with a less absolutist viewpoint. What our society needs today is a system that contains the best of all possible ways of doing things – not knee-jerk reactions, but thought-out strategies. In many countries around the world, a combination of capitalism and socialism works very well for the good of most of the population. The production and distribution of goods is based on the structure of capitalism, but the governing bodies know that their countries will be more productive and happy if healthcare, good education and good infrastructure are provided. The members of these societies are willing to be taxed at a higher rate to be sure that the same basic services are provided to all of their citizens. There are many hybrids and permutations possible that could include parts of many economic systems. But we need to stop this insane practice of attaching such an emotional charge to any one of them. It puts a damper on any discussion of what kind of system would work to provide *all* people with quality lives.

One of the biggest problems with capitalism as it exists today is that, because of the programmed emotional charge that we have allowed to become associated with it, we think we must allow all that is currently going on in our capitalistic economic system with *no questions asked.* After all, that's just the way capitalism works, isn't it? In any society that desires to remain functional, all sectors must work together for the good of the whole. Every job has its place, and every skill and passion is needed. But the people who have a talent for raising capital and manipulating money have mistakenly thought that they are entitled to keep all the money they can collect. It is their passion and goal to accumulate material wealth, no matter how excessive and ridiculous. Through their wealth they have gained control of the lawmakers, the courts and the enforcers. They have, therefore, created the very rules by which they have redistributed wealth and power to themselves. They have forgotten that, after all the time and energy spent collecting houses, hotels and railroads, the money all goes back in the box for the benefit of the entire society. For them, however, the lives they destroy are irrelevant and just a part of their game. These wealth accumulators come up with new rules and mechanisms to amass more money that most people cannot even understand. They gamble with our money using derivatives, hedge funds, credit default swaps, mergers and acquisitions, leveraged buyouts, sub-prime mortgage rates, and a lot of things most of us have no idea about. No goods are produced or services provided. They have no regard for the destructive effect of their greed on others, and they think that the rules of capitalism (created mostly by them) allow them to do this with a clear conscience and no consequences. They are like any other addicts. They are always in denial, they don't care who they hurt, and they always need more to feed their addiction. Dictators think that their power and ruthlessness gives them the right to all the marbles, while bankers and Wall Street tycoons have a huge sense of entitlement believing that, because they are working within the system – no matter how depraved it is – they get to keep whatever they can scrape off the board. Many people feel that we no longer live in a free-market capitalistic system, but that we have evolved into a *corporatocracy*, where corporate profit motives run the government, make slaves of the people and redistribute the wealth upward.

There seems to be a common but troubling attitude in our country of "I earned it, it's mine, and you can't have any. I don't want to pay taxes because you might get some benefit from what I pay. Someday I expect the American dream to be mine, and I will then own all the houses, hotels, utilities and properties. So go sleep in your cardboard box and don't bother me." I find this particularly bizarre in a country that claims such an adherence to Jesus' teachings. Mother Theresa was asked why she administered to the poor in America where there was such wealth. She said that the poverty here is worse than anywhere else because Americans have so much and look down on the poor with disdain instead of taking care of them.

New ways of living together and sharing talents and goods are emerging around the world which allow people who are willing to work, but have no access to money, to be an integral part of their society. Nobel laureate Muhammed Yunus instituted in our times the practice of *microcredit,* which has made a huge difference in a large number of people's lives. A small amount of money (usually $500 or less) is loaned to a poor person with no collateral to start a small home-based business. These small businesses have enriched many communities around the globe. In the United States and many other countries, barter is coming back into popularity. In many communities people can become a part of a collective where *local currency credits* are used. People earn local currency credits by contributing their goods or services in return for a coupon saying they have earned a certain number of "local dollars." For example, a piano teacher gives lessons that give her credits she can use to get her yard work done. There are also *mutual credit systems* that allow people to have negative balances. This means that they can get something they need now and the community will allow them to owe a balance until they can donate time or goods. *Commercial barter* is also allowing businesses to sell goods that might otherwise not be sold by trading for goods or services from other businesses or people. All these systems take down walls between people and help them to feel like a part of their community.

When I was in first grade, I learned that the population of the planet had just reached two billion. Scientists worried about what would happen if we doubled that population any time soon. By conservative estimates there are now over seven billion people on the planet, and some scientists think it is more like eight or nine billion. That means that, in my lifetime, the population of the planet has at least tripled and possibly quadrupled. With all these people seeking to have more stuff and richer lifestyles, it is going to take an immediate conscious planetary effort to not destroy our mother Earth. On a recent Bill Moyers and Company episode, Henry Giroux was talking about our current form of capitalism and said that, for many people, "...it's easier to imagine the death of the planet than the death of capitalism."

As part of our new paradigm for living together on this planet, we have to ask ourselves a few questions. Can we live happier with less? Can we quit torturing each other? Can we share the abundance we have? Can we work together as Earthlings to bless our planet with healing? The answers to these questions will depend on one concept. Can we quit seeing ourselves as separate from other humans, and can we see our individual behaviors as having far-reaching effects? Can we quit rationalizing the continuance of destructive actions in the name of economic growth? In short, can we learn to live responsibly and share?

The concept of *shared prosperity* is found within discussions of many types of economic and social systems. It is what Jesus, the Buddha, Mohammed and many other spiritual leaders have tried to teach us. It is what most of the people around the world would tell you they want if you asked them. But it is one of the most difficult of all things to achieve. It requires a highly evolved society of people who have learned to live outside the influence of their egos. It demands personal responsibility and integrity from each person to contribute to that society all that he can and trust that others are doing the same. True shared prosperity is created from love, not legislation. Whether or not we can create such a society at this moment in our evolution is the big question. I think we can. We can all kindle the fires of change by generating the energy of shared prosperity as we develop a real concern for our fellow human beings – a concern that is reflected in our actions.

Quantum physics is showing us what many people on the planet have always known. We are not separate individuals isolated from the pain and joy of all other people. In the terms of quantum physics, we are all "entangled." Alpha apes torturing their underlings affect the stress hormone levels of the entire troop and, to a smaller – but perceptible – extent, the entire planet. As with the baboons, our societal traditions are passed down from generation to generation, and nothing gets better until we understand that we don't have to tolerate bad behavior, no matter how traditional or long-standing it may be. There is no evidence that validates the trickle-up effect. There is no economic or governance system that will work as long as the alpha apes are allowed to control our societies. Love and compassion and caring about other humans as much as we care about ourselves are the only things that can create a system that works. If we can collectively put enough high-vibration energy out there, the alpha apes will still jump up and down and pound their chests, but their destructive power will be minimized.

Chapter Twelve

HEALTH AND WELL-BEING

The History of Medicine:

2000 B.C. – Here, eat this root.

1000 A.D. – That root is heathen. Here, say this prayer.

1850 A.D. – That prayer is superstition. Here, drink this potion.

1940 A.D. – That potion is snake oil. Here, swallow this pill.

1985 A.D. – That pill is ineffective. Here, take this antibiotic.

2000 A.D. – That antibiotic doesn't work anymore. Here, eat this root.

Source Unknown

In the Amazon rainforest a young shaman applies a sticky black salve to a wound on a young man's leg. In China an elderly woman gets an acupuncture treatment for her back pain and is then handed a bag of custom-mixed herbs to treat her heart condition. In Canada a woman is being draped in a surgical suite in preparation for a hip replacement. In Japan a man is receiving a Reiki treatment for stomach problems he has had for several weeks. In India an Ayurvedic practitioner tells a woman she has too much heat in her system and gives her a diet to follow and recommends yoga and meditation.

How people deal with their health issues is changing all over the world. In Eastern countries Western medicine is finding its way into the treatment of many illnesses. In Western countries, alternative or complimentary therapies are becoming more popular every year. In China the use of antibiotics, heart medications, and even antidepressants has become standard therapy. In the USA acupuncture and herbal medicines are being used alongside standard drug and surgical therapies. People around the world are starting to believe more and more in the power of spiritual energy and positive thought processes to heal the body and the soul. And yet there is a strange phenomenon occurring amidst the emergence of the acceptance of new health and wellness principles.

Instead of taking the best from all worlds, many people have become fixated on one narrow aspect of healing and have rejected anything at all from any other practice. Many Americans have become totally disillusioned with Western medicine and refuse to take even an aspirin to relieve pain. There are those that will only use herbs and those that only believe in homeopathic preparations. Some believe that spiritual healing of one type or another plus a few supplements will cure any illness and they refuse any surgical or medicinal intervention. And still others believe that only FDA approved medications and procedures can have any efficacy in the healing process. With so many wonderful possibilities to choose from, why do people limit themselves to one narrow alley of therapeutic options? Why do they opt to stay in the tiny box of absolutist thought processes when it comes to their own health and well-being?

For some it is necessary to have scientifically tested and approved therapies since nothing else can be assured to work. However, let's look at the testing and approval process to see what really happens. A pharmaceutical company will usually spend between $500 million and $2 billion[1] to get a new substance through the FDA approval process. They must, therefore, have the reassurance that they will recoup their investment and pay their stockholders dividends on any drug they take through this validation process. It can be a tricky thing to know which compounds to go with and which ones to abandon. What may look very promising at first may turn out, upon broader testing, to have too many side effects to be marketed. Until a drug is in widespread use, its deleterious attributes may remain unknown. With such a large investment in developing testing protocols, finding doctors and institutions willing to do the testing, and hiring companies to monitor the testing records, it is a disastrous day when a new drug has to be dropped before it is approved and has made money for the company.

This limits the number of substances that will ever be tested through the FDA approval process. A substance such as a vitamin or herbal supplement will never go through this very expensive process. Anything that is readily and cheaply available and is not patentable is not feasible for this kind of testing. In order to remain profitable, drug companies can only test and market molecules that they themselves have developed or bought from other biotech companies. A good example of this is the highly controversial substance, marijuana. Many studies have been done confirming the medicinal benefits of the marijuana blossom. It has been found to reduce nausea/vomiting and increase appetite in chemotherapy and AIDS patients, it reduces musculoskeletal spasms and pain, and it has many other therapeutic benefits. Yet it has still not been approved by the federal government to be used in even the sickest of patients. However, a synthetic THC-like molecule called dronabinol (Marinol®) was approved over a decade ago. The active ingredient in Marinol is a synthetic molecule similar to delta-9-tetrahydrocannabinol (delta-9-THC), a naturally occurring ingredient in the marijuana plant. However, natural marijuana has more than 40 other active ingredients, many having effects that Marinol does not have. Many patients do not care much for Marinol since it has such a long half-life and it leaves them stoned most of the day. And as many people know, one gets the munchies when pot's effects are wearing off, thus benefiting those who have poor appetites. Most patients who have used Marinol and marijuana much prefer the natural substance. But, as we all know, the synthetic molecule is the only one approved by the FDA, and the natural substance is still illegal by federal decree, which trumps legislation by individual states.

It is easy to understand that herbs, vitamins, and other supplements are not likely to be tested and approved for therapeutic purposes by the FDA. Fortunately, a number of scientific institutions are beginning to test promising supplements for efficacy in treating a number of illnesses. Even the NIH (National Institutes of Health) has created a section for testing alternative therapies. Other countries such as Germany and Japan have done intensive research on herbs and other alternative therapies for many years. I once visited Professor Josef Hoelzl at the University of Marburg in Germany who was the world's most knowledgeable person on Saint John's Wort (an herb often used for depression). Just as is possible with antibiotics and other drugs, he was able to measure St. John's Wort's strength in supplements and in ones blood and could tell you all known properties of this plant extract. This kind of knowledge regarding alternative therapies is just now beginning to permeate American society. In the appendix, I have listed a few good resources for finding useful information regarding alternative therapies.

The Western concept that the body, the mind and the spirit are separate entities is gradually giving way to a new unified vision. Research now demonstrates the benefits of meditation, thought control, moderating your emotions and stress reduction. Research is also helping us understand the way the body, mind and spirit work together. In her audiobook *Your Body is Your Subconscious Mind*[2], Dr. Candace Pert explains how neurotransmitters and cell signalers interact with receptor sites on every cell in the body to react to emotions and thoughts. Since that is true, we can no longer think of the brain as acting separately from the rest of the body – taking in stimuli about the environment, making decisions about these stimuli and sending signals to the body about how to react to the incoming stimuli. Every cell in the body participates in this process. This explains why every tissue in the body can be affected by stress and negative emotions and thoughts. As we free our minds from conflicts, anger and resentment caused by judgment, all of our body's tissues benefit.

The prefrontal cortex differentiates man from all other species. The prefrontal cortex of the brain is the Chief Executive Officer. It filters out extraneous stimuli to help us determine which things are worthy of our concern and which things are not. If we allow it, the prefrontal cortex can be programmed by others' expectations, random incoming thoughts and experiences, and predetermined emotional reactions so that it lets in continuously distracting stimuli instead of filtering them out. We process these stimuli in a way that is detrimental to our physical and spiritual health. If we can learn to control our thoughts and emotions, we will begin to reprogram our prefrontal cortex to deal with the things we encounter everyday in a more constructive and less damaging way. There will always be plenty of dangerous situations going on around us, but we have a great deal of control over the level of fear that arises. There will always be opportunities to be angry or hurt by what others say or do, but we have the choice to react viciously or unperturbed. To react in ways that are not customary takes some insight and self-training.

Some good techniques for doing this reprogramming are meditation (mindfulness), biofeedback, binaural beat therapy, relaxation and guided imagery techniques, self-help books and any other process that helps one control one's reactions to everyday occurrences. We now use the word *mindfulness* in the United States to eliminate the religious associations that exist with the word *meditation*.

The more we learn to choose and be mindful of our experiences and thoughts, the more we contribute to the development of healthy joyful mind/bodies. If we choose to be entertained by violence and conflict, that kind of energy will be incorporated into our mind/bodies. If we learn to think critically and really evaluate information and circumstances free from emotional charge, we can expand our thoughts into those that are helpful in creating a better perception of the world and ourselves. Therefore, eliminating our absolute thought processes can help us heal our mind/bodies.

* * * * *

Mavis was a patient of mine with numerous problems. She was considerably overweight, her knees and ankles were deteriorating with osteoarthritis and she had difficulty exercising in order to lose weight. Her cholesterol and triglycerides were quite high and she was at risk for developing diabetes. She was a working mother, her only children at home were, as she called them, "typical teens." Her job was full of stress and her coworkers caused her a lot of anxiety and did not seem to respect her abilities. Her husband was always on her case to lose weight and she was suffering from many symptoms of depression. She had been on every diet she had come across, but any weight loss was never permanent. She had never tried antidepressants because she had heard of numerous side effects. As she gave me her history, I could tell that she was close to tears much of the time.

I began to talk to her about a possible different approach to her life and her health problems. I talked about learning to meditate, possibly starting with binaural beat therapy. I told her that there were other ways to exercise than walking or running, which can be hard on arthritic knees. Symphony conductors seem to live long lives whether or not they walk or run daily. Perhaps the upper-body exercise they get is more than adequate. I recommended to her that she "direct" the music on her television or CD player, possibly with small weights in her hand. I told her about some supplements and dietary changes that have been shown to help reduce cholesterol and help her lose weight. I told her that her issues with food needed to be dealt with in different terms than the latest dietary fad and that she needed to become aware of her relationship with food. I also told her that getting some counseling could help with her familial relationships and those with her work colleagues. I even mentioned the possibility of a short course of antidepressants to help her get a different perspective.

At first she was resistant because she had grown up in a family that made her feel that needing counseling was a sign of weakness and that faith and prayer should solve all problems. Meditation belonged in Eastern religions and not in Christianity. And she had always believed that only standard allopathic treatments were properly tested and therefore useful in treating ailments of any kind. But she was feeling a great deal of pain at this time and I eventually convinced her to try some of these alternative things. She even agreed to try a course of antidepressants until she had her life in better perspective.

Over the next few months she began to use the meditation CD's and got counseling to help her understand how to deal more effectively with the problems in her life. She started "conducting music" and soon realized that she was breathing hard after only a few minutes. As she became more conscious and aware, she concluded that she actually had a food addiction, with food serving as a temporary escape from her unhappy situation. Knowing this, she began to change her relationship with food and gradually began to eat to live rather than live to eat. Her cholesterol came down and she began to lose weight. Now and then she would revert back to her old ways of thinking and would lapse into old behavior. I explained to her that this was normal to occasionally get off the track and that she should not feel bad about it but just get back on track as soon as possible.

As with anyone, the path to new thought processes and behaviors was a bit of an uphill climb and went slower than she would have liked, but each success led to new insights and made the journey easier. She eventually admitted that learning the concept of combining a number of useful therapeutic options from different disciplines was something that she would use the rest of her life.

* * * * *

Just as we accept that there are many opportunities and options for healing our bodies and spirits, we must realize that there are also many ineffective therapies that are hyped and advertised. How do we know what will work for us and what will not? How do we know what to combine with what and how effective any combination might be? The first thing to understand is that, like everything else, there are no absolutes in medicine. Every disease varies from patient to patient in how severe it is, what the symptoms are and how it will best be treated. No supplement or FDA-approved drug has absolute efficacy or is absolutely free from side effects. The same is true for any other therapeutic options. Even if a treatment is shown to be 95% effective, you may still be in that 5% for whom it does not work. Or the opposite might be true. You could be in the 5% for whom a therapy *is* effective. So how does one navigate through all the available therapeutic options? Here are a few ideas that should be helpful.

First, do your homework. With the Internet, there are limitless options for looking up your problems and possibly helpful therapies. In the appendix you will find some resources that are currently available online, but there are many others. Although often difficult, determining your diagnosis is the first and most important step. The doctors you see won't always be familiar with the problem you have. I treated a lot of ME/CFS (Chronic Fatigue Syndrome) patients when I was in practice – I call ME/CFS, fibromyalgia, gulf war syndrome and others the *mysterious illnesses*. Many of these patients had seen many doctors before me. Most often, the doctors had ordered a few basic tests normally done when a patient complains of fatigue and other vague symptoms. When nothing definitive showed up, the patient was treated for depression. Because I was familiar with these mysterious illnesses, I would hear two or three of the patient's symptoms and would be able to describe most of their other health challenges. Often this would bring them to tears because they finally felt validated and relieved to know what was wrong.

It's important to understand that you must always be your own healthcare director/patient advocate. It may seem strange to hear a doctor saying this, but you cannot leave your health in the hands of healthcare professionals. They may or may not do the right thing for you. Many times it will take awhile to find a physician with expertise and an understanding of your problems. You may need to do a bit of research first. There is a plethora of books and newsletters about available alternative therapies. You can use search engines to look up a variety of opinions about any therapeutic option you might be interested in. You will hear and read many differing opinions about any of these therapeutic options.

This is an opportunity to develop your evaluative thinking abilities. In looking at health and wellness modalities, you really have to back away from the mural and look at the entire picture. I have treated many HIV/AIDS patients and was often surprised by some attitudes I encountered. Patients who were getting very sick would refuse to take the available antiviral medications because they had heard of some short-term or long-term side effects. I explained that the untreated virus was creating much more serious side effects than the medications would. Look at the pros and cons of side effects vs. benefits of a treatment. How expensive is it? Can cheaper therapies be just as effective? Is the therapy likely to cause harm? Could a combination of therapeutic modalities be more effective than a single modality? For example, would a person with high blood pressure do better with medications, meditation and moderate exercise than with just medications alone? Evaluate the source of the information. Is it a source that has a good track record? Does the information seem unbiased? Is someone making money by giving you information about their modality (that's not always a bad thing)? Have you heard good personal reports (not just testimonials) about it? Have you looked for support groups or web discussions of your problem? You can get more objective opinions in these groups. You can also find names of physicians who might be more familiar with your condition. Weigh all the information you can gather and make some decisions.

Second, try it. There are two types of therapy – one is for a condition you currently have and the other is for achieving and maintaining good overall health. Medications from your doctor will usually be to treat a specific condition such as diabetes or high blood pressure. Supplements such as vitamins and antioxidants may be used for treating specific conditions or for long-term health benefits. Medicines, supplements and other therapies take variable amounts of time to show results. Always check on known interactions with other medications and modalities before you start. I always recommend giving a therapy (such as a supplement to treat a specific condition) at least two months before deciding about its benefit, unless its side effects make it intolerable for you. When trying to determine which supplements will give you the best long-term health effects, try to find studies that show benefit rather than just listening to the hype. Otherwise you can spend a small fortune on supplements. Some things such as meditation, yoga, dietary changes and exercise take more time to be properly evaluated. Always consider the possibility that a combination of things may be necessary to accomplish your healing.

Third, keep a record. Every person should have a copy of his medical records as far back as possible. Parents should have records on all their children. You have a right to your medical records even though people may try to convince you otherwise. Keep your records locked in a filing cabinet and update them regularly. This may seem silly, but it is really vital. In my area a local healthcare facility went out of business and people couldn't access their medical records. My niece couldn't get into college without a record of her immunizations. Also, if you have your records, a new doctor can see exactly what you have done in the past to determine what might be helpful again.

Keep a personal health journal. If you are generally healthy and feel fine, you won't have much to write. If you are dealing with poorer health or have a chronic condition, you may be writing a lot in your journal. Journaling makes it is easier to see the effects or consequences of any new therapies you start. It can also be useful to help you remember what you have already tried and which combinations are most effective. Once a month write everything down that you are currently taking or doing. Daily, or as often as possible, write down how you feel, other things that might be affecting you, and any changes you make in the regimen. You might even create a 1-10 type scale to use in different areas (e.g. – energy level, pain, mood or other important measures of how you are doing). Data such as blood sugars, blood pressures and temperatures should be recorded. Every so often go back and look at your journal to see if you find any patterns or interesting observations.

Finally, the United States has the most expensive healthcare system in the world and is 37th in healthcare outcomes such as infant mortality, life expectancy and the overall health of its people.[3] We cannot expect to improve the health of the nation if we continue to allow Big Corporate Healthcare and Big Pharma to run our healthcare system. We have, unfortunately, let ourselves be brainwashed into thinking that a national healthcare plan would be terrible, that we would have to wait inordinate periods of time before seeing a doctor or having a procedure, that it would mean euthanasia for the elderly, that it would take away our choice of doctors and that bureaucrats would be making decisions that should be between doctors and their patients. Right now Big Corporate Health is making those decisions for you, if you are lucky enough to have healthcare coverage at all. Healthcare insurance companies play no useful role in the healthcare process, and they cost us a huge amount of money that goes to stockholders and corporate executives instead of doctor/patient benefits. A national healthcare plan has the potential to change the focus of medicine and provide affordable healthcare to all.

Big Corporate Healthcare has spent billions of dollars over the years trying to keep the status quo. When Medicare part D (the prescription drug benefit) was passed with much ado, it was not even considered that Medicare could negotiate large volume drug price discounts as is done in other countries. Big Pharma had lobbied that out as a possibility. United States patients subsidize cheap drugs for the rest of the world in that we pay much more for our drugs than people in other countries where the government can buy pharmaceuticals at quantity discount prices. Many people still order their medications from Canada or Mexico because it is cheaper than buying them here – and Big Pharma is trying to stop that from happening. While President Barrack Obama tried to get Congress to pass a healthcare reform bill, Big Corporate Health was spending $1.4 million per day (taken from your healthcare premiums) to lobby congressmen to do nothing. They organized obnoxious disruptive groups to create chaos at town hall meetings with our congressmen so that beneficial discussion could not occur. They spent millions on fear-based television ads. And we fell for it, as we often do.

We continue to allow our government to spend trillions of dollars to expand our military industrial complex, but we lack a national healthcare plan because of corporate interests. If we do not allow ourselves to look outside the box and consider any other healthcare options than those we currently have, the health of our people will continue to decline while we are still erroneously convinced that "we have the best healthcare system in the world."

Chapter Thirteen

HOORAY FOR HOLLYWOOD

We must get the American public to look past the
glitter, beyond the showmanship, to the reality, the
hard substance of things. And we'll do it not so much
with speeches that will bring people to their feet as
with speeches that bring people to their senses.

Mario Cuomo,
52nd Governor of New York

We had all gotten to work a little late that Election Day morning. We had our "I Voted" stickers on our clothes and naturally began to discuss politics and who had voted for whom. This year a very well qualified woman with a deep voice named Carolyn Warner was running against a car dealer named Evan Mecham. Most of us had voted for the more experienced woman, except for June, the back office nurse who also had a very deep voice. "What made you decide to vote for Mecham?" we asked. "Oh, I don't know," June said. "I just couldn't vote for someone who has a deeper voice than I do."

I have canvassed for a couple of political candidates in whom I believed, which meant I got to talk to a lot of people about why they were voting for this candidate or that one. I have always been amazed at how little people know about the candidates or their platforms and how much importance they put on their appearance, charisma or ability to deliver a speech. We seem to care too little about the substance of a message and too much about its presentation. This is true about most aspects of American life. We seem to be a *Hollywood society*.

Here in America we have some of the most talented moviemakers, television producers and entertainers in the world. We have come to expect that all we watch or listen to will be presented in an entertaining way. We make judgments and form opinions on important topics based more on entertainment value than the information itself. Huge amounts of money are poured into election campaigns. The ads are so negative and irrelevant that one scarcely knows what the real viewpoints of the candidates are. There is certainly nothing wrong with enjoying information that is presented in a well-organized and entertaining fashion, but how much important and useful information do we miss when it's presented by someone who is not a great entertainer? How often do we let the charisma of a religious or political person influence our opinions about what they tell us? How often does a good idea go undeveloped because the one with the idea happens to be a mild mannered person who can't present it with enough gusto to grab the listener?

Noam Chomsky is an example of a speaker with fascinating things to say but who speaks in a monotone. His knowledge and analysis of events is so far from standard thinking that I gain new insights every time I hear him speak. He is, by his own admission, a very bland speaker who talks in a matter-of-fact monotone voice and just tells it like it is. That is his natural style. It takes effort to listen to him, but if you do, you will learn things about historic and present day events that will change your views, perhaps profoundly.

On the other hand, men or women who have the gift of charisma and showmanship and who are powerful speakers can often convince us of things that have no basis in truth. They know, as Joseph Goebbels did, that a lie told often enough and with enough passion and theatrical flare will often be accepted as truth, even when people intuitively know it is not. They have the ability to inflame our passions and bypass our ability to reason with their skillfully-contrived rantings and ravings. For the last decade or more the "Shock Jocks" of radio and television have had to become more and more outrageous and inflammatory to ignite the emotions of their viewers and listeners. Once they hook a listener, they can say the most absurd and idiotic things, and the outlandish points they make will never be questioned or evaluated critically by their fans. They simply spew it forth with the credibility of the most respected investigative reporter. Unfortunately, this erroneous information will be passed on to others who are also prone to accept things unevaluated until ridiculous ideas often gain a historic place of their own.

* * * * *

Johann Friedrichs was living in Atlanta in 1979 when he told a friend of mine why he had come to America. He had lived in Berlin as a young man and had witnessed the stormy rise of a fanatical young man named Adolf Hitler and heard him give powerful speeches on the radio. One day Johann heard that Mr. Hitler was going to be the featured speaker at a huge political rally in the city's largest stadium. He decided he needed to go hear this man in person to determine what he really thought about his politics. The stadium was packed with people eager to hear the man speak who would someday be known as "Der Fuehrer" (The Leader). Johann listened intently to what this man had to say, mostly about the threat Jews and other "undesirables" posed to German society. The crowds roared at the end of each bellowed statement. The excitement was palpable and this man Hitler had an uncanny ability to use the German language to persuade people and incite their rage and passion.

As Johann walked home from the rally, he found himself very moved by Hitler's words and was furious about the Jewish threat to German society. Then he stopped dead in his tracks and choked as he said to himself, "Wait a minute, I'm a Jew!" His heart pounded and his mind raced as he began to understand the power of language, group incitement and unquestioned patriotism to create a national enemy, and Johann decided to leave Germany at once and came to the U.S.A., thereby escaping the Nazi atrocities. True story.

* * * * *

Religious organizations gain large congregations if the production aspects are good. Musical numbers must be more and more phantasmagoric with orchestras or rock bands to accompany the singing. Ministers seem to be more passionate Shakespearean actors than bearers of the good word. The more charismatic they are, the more they can produce strong emotions in their congregations, and the larger these congregations grow; these larger congregations seem to be able to draw more people into them.

Lawyers seem very often to be frustrated thespians whose ability to sway a jury is often based more on performance art than on evidence. And, unfortunately, their tactics work all too well on juries who may be confused by the presented evidence and complicated laws, and they are swayed by an Oscar winning performance that makes a lawyer's argument seem more valid. With the use of DNA evidence, we now realize that many innocent people have been imprisoned and even executed, and many who were judged innocent have been found guilty. When judges instruct jurors regarding what they can and can't consider in reaching a verdict, jurors should know that they are, nevertheless, allowed to make their own decisions based on logical evaluation of the evidence and even on what their instincts tell them. It is often difficult to reach a verdict based purely on evidence, but good acting should have nothing to do with the important verdicts that impact people's lives so deeply.

Like lawyers, legislators are people who seem to be aspiring orators. After political debates, post-debate analysts talk about body language, eye contact, faux pas, manner of dress and whether they looked into the camera. We know little about what they would do to change our government for the better, but we do know who wore an American flag label pin and who didn't. With all the respect that we usually give Senators and Representatives (well, not so much currently), one would think that we could rely on the information they give us as being well researched and correct. However, as we have seen for so many years now, their information very often comes from the influence of skilled lobbyists who give our legislators "talking points." Usually the views of politicians are colored more by contributions from big business than by factual information. They choose "facts" that support their viewpoint and spin information in a way that makes the other guy look bad and them look good. They find out what the viewpoints are of a crowd of people to whom they will speak and tell them just what they want to hear, not concerned with the fact that it totally contradicts what they said to different crowds. This makes it difficult to determine what candidates will most likely bring to the legislative process. Will it be cooperation in working for the common good of all people, or will the candidates impede the legislative process by supporting the wealthy corporations who fund them? It is too often the latter, allowing corporations to buy those who are supposed to represent the interests of their constituents.

The main purpose of the mainstream media seems to be to distract us from the real problems that we should be working on. "If it bleeds, it leads," has been the media's motto. We see few examples of good things that are happening and even fewer possible solutions to the real problems that need to be addressed. We were furious when the banks had been so unscrupulous that we had to bail them out with taxpayer money. They caused so much economic and psycho-emotional grief in the country that the Occupy Wall Street movement emerged – and this time we were going to take the banking system to task. But then our attention was drawn to the mass shooting of white children and we were distracted from economic corruption, determined that this time would be different and that we would push Congress to get some gun legislation passed. But Congress did nothing and we were distracted again by new revelations that our government is spying on us as well as the rest of the world, and gun control legislation was forgotten about until the next mass shooting. The 24-hour news cycle gives us endless things to worry about and be afraid of, and the newest story grabs our attention away from the last thing we were outraged about. We seem to be in a state of societal attention deficit disorder ("Oh look, a shiny new frightening object!").

Some people seem to be addicted to this fear-based reportage, but it only adds dark energy to their psycho-emotional status. How can it do anything to relieve the stress of one's day to come home and watch the news for the rest of the night? There are other options (albeit few) in your television programming that will uplift you and better inform you. Seek these out and let the "bleeding" alone. "But I need to know what's going on. How else will I fight it?" you might say. The reality is that very few people who get programmed with fear will ever become activists to change society for the better. Fear is a tactic used to control the masses so they will allow the powerbrokers to do whatever they want. It is impossible to fight fear with fear – you only get greater fear. The best thing we can do to counteract fear, anger and violence is to keep our lives filled with love, gratitude and compassion regardless of negative world events. This is hard to do with a constant diet of fear-based news. Only light energy can supplant the dark energy. The best activism is always born of love. Mother Teresa said that she would never speak at an anti-war rally, only at a peace gathering.

The 24-hour news cycle has also created a most disturbing atmosphere of contentiousness and irrelevance in covering politics. Instead of reporting relevant and useful information, they spend their time blathering on about he-said-she-said stuff, trying to catch people in word traps, making mountains out of molehills and sensationalizing everything possible.

"Obama said the mind meld came from Star Wars instead of Star Trek."

"Candidate X said..., but two years ago he said... What a flip-flopper!"

"Can you imagine anyone wearing a dress like that to the debates?"

"He didn't look into the camera and had very little charisma." (But what did he say?!)

The Citizens United decision from the Supreme Court allows enormous amounts of corporate money to be donated anonymously to campaigns that serve corporate interests. Our elections have become clown shows with a focus on negative campaigning making it nearly impossible to not be disgusted by it all. Since the public's vote is so strongly affected by negative but effective ads, these ads will proliferate like cockroaches. It is apparent that campaign reform, including public financing, will never occur until we have a constitutional amendment, taking corporations out of the same category as human beings. Since there is little chance of that happening until people understand that it can, the best thing we can do is minimize the effect of political brainwashing by not tuning in to it.

Edward Bernays was the American nephew of Sigmund Freud, the founding father of psychoanalysis. Although Bernays is almost completely unknown today, his influence on our society is probably greater than Freud's. Like Freud, Bernays was convinced that humans were driven by irrational forces and could never be allowed to fully express themselves, and that they must be tightly controlled and would always be discontented. Bernays used the new science developed by his famous uncle to manipulate the masses. He invented the profession and the term *public relations*. He worked for most of the major corporations and advised politicians on how to win favor with the public. By stimulating our inner desires and then sating them with consumer products, he believed he could manage the often-unpredictable behavior of the masses. He understood that humans make decisions based as much on emotions as on information. Today's advertising and marketing companies rely on the principles of Edward Bernays to sell products, sway public opinion, get politicians elected and assuage the outrage of the people when those politicians misbehave.

Advertising is a multi-billion dollar business that produces the most persuasive messages and the best sound effects, images, music and jingles to sell products and ideas. Advertisers develop messages and presentation techniques from intense studies they have conducted by polling focus groups and the public in general. They also mine a huge amount of available data about people's buying habits through credit card records, supermarket bargain cards and Internet social sites. Their goal is to persuade consumers to buy products or ideas by creating an emotional reaction that they are not even aware of.

When we choose to be entertained by movies, television or video games, we must then make the choice of what kind of energy we will bring into our lives. The debate goes on about whether violent video games cause shootings or other violent events. Two large meta-analyses (analyses that look at many studies for overall trends) including data from over 134,000 people have concluded that violent media causes more aggressive behavior in real life.[1] Whether violence in the media, especially video games, is solely responsible for mass shootings is doubtful, but, together with isolation, maladjustment, bullying and other risk factors for violent behavior, media violence does add in to the total equation. These games make expendable targets out of what are represented as human beings on the screen. They certainly smother our reverence for life and instill the concept that there are always enemies to be dealt with violently and that might always makes right. There is rarely a day that passes in this country where an argument or a perceived threatening situation does not result in someone getting shot with the excuse of self-defense or "just standing my ground." Totally crazy!

All the books, movies, television shows and video games we choose have their own energies. Video games like *Call of Duty, Medal of Honor, Battlefield* and the U.S. Army's own *America's Army* seek to glorify war and make their games as lifelike as possible, but certain realities are omitted. No one leaves the game missing arms or legs or having sustained serious brain trauma. Severe post-traumatic stress disorder does not often occur with video games and no one is left disabled and unable to provide for his family or needing to deal with the Veteran's Administration for the rest of his life. One simply pushes the ESCAPE button and reboots for another game. The adrenalin rush is addictive and no one believes that mindless fun can have any detrimental effects – but they are wrong. Entertainment and reality are confused, stupidity is often mistaken for courage, and our youth are being programmed to support the ongoing war machine. If they get onto the real battlefield, however, they find the situation is very different – but, by then, they are committed. We need to seriously consider the energy that is brought into our societies by what we choose to be entertained by.

When we participate in acts of kindness, either giving kindness or receiving it, serotonin levels go up in our brains (which makes us feel better), and our immune systems are strengthened. More surprisingly though, just observing acts of kindness and compassion increases serotonin levels and improves our immune functioning to about the same degree as being involved in such acts. Observing acts of violence and aggression affects us as well – but in the opposite direction. We are taught that being a man is all about aggression and power, but we *do* get to decide whether we believe this is true. Whether we choose degrading entertainment or entertainment that fills us with love, our choices will determine whether we actively emit darkness or light, and that energy adds to the total energy equation for the planet. Everything we expose ourselves to creates attitudes and emotions about everyday life, and the sum total of these attitudes affects the energy and behavior of a society's people. Energy is everything!

We have the ability to determine what will be presented to us in the media. I have a friend who decided to vote against the candidates who had the most negative ads in the last election. We also vote every time we buy something. When we choose not to buy something because the company it comes from supports issues we don't agree with or advertises on programs full of violence and fear, we make our desires known in the strongest way possible. Companies want to sell their ideas or their products. Letting them know that we will not be purchasing them because of their policies speaks louder than anything else we can do.

Having thousands of entertainment options is a relatively new phenomenon. A century ago, there were a few radio stations. A half-century ago we had three or four television stations in addition to radio programming. Now the fight for consumer dollars and for the minds of men has created a monstrous conundrum. News has become nothing more than entertainment. Most news sources are owned by large corporations and what we see on the news generally benefits the wealthy few. It is easiest to believe that which is presented in an entertaining and convincing way, whether or not it is true. Being entertained is not a bad thing, but we must be cautious to separate the theatrics from the message. There are many good messages and concepts that will be missed if we tune them out because they are not presented in an entertaining way. Likewise, we must be careful not to allow others to program us for war, consumerism, intolerance and fear by hiding their messages in well-produced spectacles.

Chapter Fourteen

MONDAY MORNING DIETS

I can resist everything except temptation.

Oscar Wilde

Your class reunion is only two months away. You would like to be forty pounds lighter when your old classmates see you. So the diet must begin right away. You know that Monday morning is always the best time to start a diet. So you get your diet all planned out and your determination is going to help you succeed this time. Monday goes well. Every meal is just as you planned. Tuesday cruises along nicely. Your success so far has inspired you to stick to your diet with perfect control. Wednesday is a little tougher because you are getting pretty hungry by the end of the day, but you do it! Thursday arrives and all is going well until they celebrate Julie's birthday at the office. Oh nooo! Pam has made her famous German chocolate cake. Well, nobody knows you are dieting, so you just *have* to have a piece of your all time favorite cake. That night when you arrive home, you are hungrier than ever because of the sugar crash, and you are quite discouraged that you had that piece of cake at the office. So dinner becomes a bit of a pig out. Totally discouraged, you realize that you have blown your diet so badly that you're going to have to start all over again. But the weekend is coming up, and everyone knows that all diets start on Monday mornings, so you revert back to your old eating habits for Friday, Saturday, and Sunday. On Monday morning, it all starts over again.

Whether it is dieting, exercising, quitting smoking, staying away from video games and the Internet, keeping the house clean, or any other thing you feel you need to change, the "Monday Morning Diet" scenario often comes into play. And the all-or-nothing way of thinking is what keeps us stuck in this pattern. "Winning isn't everything, it is the only thing," has become our motto (I never really figured out what that meant). So failure is no option. This is really an absurd and very destructive way of thinking. If we regard every lapse in behavior as failures, we begin to think of ourselves as failures. This sets us up for further failure. There has to be a better way to create desired changes in our lives.

Perhaps we need a different perspective. We didn't develop bad habits overnight, and we will not fix them overnight. Our first mistake is setting unreasonable, unrealistic goals. Before attempting to change our behavior, we need to analyze to the best of our ability the causes of that behavior. Most compulsive behavior results from an unconscious need to relieve stress or boredom or to provide pleasure. Each time the behavior is repeated, it takes us closer to a state called addiction. Most often addiction is thought of as being related to drugs, but we can become addicted to almost anything. Food, sex, exercise, video games, television, and mood altering substances are certainly not negative things in and of themselves, but when they become habitual escape routes, they become addictive. Even our emotions can be addictive, as will be explained later.

Doctors no longer look at addiction in a strictly physiologic way. Stopping the substance or activity does not have to cause withdrawal symptoms. We now look at addiction in the light of its effects on our lives. Does looking at porno or playing video games interfere with the relationships in your life? Does using food to escape boredom or deal with stress cause health and self-image issues? Does watching too much television or spending a lot of time on the Internet keep you from interacting with friends and family or keeping your house clean? Does alcohol or pot numb you out to the point that things don't get done or cause you to lose your job? Addiction can be stark or subtle, continuous or binge, very destructive or just moderately disruptive. Clearly it is one of our greatest learning challenges. It is one of the things we have to deal with effectively if we are to have the best life possible.

At one time an addicted person was considered simply a weak person – whatever that means. Now we understand the biochemistry of addictions of all kinds. We now know that all the cells of our bodies have receptor sites for hundreds of small proteins called peptides. There are endorphin receptors that can decrease pain perception when endorphins attach to them. Every emotional state is associated with certain neuropeptides, including our perception of pleasure.

There are also networks of nerve cells that fire together throughout our brains. These nerve pathways (neural nets) bond together when activities or emotions are repeated regularly. While they are strengthened by repetitive patterns, they can also be disrupted when these patterns are discontinued or altered.

Human beings are wired to seek pleasure, or at least relief. Addictions are usually an escape, sometimes from the mundane and boring, often from the painful and scary, and always to a place we'd rather be. Instead of doing the dishes or homework, we escape to television or the computer. When anxiety or boredom hits, we might escape to the taste and texture of ice cream. When our lives seem out of control and frightening, we may seek to escape with the help of chemicals such as alcohol or prescription drugs. We usually don't intend to become habituated, but every time we decide to escape "just this once," the behavior, substance or emotion becomes more strongly wired in. Sometimes we try a drug like cocaine or meth because someone else has told us what a rush it is. That rush happens because these molecules bind to the same receptor sites as the endorphins or other neuropeptides (nervous system molecules) that are made naturally in the body. But these chemicals bind more rapidly and more tightly than the natural neuropeptides do. It creates a very strong event memory and, even though we might fear becoming addicted, every cell in our body eagerly anticipates the next rush.

The larger events in our lives are always associated with strong emotions, and these emotional imprints help us to remember these events. "Unforgettable moments" are always events that were full of strong feelings, whether positive or negative. Every time the remembrance of these events is triggered, the feelings associated with them are reignited. These strong emotions, in turn, strengthen the imprint of that memory in our minds. As we remember the event with its emotional charge, it gets even more deeply imprinted, which makes it even more memorable – the so-called *vicious circle*. In the case of addiction, the high (or momentary pleasure) one gets from the addictive behavior reinforces the craving for that addictive behavior; i.e. – the memory of how one feels on alcohol instantly comes to mind when the stress of a current situation creates discomfort that needs to be relieved. Every time one takes a drink, the feeling of relief or numbness reinforces the desire for more alcohol. However, every time one denies the addictive behavior, the neural nets associated with it begin to break down.

The concept of *assigned values* was discussed in an earlier chapter. This principle says that every event in our lives – every occurrence, every circumstance, everything someone says to us or does to us – has only the value we assign to it and therefore has only the emotional charge we give it. In other words, a situation is just a situation, and it is how we interpret it that causes our feelings about it. This concept is all about perception. We have been conditioned to think, for most situations, that there are standard reactions. We *must* feel insulted and hurt when someone says something that could be perceived as derogatory. What reaction other than fear is possible when we see something threatening on TV? How could anybody respond to certain unfortunate circumstances with anything but depression? But we all have the option of assigning non-standard values to the circumstances of our lives, thereby perceiving things as less traumatic, less stressful or less unfortunate. We can see the death of a loved one as something we'll never get over, or we can appreciate the beauty that person brought into our lives every time they come to mind. We have thus assigned a positive emotional charge to the memory of that loss rather than a tragic one.

Psychologists often use the principle of *assigned value* in what they call *rational emotive therapy*. We interpret situations in our lives, and that determines how we feel about them. If the feelings our interpretations cause are uncomfortable, we may try to think of something that would take us to a happier place – like eating a piece of cake, taking mood altering substances, or going to our computers. Some people think that it is the emotions that are addictive, and others feel it is the behaviors these emotions lead to that are addictive. But it is clear that giving a positive or neutral value to an event, circumstance or thought will lead to a more positive emotional charge. This will, in turn, lead to feelings and behaviors that make our lives better. This is not easy to do because we are so strongly influenced by the way we have interpreted events or thoughts in our past. But that is what becoming conscious and aware is all about. We consciously notice the situations that confront us every day and make willful choices to interpret them in a more positive and beneficial way, thus creating a more positive – or at least neutral – emotional charge.

Addiction is usually caused by an unpleasant emotion coming up (boredom, anger, anxiety, depression or maybe fear). This unpleasant emotion then needs to be replaced by a happier one (relief, enjoyment, euphoria or even numbness), and this desire for a happier emotion leads us to the addictive behavior. If your boss at work is always in your face and criticizing your work, you may interpret his or her behavior as totally unappreciative of what you do. You may even believe that you have all the terrible traits you're being told you have, and that you are far inferior to other employees and other people. This interpretation will lead to unhappy feelings of anxiety, not being appreciated, anger and depression. You may feel you have no other option than to tolerate this behavior because you need the job. If you cannot leave these feelings at the workplace, you will likely need some way to dissipate this stress after work. And, besides the addictive behaviors used to get rid of the stress, you often take out your frustrations on those who don't deserve it. Since your situation is about the same each day, your dependence on these things for relief will eventually cause habituation. Eventually you get to the point that the addictive behavior doesn't even need stress or boredom to trigger it; it's now automatically what you turn to no matter what is going on in your life.

Addiction can be dealt with at any step in this process. You can avoid thoughts or situations, when possible, that would make you uncomfortable. Since changing jobs is not so simple these days, you may need to assign a different value to your boss's behavior that makes it meaningless and non-hurtful. You can say to yourself, "I'm doing my job to the best of my ability. I don't know what factors influence his or her way of treating people, but I wish this person well in becoming a more enlightened human being."

If your emotions are affected negatively anyway, you can say to yourself, "I don't like being hurt and depressed, so I will find something else to dwell on." Replace the unpleasant things that were said with thoughts of something that brings you joy – a favorite pet, a great song or a good friend (unless that friend is booze or other problematic things). You could even try thinking about what positive things you could do to keep your boss more pleased with your work.

Finally, it is important to understand that any particular feeling does not have to lead to a predictable behavior. If you're feeling hurt and depressed, you don't absolutely have to reach for the alcohol. You can go for a brisk walk humming the *Stars and Stripes Forever* instead. If that little happy feeling comes that reminds you what it would feel like to use meth, cocaine or pain killers, remind yourself that their usage would just reinforce a habit that is destructive and that needs to be given up.

We don't have to like an emotion to become addicted to it. A person who suffers a setback may automatically experience feelings of depression or victimization. Another person may react differently to the same setback and even become excited at the challenge of finding a good way to deal with it. It has a lot to do with what we've learned in the past and what secondary benefit we get from an emotion. The feeling of being a victim is extremely addictive since the victim stance has a very strong secondary benefit. If everything is someone else's fault, then the victim is not responsible and has no real action to take – nothing to change in his own life. The victim believes that others must change in order for the victim to become happy. Similarly, if a person experiences a lot of anxiety and/or depression, it often comes from having the perspective that they have no control over their life – a bit like victimhood. Feeling angry, emotionally hurt, bitter or sad can be every bit as habituating as overeating or drinking too much alcohol. "But I don't want to feel this way; it just comes over me," is the natural reaction of a person who is told that he or she is addicted to his or her automatic emotional responses. Emotions do seem to wash over us, but we must let the negative ones run off us as water runs off a duck's back instead of absorbing them like a terrycloth towel.

People can become so immersed in their emotions that their feelings begin to determine how they view their lives. If they're feeling bad, they must be having a bad life. Many people truly want to get rid of dark emotions, but they feel stuck with them. When we revisit a hurtful moment in our past, we feel the same painful emotions we had at the time it happened. Thus we allow our past to create the way we feel about our lives right now. We need to remember that we always have the option of choosing what we focus on *right now* – revisiting unpleasant moments or focusing on more joyful times. We really *do* get to choose which thoughts to let stay in our minds and which to drop. Often we perseverate on painful events thinking, "I really wish I could have thought of something vicious to say back to her at the time." Or maybe, "That was such a stupid thing to let myself get into. How did I ever let it happen?" The more we practice choking these thoughts off as soon as they enter our minds, the less the unfortunate events in our lives will be able to rob us of our joy, and the less they will re-imprint themselves in our minds. Trying to numb these unhappy feelings rather than replace them with better ones can lead to cravings and addictions. You may have to tell yourself a hundred times, "Let it go, leave it alone." By paying attention to what we are thinking and feeling all the time, we give ourselves the opportunity of choosing the thoughts that will create the happy life we are looking for and we will be plagued with much less addictive behavior.

We have come to desire, and even expect, quick fixes for everything. When I told my patients that they had to eat better, cut down their stress and get some exercise, they would often say, "Isn't there a shot I can get instead?" We are not used to working on things long term, but there is no other way to get rid of the Monday morning diet trap. It may not be as hard to do as we expect. It just requires a new and different perspective of what life is. When we think of life as a series of goals to be achieved, it can be very depressing when we seem to be missing the mark all the time. But when we think of life as an evolutionary journey in which we pay attention to everything and learn from every bump in the road, it becomes much more doable in a series of gradual steps.

* * * * *

I was one of the first doctors in the Phoenix area to accept an AIDS patient into my practice. It began when one of my regular families discovered their son had contracted a strange and frightening new illness and was moving back from California to live with them. I didn't know much about this illness, but I wasn't about to turn him away. It wasn't long before a large part of my practice was devoted to the treatment of HIV disease. I became close friends with many of the patients that I saw often. One by one they became sicker and sicker and began to die. I was devastated, exhausted and depressed to the point of tears. I saw so many of my patients as people who were bright lights in a dark room, but I could do little or nothing for them as their lights went out one at a time. At the same time, it was a magnificent learning experience. Some of them had been abandoned by their families and came to live in my basement. Others had been lovingly taken in and cared for. I had pulled a number of them out of the grasp of death, but I had also been sued by the relatives of a woman who had asked me to help her with an alternative therapy when her immune system had been completely destroyed and she was near death. I was devastated by the continuing loss and had very few days when depression did not haunt me.

When I realized my depression was interfering with my ability to help my patients, I became determined to get rid of it. I knew it came with the territory, but *I did not like being depressed*. It made me angry that this ugly monster hung around so much of the time. I found that anger at my depression could occasionally be a useful tool. When the depression hit, I would just tell it – often furiously – to *just go away!* Then I would think of one of the wonderful interactive moments where I had really made a difference to someone. At first the depression just laughed at me and seemed to say, "Yeah, right." But after telling it to leave a hundred times, it began to understand that I was serious. After a thousand times it showed up far less often. And after ten thousand times, I saw it only rarely. I had finally broken up the neural net that had made depression such an integral part of my life. Of course I have been depressed by certain situations since then, but I decided a long time ago that I really don't like the dark feeling of depression, and it always has to leave after a very short time.

* * * * *

Bad habits, addictions – whatever you want to call them – have to be dealt with using certain tools. The first is *awareness*. When you slip off your diet on Wednesday, detach yourself from the depressive emotional charge that wants to be associated with falling off the wagon. Just observe the moment and ask yourself what just happened. Is there a different way you can look at things? Was there a certain trigger that could be avoided next time? If anxiety or boredom caused you to slip, can you deal with it differently? Can you just breathe deeply next time and let it pass? Can you just observe it without assigning any judgment or emotional charge? After reflecting for a moment, get right back on your diet and be happy for what you have learned. As a side note, I hope you really enjoyed that piece of cake, because research has shown that something delicious eaten with guilt actually depresses your immune system while true wondrous enjoyment boosts it.

The next tool is *persistence*. The quick fix just doesn't work. It has taken a long time for the neural nets associated with unwanted behavior to form. It will take a while to break those neural nets and create new, more functional ones. View your life as a path, not a goal. Pay close attention to every moment and, with patience and determination, try to control your thoughts all along your journey. Remember that the future can be nothing more than the sum of all your now moments. When alcohol or food or the television calls to you, stay in the moment and say to your destructive urges, "I've told you before, no thanks. That's only my receptor sites calling, and they're just going to have to quit bothering me." Each time your receptor sites don't get fed, they get less and less demanding and begin to decrease in number. You are forming new neural nets that you'll be much happier with.

There are also those strange times when moments of joy or accomplishment can actually trigger the same urges that anxiety and boredom have been causing. You're high on life, you're in a good moment, and you keep thinking that you'd like to take it up a notch or two. You feel like celebrating, but it certainly doesn't make much sense to say to yourself, "I'm going to celebrate my sobriety with a drink." Perhaps you can celebrate an occasion with a small piece of cake, as long as those occasions don't come too often. However, other more powerful molecules like alcohol, meth, cocaine and narcotics can affect your receptor sites so strongly that someone with abuse problems can't even use them "just this once" or "just a little bit," or they will bind rapidly and tightly to these receptor sites and that person will be in full-blown addiction behavior again. Learn to be happy in the warm glow of the moment, appreciate it, and quit looking for a higher high or a more joyful joy outside of yourself. Let your own endorphins fill up your receptor sites. And, if you slide off the path occasionally, just notice where the muddy spot was, wipe the mud off your feet, and get right back on the path without discouragement or despair. Just see it as another opportunity to learn about yourself. Persistence is hobbled by discouragement and feelings of failure. You have to take the emotional charge out of the picture.

One of the strongest and most useful tools in controlling addictions and bad habits is the practice of meditation (or *mindfulness* as it is often called here). Meditation is the practice of clearing ones mind of the constant chatter that goes on there. It works primarily on the frontal lobe, which is the center of thinking and decision-making. Mindfulness helps you to become more aware of what is happening moment to moment. The more you meditate, the less likely you will be able to do things that are not in your own best interest. Transcendental meditation is one of the most common forms of meditation, but it can take a long time to master. Another form of meditation that I have found to be very useful for breaking undesirable habits is *binaural beat therapy*. You put on headphones, try to clear your mind, and let the track on the CD run. It seems to take effect more rapidly than other methods. But consistency is the key with any type of meditation. When you begin to see results, stay with it and the benefits will increase over time.

One thing that seems like a no-brainer, but isn't always, is to keep temptations as far away as possible. If you don't bring the wrong kinds of food home, you can't eat them. If you have problems with substance abuse, you are going to have to remove yourself from the people and places that draw you into using these substances. This can be difficult because it may involve your friends and family. If undesirable emotions keep bugging you, try to identify any person or situation that seems to bring them up (there *is* caller ID). Then just keep persistently ejecting these emotions from you by replacing them with better ones.

Yes, I know. Changing habits that hinder spiritual progression is not so easy that it can be put in a few paragraphs and accomplished quickly. Sometimes we need to get help and support. A visit to the doctor may be helpful. But, when we slip – and we will, let's avoid the all-or-nothing attitude that stops us in our tracks and leaves us searching for a new start time. The next minute should be our new start time, if we want to wait that long. Our lives are evolutionary learning processes, not a series of goals that must be reached for us to be happy. Our continued persistence and focus will eventually cause the old neural nets to rewire and form new circuits that will help us slip from the clutches of our addictions.

Chapter Fifteen

TEMPERAMENTS AND COLORS

*Children are different from one another, especially
in temperament. Some are shy, others bold; some
active, some quiet; some confident, others less so.
Respect for individual differences is, in my view, the
cornerstone of good parent-child relationships.*

Sandra Scarr, developmental psychologist

"Why does she always have to be so silly and frivolous? Can't she ever be serious?"

"Tom always has to know exactly what we're going to do and how much it will cost. Can't he just be spontaneous and play it by ear?"

"She is the bossiest person I know... always has to be running the show... never can relax. She needs to give it a rest!"

"He seems really laid back, but push him a little too far and you're going to see another side of him."

Do you ever encounter people whose behavior you just can't understand? The circumstances at the time seem to demand a certain type of behavior, yet this person often acts in a way that seems to you totally inappropriate for the situation. If something needs to be accomplished, that person is always telling stories or being light-minded and never takes your instructions. Or perhaps you're the one who can't get excited about someone else's intense need to organize a situation and make worker bees out of a lot of people who don't seem to care that much about the project. Or you could be the one who thinks that the costs and time constraints need to be considered more completely before an activity begins.

"Why can't everyone be more like me?!" is a question that gets asked a lot. But most people don't really want an answer; they just want to express their frustration.

The most basic way to answer that question is that they *can't* be just like you because they were not born with the same temperament or personality as you. In the same way that we tried for years to attribute sexual orientation to chosen behavior, most people believe that a person's temperament is something they choose and therefore could easily modify if they could just understand why they needed to. We now understand that both assumptions are false.

A person's temperament is defined as his characteristic or habitual inclination or mode of emotional response. It is the root of one's personality. It is the way a person reacts to the events, circumstances and people that come his way. There are many ways to divide personality types up, sometimes ending up with as many as sixteen. The four most commonly described temperaments are sanguine, melancholic, choleric, and phlegmatic. In Dr. Taylor Hartman's book, *The Color Code*[1] (now available as *The People Code*), these four temperaments are metaphorically represented by red (choleric), blue (melancholic), yellow (sanguine), and white (phlegmatic). I am going to use the metaphoric color code to talk about the temperaments in this chapter. Using words like phlegmatic and melancholic doesn't really convey the temperaments as well as their representative colors do.

When I first began to understand the temperaments, it was one of the greatest aha moments of my life. It immediately began to decrease my judgment of others and allowed me to appreciate each person for what he or she brought to my world. An understanding of the basic personality types will give you amazing insight into why you, your friends and your relatives behave the way they do. In the end, I hope you will also understand why it would *not* be a good thing for everyone to be just like you.

Before discussing the color code, it is important to understand that very few people are completely one color or temperament. Most of us have a foundation of one personality type with shadings of another color, but many of us will see at least a little bit of each color within our personalities. Nothing is absolute. We are all much more complex beings than that. We may see ourselves much differently than others see us. We may wish we had more traits of certain colors than we do and less of the ones we have. But, if we understand the basics of each personality type, it will take us a long way toward helping us get rid of our unrealistic expectations of others and even of ourselves.

For each temperament there are strong points and problematic points. Even the strengths can be problematic and annoying under certain circumstances. You just have to accept a person's problematic points along with his strong points unless he has become aware of what bothers other people and has done some work on these issues. You can point out people's weaknesses until you're blue in the face, but you are not any more likely to get them to change for you than they are likely to get you to change for them. It's as much the way we are born as the color of our eyes. Any parent with more than one child knows that every child has its own personality from the earliest days. The best we can do is get some insight into everyone's makeup and try to capitalize on each personality's strengths. It is counterproductive to choose a Yellow to fulfill a Red's role. Here is a very abbreviated description of the strong and problematic points of each color.

REDS – Red people could be considered to be the Indian chiefs. They like to take charge, organize, and get things done *the right* way – *their* way. They are highly motivated and like to keep things moving efficiently. They seek positions of leadership and they like to be respected for their knowledge and logic. But they have little concern for the feelings of others and often don't have the time or patience for "silly emotions." They can seem arrogant and insensitive, controlling and manipulative and, if you don't understand their motivations, they can seem very uncaring.

STRENGTHS – Reds are active and productive, confident and usually right, competitive and bold. They are strong-willed, highly disciplined, logical, direct, honest, and great in crises and emergencies. Reds are resourceful and self-reliant and relentless with causes they believe in. They are loyal partners in relationships.

PROBLEMATIC TRAITS – Reds can be insensitive and selfish, arrogant and tactless, demanding and critical, tenacious and taxing, controlling and manipulative. Their need to be right is much stronger than their need to be kind. They are highly biased and reactionary in their judgment of others. Even though they are aggressive and strong-willed, their behavior may mask a great deal of insecurity.

BLUES – Blues are often referred to as the "do-gooders." They are deeply committed and fiercely loyal to people, and they tend to have committed relationships. They are very emotional and so giving and sensitive that they often ride an emotional roller coaster, and they are very often depressed. They often allow their hearts to rule their minds, and they often think and act irrationally. They will always remember insults and tend to hold grudges. Blues are very creative and are usually perfectionists and are the classic neat freaks. Unlike Reds, who tend to just charge into a project, Blues are the bean counters who will tell them what their project will cost in time and money. Blues always seek purpose in their lives, and they provide the best shoulders to cry on.

STRENGTHS – Blues are self-disciplined and stable as well as steady, ordered and enduring. They tend to be perfectionists and are generally tidy and organized. They are analytical (especially in watching how people behave), and they like to count the costs versus benefits of almost everything. They are self-sacrificing and nurturing, appropriate and sincere, purposeful and dedicated. Blues are obedient to authority and are loyal to their friends.

PROBLEMATIC TRAITS – Since Blues are perfectionists, they tend to have very high expectations of others that are often not met. They don't trust others to do it right. They can be critical of self and others and are sometimes quite controlling. Blues always remember and can be unforgiving and resentful; they hold grudges and often have the need to get even. They are easily filled with worry and guilt, they are moody and complex and therefore unpredictable in their responses. They expect others to read their minds and can be skeptical and self-righteous. Blues are often their own greatest enemies. They are highly emotional and intense and often lack the ability to relax. Their motto often seems to be, "Life's a bitch, and then you die." They often blame others for their unhappiness and are the ultimate martyrs and victims. Blues tend to love with strings attached and may often be heard to say, "If only you would…"

YELLOWS – Yellows just want to have fun. They are spirited, exciting and happy, and they appreciate what they have. They seem to be lucky – maybe because they just always expect it. Many Yellows are talented and would love the praise of others, but they are often unwilling to make commitments of time and effort needed to develop their talents. They may too freely abandon tradition in favor of personal gratification, and they prefer not to be bothered with the details of life. Yellows always seem to have friends, they love to talk and tell stories, they love the limelight and are usually looking for some adventure in their lives. Yellows usually prefer to provide the entertainment when there is work going on. They tend to provide lots of talk with little action.

STRENGTHS – Yellows are spirited, exciting, playful, enthusiastic and happy, and people like to be around them. They are carefree, easily discard any baggage, and they make life seem fun. Yellows are usually non-judgmental, forgiving of self and others, and they have few expectations of others. They are charismatic, popular, generous, naïve and trusting, and they are rarely depressed. A Yellow can turn a crisis into a comedy. Yellows are flexible and don't really believe there is only one way to do something. Yellows are talented and creative, especially if there is a Red or a Blue to carry out the ideas created from that creativity.

PROBLEMATIC TRAITS – In spite of their talents, Yellows are often uncommitted, irresponsible, unreliable, and they rarely go the distance. They are disorganized and tend not to complete tasks. Yellows are generally impulsive and undisciplined, and they usually cut corners where possible. But when things don't get done right, they are the first to blame others. They often have a difficult time keeping a stable income, but when they do have money, they love to spend it fast. Yellows tend to be self-centered and superficial, and they resent authority and discipline. Others see them as lazy, but Yellows just don't see the point in a clean house or putting in endless hours at work. What fun is there in that? Yellows love to talk but are poor listeners and are often interruptive and hog the conversation. After all, what they have to say is way more entertaining than what others come up with. They are undependable in a crisis and don't like the responsibility of dealing with one.

WHITES – Whites are the peacekeepers. They desire to promote cooperation at all costs. It is difficult for them to assert themselves, and they usually find it easier to let someone else have their way than to fight for something they want. This is partly because there are very few things they feel strongly about. They have a terrible time making up their minds because everything seems equally acceptable to them. They tend to be overly nice and often get trodden upon and taken advantage of. They can be timid and shy, and they experience their value and self-worth through others. But don't be surprised when you suddenly meet a stubborn streak like you have seldom seen. You can push a White just so far – then watch out!

STRENGTHS – Whites, as peacemakers, are tolerant and patient. They are gentle, even-tempered and accepting, and this makes them compatible with most other people. They are easy to get along with, they are sincere and genuine and usually very likable. Since they are often shy and introverted, they can be hard to get to know at first. They listen with empathy and observe everything and respond with words that seem to heal. They are calm under pressure and do well in a crisis. They are non-conformists and are not terribly concerned with what other people think.

PROBLEMATIC TRAITS – Whites tend to keep their feelings to themselves and can be difficult to read. They can be very clingy and needy, doubtful and dependent. They are timid and emotionally unsure, and it takes time to build their trust. They may seem boring and lazy because they are not highly motivated. This makes them unproductive dreamers, and they may seem aimless and misguided. Whites are the infamous silent but stubborn people. You may think you are walking all over them just to find that your boots are stuck in mire. White people are indecisive and may make you crazy trying to get a decision out of them (don't ever go shopping with a White!).

There are tests in Dr. Hartman's books to find out what your primary and secondary personality types are, but you should be able to get a good idea from just reading the above descriptions from an objective and honest stance. Most people read their strengths and say, "Oh yeah, that's me." But then they read the traits that can be problematic and tend to think they may not really be that color after all. However, whether or not you recognize your own problematic areas, they will irritate other people. These may be things that affect relationships with spouses, children, friends and coworkers. The strengths of your particular temperament may benefit you in life, but the problematic areas are going to hold you back if they are not dealt with appropriately as early as possible.

Your personality/temperament is innate. It comes with you and may seem to be in control of you most of the time. But what you do with the personality you are born with is your *character*. If you know you are a talented and creative Yellow, but that talent never seems to get very far, just understanding that this is a problem for Yellows can be helpful. You can tell yourself that just having fun and having people like you is not going to make up for wasted talent or poor work habits. You can then work on strengthening your self-discipline and tell yourself that there is no play until the necessary work is done. Just being conscious and aware of your weak areas will help you temper them so they won't overshadow your strengths.

* * * * *

The new school year had just started and Jill Crenshaw was eager to put into action a new concept she had just read in Florence Littauer's book called *Personality Plus for Parents: Understanding What Makes Your Child Tick.*[2] It was a course in the different personality types and Jill was excited to see if knowing these principles would help her get the best from her students this year.

It was easy to tell who the Yellows were. Fred, Ralph and Pedro were the entertainers and it was hard to get them to get serious and quit talking and let others do their work. Kathleen was always the first to raise her hand and was happy to let everyone know what they should be doing in any given situation. Sarah was quiet and shy, a good student, and seemed to avoid confrontation and conflict. Jake seemed fairly serious and conscientious about his work in class. He also liked everything well organized and did not take criticism well.

Despite being well liked, Freddy was not doing well in reading and some other subjects. The class play was coming up and Ms. Crenshaw saw an opportunity to use Freddy's outgoing entertainer skills, which would also necessitate him using reading and memorization skills to learn the part. Kathleen was given a role where a strong presence and well-projected voice were important. Her organizational skills and lets-get-it-done attitude made her a good person to put in charge of ticket sales. Sarah did not want to be in the play initially, but Ms. Crenshaw thought that the role of narrator might help her feel included without being too intimidated. Jake had shown a lot artistic talent and was very excited to work with the art teacher in creating the scenery.

Ms. Crenshaw also wanted to help her students work on their weaker points. Freddy was reminded that he would have to buckle down and learn his part if he wanted to have such a prominent role in the play. He also had to learn that his constant joking around was disruptive and could not be tolerated if the play was to be ready on time. Sarah had to be encouraged to speak loudly and enunciate and make eye contact with the audience. Jake, a perfectionist, wanted to spend far too much time on every detail of the scenery. The art teacher helped him understand that scenery was more about the overall impression than obsessive attention to detail. Ms. Crenshaw tried to teach Kathleen that patience and tact were important in getting people's cooperation for selling tickets.

The night of the play arrived and the performance went quite well with only a few minor glitches. Sarah had gained enough self-confidence to keep the show together with her narration during the few rough spots. Freddy had been serious about learning his lines and had gotten lots of laughs, which he relished. Kathleen got an opportunity to shine in her role and had learned a lot about working with people. Jake got many compliments on the scenery and his parents assured him that they did not notice any of the flaws he had talked to them about.

When the play was over, Ms. Crenshaw commended Freddy on his self-control and the accomplishment of learning his lines so well. She also complimented the other students for working hard to overcome things that they had difficulties with. The school year gave her plenty of opportunities to notice the different temperaments of her students and help them shine as well as encourage them to work on the problematic components of their temperaments.

* * * * *

In relationships, especially with close partners, an understanding of the temperaments is very important in avoiding serious damage to the relationship. A red husband with a white or blue wife can cause a lot of hurt if he just barges through life taking control and barking orders. A yellow husband with a blue wife may need to hand over the checkbook to her to keep himself from spending his paycheck before it gets in the bank. Parents need to realize that each child will have his or her own temperament and that a tailored interaction for each child will work best in raising their family. The same holds true in the workplace. Knowing about the temperaments helps coworkers treat each other in a way that will foster a less contentious and more productive workplace.

We have all heard people say, "I can't help it. That's just the way I am." This is the easy way to go through life, but there is little growth in it. People of character will recognize their weaknesses and work to diminish them. This will require stepping out of the comfort zone of their innate personalities and working to develop traits that will improve the quality of their lives and the lives of those around them. Their strengths will shine brighter and they will progress through life much more easily by continuing to work on their problematic areas. There will always be a fine line between needing to work on a trait because it is inhibiting *your* life and working on it just because someone else has a trait that clashes with it and they want you to change. Communication and compromise on the part of both individuals will be necessary. But, if you spend more time looking for something fun to do than keeping food on the table, *you* are the one that needs to work on that particular problem.

Some people just can't see their problematic areas, and others do see them but have a terrible time making necessary changes. Counseling, meditation, and self-help books and courses can be very useful here. However, sometimes its just takes a consistent determined effort to change something that has been so much a part of you for so long. If you are a Blue and tend to be easily hurt and hold grudges causing you to get depressed frequently, you will just have to remind yourself over and over again that the other person may not have meant to hurt your feelings and, if they did, their rudeness is *their* problem to work on. Turn your ego off and let it go! Holding a grudge against someone is like *you* taking poison and waiting for *him* to die. Your depression over the event only harms *your* immune system and ruins *your* day – not his. It may take thousands of times of telling yourself to let it go before you really make it stick. But, as you do begin to get control of your problematic issues, you will feel very triumphant as your character builds and you feel the joy and rewards of avoiding things that cause strife and pain for yourself and others.

This is just a brief discussion of the temperaments and character. Most people find these concepts useful in understanding themselves and those with whom they relate. These are not the only tools we need, but perhaps they will help us be less judgmental and more understanding of others who aren't just like us. The Color Code can help us be more compassionate and celebrate our differences rather than see other temperaments as better than or less than. When we notice others making an effort to work on their weaknesses, we should be complimentary and supportive instead of saying, "It's about damn time!" For that person, improving problematic areas may be a remarkable achievement.

Let us be very honest and objective in evaluating our own personality traits. Is it more important for us to be right than to be kind or cooperative? Do we need to communicate with others in a way that says we honor their views and feelings? Do we approach others in the spirit of compromise with a willingness to occasionally give up our temperament's need to do things our way? And, when necessary, can we commit to an important cause and stick with it until it has been accomplished? Most importantly, we should recognize that the presence of all colors is what makes a rainbow so beautiful.

Chapter Sixteen

IT'S A GRAND OLD FLAG

*A nation that continues year after year to spend
more on military defense than on programs of
social uplift is approaching spiritual death.*

Martin Luther King, Jr.

For some reason I had been selected to give the July 4th Men's Group lesson at the church I was attending. This particular lesson I had decided to really make the gentlemen think about the subject of patriotism. I asked the question, "What is the one-and-only, nothing-else-but, sole, complete and total reason for patriotism?"

After a few seconds of thought, a hand came up and the answer issued forth, "To unite the country."

"To unite the country for what purpose?" I asked. "Do we see people volunteering at hospitals or food banks because of patriotism? Does patriotism generate support for better schools or help for the homeless? For what purpose do we need patriotism to unite us?"

A few more moments of thought went by with only silence. Why was this such a hard question to answer? Certainly everyone there considered themselves to be patriotic. They must have known what purpose their patriotism served. Finally I dropped the bombshell and said, "Throughout history all political leaders have known that the sole, total, one-and-only purpose of patriotism is to rally the troops for war." Sounds of disbelief and disgust were heard as the group took in this statement.

"Sometimes we need to be united for war to defend our country and our freedoms from being attacked," one brother interjected.

"When was the last time we were attacked in this country which required that we defend ourselves against aggressors?" I questioned.

"World War II," came the answer.

"And how many wars have we been involved in since World War II?"

"Numerous."

"Then what was the purpose of becoming involved in all those other wars?" I asked.

"Sometimes there are threats to our freedom that don't come and attack us on our soil here and now, but might later – like communism and socialism," came the answer. "Sometimes we have to fight those threats in other parts of the world."

"How do we know which of these threats will attack us if none of them has so far? And who tells us that communism and socialism are anything more then some countries' ideas of good ways to live together? Why should we fight a war over ideas and abstractions in which real live humans get harmed and killed?" I was trying to dig a little deeper here, but it was not going well.

"We can look to our leaders to let us know when there are threats to our freedoms and where there are things to fear. They know a lot better than we do."

This was starting to scare me now. Throughout the rest of the discussion the concept that the only real purpose for patriotism (also known as nationalism) was to rally the troops in preparation for war was a hard one to sell. Surely there must be other reasons for something that is so pounded into the very depths of our souls from the first days of our conscious existence. We begin to learn at a very young age to honor the flag when it passes in front of us by putting our hand over our heart. One of the first memorized pieces we learn (besides the Happy Birthday Song) is the Pledge of Allegiance. It seems to be the same thing as encountered with religionism. To even question why one is patriotic makes you unpatriotic; and everyone just knows instinctively that it's wrong not to be a patriot. Except that it isn't instinctive. Usually the people who pound patriotism into our heads do not know why they are programming us any more than the people who pounded it into them knew. Patriotism is one of the strongest memes that invades any society. Mark Twain defined a patriot as, "...the person who can holler the loudest without knowing what he is hollering about."

Whatever the reasons for our blind unquestioning devotion to patriotism were, it led to a very lively discussion that Sunday. But a couple of months later on September 11, 2001 (the infamous 9/11) the issue became clearer. By September 15th, a large number of cars had a flag (or two... or three) flying from their antennas or decals of the flag on their windows. But only one of the brothers present at that discussion commented to me about the sudden proliferation of flags and patriotism after it appeared that we had been attacked by someone outside our country.

From the beginning of civilization, every society or country that has had armed forces has used the excuse that these armed forces were to protect that civilization from "bad" people or "bad" countries coming over and beating them up and taking their stuff. And likewise, the countries against which they were supposedly protecting themselves saw the making of arms and training of troops as an immediate threat to them, and they began the same processes. Therefore the war machine became an integral part of almost every community from the beginning of time. And when a community has spent so much time, energy, thought and so many human resources creating their military, it is not likely that this war machine will go unused for very long. Its existence must be justified and the training of its participants must be tested. From this need to test military capability, the concept of preemptive warfare evolved – beat the other guys up before they can do it to you. Once this mentality has taken root, this rationalization can be extended as far as one's armies can march until expansion of the empire is more the objective of war than self-protection.

To create a really great war machine, the alpha males who want to give the war need to recruit soldiers to fight while they, the alphas, give the orders. So the problem for those who are in the top dog positions is how to get those who are not really that enthusiastic about war to become part of the war machine. Over the centuries some techniques for doing this have evolved that seem to work well even in our day.

The first of these is to create fear. Fear of a common enemy will work better than anything else to create armies. Clever politicians have learned that they must have effective ways to demonize and dehumanize whomever the chosen common enemy might be. In Hitler's Germany, the Jews were chosen as the first common enemy as there was already animosity toward the Jews in a large part of German society. This made them an easy target. They were portrayed as heartless predators without morals who wanted to take over all banking and industry in German society. Caricatures portrayed them as weasels or rats. Later, as Russians became more the common enemy, they were portrayed as ignorant barbarians and toothless wonders whose intelligence was far less than German intelligence.

We are taught to hate people our government tells us are despicable. These people's governments have painted us as barbaric Neanderthals at the same time. If our patriotism did not require that we despise those whom our governments call enemies, we would most likely be able to intermingle with these so-called enemies and find amazing friends among them. It is hard to fathom that we give such unquestioned power to the alpha males to create terrible animosity between people who might otherwise live together in peace and mutual benefit. We the people need to quit being so easily programmed.

The United States has found numerous rationalizations to use its military/industrial complex throughout the years. Whether to protect the world from the spread of communism or the supposed threat of terrorism, our leaders have found plenty of reasons to rally the troops. And, in every case, the reason for going to war was fear-based, rarely real and always very profitable for a certain few. Today communism has pretty much burned itself out. By waging war on Islamic nations, we have only increased the terrorist threat by inspiring more young Islamic people to take revenge on those who killed their families and destroyed their homes. You can be assured that there will always be a good fear-based reason to use the military monster that we have equipped and trained so well.

The second tool used to build the military complex in all societies has to do with the image of manhood. Young men in all cultures throughout the ages have been taught, directly or indirectly, that might makes right. To be a virtuous male, one must be strong and brave. The greatest of all legendary heroes is not the scientist, the negotiator, the healer, the artist or the spiritual leader. No, it is the warrior marching with spear and club, with his sword and shield astride his horse, or shooting a thousand rounds a minute from his helicopter. He is the one females will be attracted to, the one that will be given the greatest honors, and the one whose legacy will be made into movies.

We teach our young males not to be sensitive or cry. We teach them that any dispute can easily be decided by duking it out. We teach them that to be respected really means to be feared. And we teach them that the highest honor they can achieve is to fight and die for their country. Rarely do we teach them the art of negotiation, how to think critically and question what they are told, or that all human beings are just like them in the very most basic ways. That would be counterproductive to the unquestioned obedience to authority that is necessary to create a good war machine. This mentality also creates bullies and abusive husbands or boyfriends. Unfortunately, fathers almost never think of what they are teaching their sons when they teach them what it means to be a man. Again, they only pass on what they learned from their fathers and peers.

The third tool that is used to promote patriotism is the concept that a certain geographical area governed by a certain group of individuals (i.e., a country) is superior to another and deserves to be dominant over other areas because of its superiority. This is often called *exceptionalism* ("This is the best country in the world."). We have anthems, flags, symbols, and languages to help us differentiate one country from another. Even sporting events, chess tournaments and races into space are extremely important in helping us to feel superior to and separate from other groups of people. And we do get passionate about all of these things, a passion that is scarcely seen in any other aspects of our lives. We often use sporting events as more suitable outlets for this passion rather than actual war. But even here, what starts out to be friendly competition can turn into bizarre behavior with crazed fans becoming violent mobs and people getting injured or even killed. What kind of insanity is this?

Perhaps it is this passion that makes patriotism/nationalism so important to us. The human soul loves to feel strong emotions. Often it doesn't seem to matter whether the emotion is joy/gratitude/love or rage/hate/revenge. Even though the great religions of the world claim to teach the principles of seeking joy/gratitude/love and removing rage/hate/aggression from our lives, religionism has engendered equal passion on either end of the spectrum. And so it is with patriotism. The patriotism that should create joyful feelings of connection and gratitude for a great place to live usually creates animosity, distrust, anger and aggressiveness toward others instead.

In addition to the factors listed above, young men and women are idealistic and yearn to be a part of something – something that will make a difference. While service oriented organizations such as the Peace Corps attract some young people, the military seems to hold greater appeal for most. Often it is because it is the only job a poor young man or woman can find to support a family. And just as importantly, the military gets huge exposure in the media and spends millions of our tax dollars advertising its virtues, whereas the Peace Corps gets no coverage at all. Like anything else, the military is neither all good nor all bad. Young people learn discipline, organization and how to work with other people. It is often a growing up experience for people who have yet to live away from home. They occasionally learn skills they can use later in the workplace, and they learn to care about the lives of their fellow soldiers. But these are all things that could easily be learned under better circumstances.

The actual experience of war changes human beings in most dramatic dark ways. In Ken Burns' documentary "The War," about World War II, all of the men and women interviewed who had actually been a part of the combat troops described how they were changed forever by war's insanity, its inhumanity, its violence, and its total irreverence for human life. All of these people said that they still have the scars of war's horrors even though their lives have been relatively good since then. It has been the same in every war since World War II. The Korean "Conflict," Vietnam, Afghanistan, and Iraq have all created painful, incurable wounds that will forever afflict those who survived these events. When our soldiers come home, they find that the funding for the war machine does not include adequate resources to help them cope with the physical and psychological damage created during their wartime experience.

* * * * *

The question is often asked, "Are violence and aggression genetic or learned, a matter of nature or nurture or both?" Geneticists have found a gene called the MAOA, or warrior gene, in about one-third of North Americans and Europeans. People with this gene are twice as likely to join a gang, and gang members with this gene are four times more likely to use a weapon in a fight.

Obviously, not everyone with the gene becomes violent, but, if you've had an abusive childhood or had a lot of stress in your life, you are more likely to be vulnerable to the effects of the gene. It was assumed that cultures with less violence should have less of the warrior gene. The nomadic people of the Sahara desert rarely experience aggressive behavior in their communities. In one tribe no one could remember a murder in four generations. When their genetics were studied, however, they had the same warrior gene prevalence as other groups. It seems culture may indeed have a larger influence on aggression than genetics.

Research done during World War II found that only about 15% of American riflemen aimed directly at the enemy with intent to kill. Today that number is close to 100%. What's different? When today's soldiers are trained, human-like dummies are used instead of the bull's-eyes used in WW II. Soldiers yell, "Kill, kill, kill," over and over during training and the repetition seems to make killing easier. Unfortunately, this aggressive training does not diminish the psychological scars of that killing. It is estimated that around 20% of soldiers returning from Iraq and Afghanistan have Post Traumatic Stress Disorder (PTSD), a possibly low estimate since many cases go undiagnosed and unreported. In 2012, the number of soldiers committing suicide overtook the number killed in combat. Research has shown that the single most important predictor of PTSD and suicide is whether a soldier has killed in war.

It appears that men can be trained to become finely tuned killing machines, but we apparently cannot do away with the beacon of white light inside us that causes killing, even when we are told it is justified, to leave deep psychological scars behind.[1]

* * * * *

Chris Hedges said, "The rush of war is often a potent and lethal addiction." Indeed we have seen this all over the world. During the Rwandan genocide, nearly a million people were slaughtered in about 100 days. Many of the murderers were young men with machetes who said they couldn't find enough Tutsis to quench their blood thirst. Iraq war veterans came home and told their stories of having no remorse in killing civilians in Iraq because "...it was just another dead Hajji." Hajji, in this case, is a pejorative term for an Islamic person. At Abu Ghraib, humanity slowly deteriorated into bizarre depravity where the guards were told that the prisoners were nothing more than dogs, so they shouldn't worry about what is done to them. In response to the pictures that emerged from Abu Ghraib, Vice-President Dick Cheney said, "...we have to work the dark side, if you will. We've got to spend time in the shadows." The intense environment of a war situation and the resulting adrenalin flow creates an easy excuse to go to the dark side and become a monster whom no one at home would recognize. But, if a person's patriotism causes that person to sign up for his government's war, or even if he is drafted, *he cannot lay the responsibility for what he does on anyone else.* I long for the day when the real heroes of any society will be the people who can "just say no" to the alpha apes looking for recruits to carry out their evil and destructive designs.

Now we have reached the era of "painless wars." In what seems like nothing more than a giant videogame, a soldier in Colorado can bomb a whole neighborhood in a distant country in an attempt to eliminate one or two "hostiles." In recent years our government has realized that there will be less protesting against war's horrors if those horrors are kept from the public. Currently our government has forbidden the showing on network news of caskets being brought home from the killing fields. No pictures of the mutilated bodies of soldiers or civilians. No images of the homes of civilians completely destroyed and the dead that once lived there. No film footage of children crying for their mothers who lie lifeless in the rubble. Collateral damage is a euphemism for the innumerable non-military civilians killed by indiscriminate mass bombing (the thing our war machine does best), and collateral damage is a devastating result of every war. We talk only of the numbers or *our* soldiers killed, never mentioning the massive home and family casualties suffered by our "enemies," because, of course, our designated enemies are not really considered humans.

Every leader who sends its country's young people to a war of his creation should be required to lead the charge and experience every horror that the rest of the troops endure. As long as we continue to accept the glamorization of war, the heroism of violence, and the dehumanization of our so-called enemies as shown in our television shows, movies and video games, we will never have the incentive to develop peace. For as Einstein said, "You cannot simultaneously prepare for and prevent war."

One thing we usually fail to see is that greedy ambitious men promote the concepts of a country's superiority or exceptionalism. War is highly profitable to corporate greed monsters. As we've seen with the war in Iraq, Halliburton, Blackwater (now Xe) and many other corporate interests have made billions from this insane war. The government defense contracts for war-related planes, ships, tanks, guns, bombs, remote controlled spying and bombing drones and thousands of other devices and services run in the billions or trillions of dollars. Many tanks and planes and other instruments of war are mothballed before they are used a single time – clear evidence that winning military contracts for the home state is an important thing for getting legislators re-elected. There are over 700 U.S. military bases in 68 countries with over 250,000 military personnel needed just to run these facilities – this does not include combat forces. Our presence causes great animosity in most of these places. We never seem to have the money for universal healthcare, better schools, rebuilding the infrastructure or investing in clean green energy, but we always have ever-increasing budgets for the war machine. As one bumper sticker says, "When will schools have all the money they need and the Air Force have to hold a bake sale to buy a bomber?"

Patriotism could be a wonderful tool for imbuing our society with some marvelous improvements that would make America a better place to live. We could become passionate about education, healthcare for all, the reduction of poverty and the untampered election of peace-oriented leaders. We could require corporate America to bring our jobs and our manufacturing back into this country. We could spend the current military budget on infrastructure and renewable energy resources. However, we cannot do this until we ourselves believe in the importance of these things and demand that our resources and manpower be used to accomplish beneficial activities instead of destructive ones.

To see what patriotism could do best, we need only look at what happens after a national disaster. Even though our own government sat on its haunches and did little to aid the victims of hurricane Katrina, tens of thousands of Americans sent the necessities of life, took people into their homes and helped people mop out the mud and rebuild their lives. Americans are always ready to lend a helping hand. Their hearts are large and their compassion is great. Even when there is a tragedy outside this country (such as the tsunamis), we are ready and willing to help out. Religious organizations do some of their best work in this area and should be applauded for their compassionate leadership. Isn't it pathetic that any nation's government should be far less known for helping its people than for creating havoc and destruction?

We are told that war is the only way to protect our freedom. If our leaders can find someone they can convince us could threaten us later on, a preemptive attack is justified. We hear phrases like, "They hate us for our freedom." And, when it appeared that we had been attacked on September 11, 2001, we went into fear mode (as was expected of us) and let our government take away a large number of rights so they could "protect us and keep us free." We have never tried on a sustained basis to work for peace. Instead, we go into fear mode and are easily convinced that we must go to war if we do not want to become enslaved. We are only allowing ourselves to be manipulated, and I will explain what I think would be a better option later in the book.

We now need to redefine patriotism. John Edwards said, "Why can't Americans be patriotic about anything but war?" We can no longer afford to give our blind loyalty, not seasoned by inquiry, to any ruling regime. We must instead scrutinize every action of our leadership and hold it accountable for any activity that does not work toward the greater good of the country and the planet. Patriotism should *not* be an absolute acceptance of anything our government wants to do. It should become a force that causes the leaders of a country to respect and fulfill the will and needs of the people instead of the people fearing their government and being pepper-sprayed or clubbed when they dissent. It should create better schools, good healthcare and cures for diseases, good jobs and wages for all – not just a privileged few, and a community of compassionate caring citizens who take care of each other. It should be a great force for good things to happen instead of a tool of death and destruction and unquestioned control by those whom we allow to govern us.

Chapter Seventeen

FOR THE BIBLE TELLS ME SO

Scriptures: the sacred books of our holy religion,
as distinguished from the false and profane
writings upon which all other faiths are based.

Ambrose Bierce

At the foundation of any current-day religion are the writings of ancient prophets or sages. Often these are taken literally, sometimes they are interpreted more progressively, but they are always referred to by the leaders of the various religions. For the Christians, the Bible is the basis of most religious organizations. For the Jews, it's the *Torah* and the *Old Testament Prophets*. For Muslims, it is the *Koran*. Buddhists look to the *Jataka*, which are the stories and sayings of the Buddha. For Taoists, it's the *Tao Te Ching*. These sources are ancient texts written in a time when life was very different. We would need a full understanding of the language and idioms of the day, the traditions and customs of the society, and the topics of discussion in those societies to truly understand what the writers were trying to convey. Yet there are absolutists in every society who want to take the words as they appear today as the absolute literal word and will of God, as if God had written all truth into a Word document, put it onto a data CD and sent it down directly to the publishing company for printing and distribution.

One would think that the Bible would be searched for anything uplifting, inspirational, or useful in ones spiritual evolution. But instead of seeking what is beautiful and useful from these writings, chapter and verse has been used to wage wars, to enslave other humans, to deprive certain groups of people of their rights and to help rationalize horrible hate, intolerance and violence committed in the name of God. The authors of these verses would be horrified to know that their writings have sent people to die in wars and others to hate each other. The actual theme of the New Testament, in particular, was supposed to be love and self-improvement.

We all have to make up our own minds about how we regard scripture and its role in our lives. Many people spend hours each week studying the Bible alone and in groups trying to determine exactly what is meant by each phrase. A whole study session can revolve around the semantics of one verse. If we look at the verse from one perspective, it can mean one thing; if we look at it from another viewpoint, it can have a completely different meaning. Because of the way scriptural sayings were passed on to us – starting as oral traditions and later written, rewritten and translated many times – it is impossible to know exactly what the original sayings were. I think all people who study the Bible would be helped by understanding as much as they can about its origins and subsequent development.

In *Don't Know Much About the Bible¹*, Kenneth Davis provides a unique overview of the Bible's origins. Most people have never thought about how the Bible came to us, but the "God's Computer to the Publishing House" idea would work for some of them. Some Bible readers would say that God spoke to his servants, the prophets, and the prophets wrote God's word on papyrus, leather or whatever was used in the area. These manuscripts were handed down from generation to generation and eventually compiled into the Old Testament. It is also thought that several scribes wrote down the words of Jesus as he spoke them, and four of these were preserved to become the four gospels. Add a few letters from some of the apostles plus an apocalyptic scenario written on a penal colony island (the book of *Revelations*), and you have the New Testament.

The earliest books in the Old Testament originated somewhere around 2,000 BCE (BC). The first five books in the Old Testament that most people use are Genesis, Exodus, Leviticus, Numbers, and Deuteronomy. These books are called the Pentateuch or the Five Books of Moses, and these texts also comprise the Jewish Torah. Their author was long believed to be Moses, for he does state that he is writing stuff down. Without an explanation, however, we would have the mistaken impression that these were literally the writings of Moses. In reality, all of what is in these books was an *oral tradition* that wasn't written down until around 1,000 - 1,600 years later. That means that all of these books, and most of the Bible for that matter, was told as stories that were memorized and passed from generation to generation until someone said, "Hey, these are cool stories about our heritage. Someone ought to write them down. I ought to get as many of these storytellers together as I can and put their information together. It might make a New York Times best selling scroll." Old Testament oral traditions were not transcribed for several hundred years. New Testament stories could have been written down as few as forty years after Jesus' lifetime.

Have you ever played the game *Gossip*? Someone starts the game by whispering a phrase into the ear of another person and the whispered phrase gets passed from one person to another until everyone in the room has heard it. The last person to hear it then states what he heard and compares that to the original phrase.

Sometimes it is quite funny, but seldom is it the same phrase. I can imagine that the storytellers and memorizers were much more meticulous than people playing this game, but over hundreds of years, or even fifty years, it is impossible to guarantee that the written words were exactly what Moses said – or later, Jesus.

Then there is the problem of word meanings. Anyone who has learned more than one language knows that there are words, phrases, and idioms that cannot simply be translated directly into their equivalents in another language without a knowledge of the culture, the times and the customs. You almost have to grow up in a society to really know what is meant by the idioms and phraseology of that period. Someone trying to learn American English even today would not understand certain phrases without a bit of explanation. "I ran into Joan at the grocery store today." (Was she badly hurt?) That same English learner might understand, "He broke his arm last week." But he might not understand, "She broke my heart," or "I broke my head studying for the exam," or "I'm broke until my next paycheck." Or "Whew, who just broke wind?"

Word usages changed with time in those days too. The first Latin version of the Bible was called the versio vulgata (common translation). Today it is known as the Vulgate Bible. In those days, *vulgar* meant *usual* or *common*; today it more often means *dirty* or *vile*. It's another example of shifting word meanings.

So, when you read many times in the Bible "forty days and forty nights," does it literally mean that many days and nights, or was it just their way of saying a long time? Moses and the Israelites also spent 40 years (a generation) in the wilderness. Many people try to figure out literal timetables based on the Bible. In fact, the Irish Archbishop, James Ussher, in 1650 AD calculated the ages of the patriarchs and worked out that the creation of the earth occurred on Sunday the 23rd of October, 4004 BC[2].

We have all heard many predictions of when the last days will arrive and when Jesus should return. But we have to remember that Jesus' disciples expected his return in their own lifetimes. In the Gospel of Matthew, Jesus was talking about the calamities of the days before his return and said:

Now learn a parable of the fig tree; When his branch is yet tender, and putteth forth leaves, ye know that summer is nigh: So likewise ye, when ye shall see all these things, know that it is near, even at the doors. Verily, I say unto you, this generation shall not pass, till all these things be fulfilled. (Matt. 24: 32-34) Note: All Bible quotes are from the King James Version.

Forty years was considered a generation. Jesus did not return within that time, and the people who were closest to him had apparently misinterpreted his words. It took nearly a century before his followers realized that they must make plans about how to organize themselves and continue living because Jesus had not returned to conquer the Romans and reign over his kingdom by the time they had expected. Countless Bible scholars since then have claimed to know what Jesus or John (who wrote Revelations) *really* meant with their predictions of gloom and doom. They have predicted the *real* end of days and second coming for a particular time only to find that the sun went down and came up again – and again. Hal Lindsey's popular book *The Late Great Planet Earth* postulated that the fig tree very often stood for the nation of Israel. After lying dormant for a season, it would come back to life as it did in 1948 when Israel was established as a sovereign nation. According to Mr. Lindsey's cleverly devised timetable, the second coming should have been within 40 years (a generation). So by 1988 all predicted things should have occurred. But here we are – still.

* * * * *

In the third century C.E. (A.D.) a church father named Origen made the following statement about the copies of the gospels that he had access to:

"The differences among the manuscripts have become great, either through the negligence of some copyists or through the perverse audacity of others; they either neglect to check over what they have transcribed, or, in the process of checking, they make additions or deletions as they please." [3]

The problem of differences between manuscripts became very clear in 1707 when John Mill, a fellow at Queens College, Oxford, England published his version of the Greek New Testament. He had spent 30 years acquiring and comparing some 100 Greek manuscripts of the New Testament, numerous writings of early church fathers in which they had quoted such texts, and comparisons of Greek texts with very early versions written in Syriac and Coptic (languages spoken by very early Christians). Most astonishing was a document he published with his Greek New Testament that pointed out some 30,000 places of variation between the different versions he had available. He did not include minor things such as word order. He unfortunately died of a stroke about two weeks after the publication of his work and, therefore, did not get to observe the huge controversy caused by his writings.

For the three hundred years before Mill, the *Textus Receptus* (the text that is received by all) was considered to be the uncorrupted, original, and best version of the Greek New Testament. After Mill's publication, considering Biblical texts to be the absolute, literal, and unchanging words of God was abandoned by most until the 19th century when, for some reason, this way of thinking arose again – especially in America.

Today, over 5,700 manuscripts of the New Testament have been found and catalogued. Even with computers, it has not yet been possible to count all the variations between these numerous manuscripts, but estimates run between 200,000 and 400,000. In any case, there are more textual variations in the New Testament than there are words in it.[4]

* * * * *

After we realize that most of what is in the Bible was passed on orally as stories until someone decided to write them down, we have to understand that we don't even have any original texts of these written-down stories. We don't even have copies of the originals, or copies of the copies of the copies. In most cases, we have copies that were made centuries later. And these numerous copies contain many differences among them. To understand why this is the case, we have to look at the way books were created in those days.

Bart D. Ehrman's book, *Misquoting Jesus*, contains a very good understanding of how writings came into being before printing presses or photocopiers. When Paul sent a letter to be read in various branches of the early Christian church, such as those in Rome, Corinth, or Thessalonica, the members of that branch could not just go down to Kinko's and make copies of the letter to send to other branches. Nor could they just fax it or e-mail it to Ephesus or Galatia. Everything had to be copied by hand at that time, and to find good copyists, especially early on, was not always that easy. Most people at that time, and for a very long time thereafter, were illiterate. If you could read and write, it would very often be your profession. Greek was the language of the earliest Christian texts and they were often copied in what was called *scriptuo continua*. This means that there were no punctuation marks, no distinction between upper or lower case letters, and no spaces between words. This meant that a copyist did not actually have to be able to read texts; he just had to imitate the letters in the right order. However, not being able to actually read a text made it much easier to make mistakes.

There were two basic kinds of mistakes that were made – accidental and intentional. Accidental mistakes occurred due to things like *scriptuo continua* and bad handwriting. A lot of abbreviations were used as well, and some of them were mixed up. For instance *pneuma* means "spirit," and *poma* means "drink." When the abbreviation *pma* was encountered, it's easy to see that either word could be transcribed. Paul writes in I Cor. 12:13 that everyone in Christ has been "baptized into one body" and they have all "drunk of one Spirit" – or "drunk of one drink," which was occasionally written instead. *Periblepsis* (or eye-skip) occurred when two lines being copied ended in the same words or letters. When the copyist came back to the manuscript, he would sometimes leave out the second line that ended in the same letters thinking he had just transcribed it. Another common mistake was made when one person was reading a text and several others were writing it down. Two words that sounded alike but were written differently (homophones) were often mixed up.

The other type of mistake that was often made was an intentional one. As letters and books were sent from one branch to another, the letters had to be read out loud to the congregations since most of the faithful did not read, and there were precious few copies to be had. As possible mistakes were detected during these readings, the reader would often correct the manuscript according to his own understanding. This may or may not have been an accurate understanding of what the original writer meant. Further, we might assume that all the early leaders of the Christian church were in accord with one another on the teachings of this new religion. This was not the case. For those familiar with the New Testament, you will certainly know of the several conflicts between differing camps of the church. In several of Paul's letters he chastised Peter and other members of the church who insisted that converted male members to the new Christian congregations must be circumcised (ouch). They also disagreed about whether it was always necessary to eat kosher foods and to eat only with other Jews. Peter maintained that the Jewish law was *the* law. But Paul was more lenient and said that outward signs of faithfulness were much less important than living according to the spirit of the new gospel of Jesus. Even at this early point, there was not absolute agreement among the apostles of what the gospel of Jesus was. Did it still include all the earlier Jewish laws (circumcision but no pork, strict Sabbath rules but no shellfish)? Or did the new gospel of Jesus supersede the Law of Moses in some areas? How copyists of these manuscripts understood "the gospel" in their areas determined how they "fixed" the manuscripts they were copying.

Sometimes intentional changes would be made to make passages in one book agree with passages in another. Sometimes it was to make New Testament references agree with Old Testament writings. This was particularly important when it was decided that Jesus was the Lord Immanuel spoken of in Isaiah. At other times, it was to make different books of the New Testament agree with each other. The Lord's Prayer, found in both Matthew and Luke, is a good example of this. The version in Matthew is still longer than the one in Luke, but the one in Luke used to read like this:

Father, hallowed be your name. May your kingdom come. Give us each day our daily bread. And forgive our sins, for we forgive our debtors. And lead us not into temptation.

Whenever there were differences in stories told in the four Gospels, they were "harmonized" according to the best understanding of the transcribers. Other verses were "clarified" using the oral stories about Jesus the transcribers had heard as the basis for their clarifications.

Most bible scholars believe that some of the apostolic letters included in our current version of the Bible may not even have been written by the authors to whom they are attributed. Colossians is one of these that may have been written by a follower of Paul who used Paul's name to gain more credibility. Paul himself preaches over and over of the problems with "false teachers" coming to the congregations with concepts that were not congruent with the ones he had left with them. Were these "false teachers" really trying to corrupt the church members or were they well meaning people with a somewhat different understanding of church teachings?

The Bible that we have today has evolved over the past centuries. A canon is a collection of books that Christians (or members of any religion) consider divinely inspired and which constitutes their scriptures. The Bible has not always been the same collection of books that it is now. In fact, there are a number of Christian Bible versions available today that have different collections of books. The *apocrypha* is a set of Old Testament books that are not in the Protestant Bible but many are in the Catholic Bible and most are in the Eastern Orthodox Bibles. The New Testament also evolved over time into what it is today. Books were included in certain Biblical canons because they fit with the doctrine of a certain church's leadership or excluded because they did not fit with the current teachings of those church bodies. There were many battles over what would become accepted teachings and literature for the Christian church. For instance, the book called "The Acts of Paul and Thecla" was not included in the New Testament canon because it spoke of a woman who was a friend of Paul who preached and baptized.

Women preaching and baptizing was not something church leaders in those days wanted to promote.

There are also other writings about Jesus' life that were not found until after the Biblical canons now in use were closed to new writings. The most famous of these is the *Gospel of Thomas,* sometimes known as *The Secret Sayings of Jesus.* This is a collection of the sayings of Jesus that may well have taken form before any of the traditional canonical Gospels (Matthew, Mark, Luke, and John). From the very earliest days until the present, it has been a great battle to decide what should be included in "the absolute literal Holy Word of God." Most Bible absolutists view the edition they have as the correct version. But a valid question would be, "What makes your version the correct one?"

What is important about the Bible, however, is not so much its evolution as the way people use it to justify their views on many different topics. One glaring example of this is in Leviticus 20:9-13. Many people love to condemn homosexuality using verse 13:

13: *If a man also lie with mankind as he lieth with a woman, both of them have committed an abomination; they shall surely be put to death; their blood shall be upon them.*

But no one seems to talk about verses 9 and 10 right before verse 13:

9: *For every one that curseth his father or his mother shall be surely put to death: he hath cursed his father or his mother; his blood shall be upon him.*

10: *And the man that committeth adultery with another man's wife, even he that committeth adultery with his neighbor's wife, the adulterer and adulteress shall surely be put to death.*

We are quick to condemn other religions when a few fanatical zealots use scriptural verses to justify their acts of violence and terror, but Christians have done the same thing since the early days of their existence. The Crusades, the Spanish Inquisition, the burning of "witches," and many other "putting-to-death" events throughout history have been done in the name of the Christian God.

The scriptural verses of any religion should be searched for anything that is uplifting, encouraging, filled with admonishments to be better humans, and stories of love and compassion. In an absolutist world, we think we have to abide by all verses if we accept any of them. If we did that, there would be no problem with over-population. All children that swear at or hit their parents, all people who work on the Sabbath, and all people who have sex with anyone but their opposite sex spouses would be executed. No sane person can support a God format that requires such things. Very often we allow our church leaders to tell us how we must live our lives, based on the Bible. We take their word for it and their opinions become our tribal rules. "If God says it, I gotta do it," is what many people believe. However, how we envision our God will determine what we think God requires. Perhaps we can actually think of God in a completely different way without losing our connection to God's Spirit. This *is* an option. Read on.

Chapter Eighteen

THE GOD FORMAT

If you don't believe, you can't have all *the answers.*
*But, if you <u>do</u> believe, you can't have **any** questions.*

Source Unknown

In the east there begins to be light and, even before the glowing orb we call our sun rises over the horizon, the clouds are glowing with shades of orange and pink and the sky turns from deep indigo to a brilliant blue. The sun appears every day and has since man has existed. Yet early man did not understand why it appeared and why it slipped away just as mysteriously. So amazing was this daily occurrence to early man that he gave the sun the honor of godhood. Humans worshipped the sun, gave it gifts (including human sacrifice), and hoped to continuously find favor in the eyes of this great god so that it would surely appear the next day.

There were myriad things that man did not understand, and he created gods that needed to be pleased and praised in order to have plenty of rain and a good harvest, to be blessed with healthy children, and to be protected from his enemies. There were gods for thunder and lightning, forests and oceans, astronomy and irrigation, love and passion. Great myths arose detailing the bizarre lives and interactions of these gods with earthlings – Osiris, Thor, Jupiter, Zeus, Apollo and many others. Eventually the concept of a single omnipotent god began to take hold. In many parts of the world people began to revere certain spiritual leaders as spokespersons for the one god. The sayings of these enlightened spiritual leaders eventually became scripture and the world's religions began to take form.

It is somewhat difficult to define what constitutes a religion. Do the sayings of Confucius constitute an actual religion? What about the teachings of the Old Man of the Tao? Did the Buddha expect that his words of enlightenment would become a world religion? In any case, religionism (the practicing of a certain set of religious teachings) often arose out of a desire to lift oneself to a higher spiritual plane. In other words, people wanted to move from darkness into the light. Many enlightened souls began to understand that the accumulation of possessions, the need to feed the ego, continuing in their addictions, and judging their fellow humans were not bringing them happiness. Such people were naturally drawn to the teachings of Jesus, the Buddha, Mohammed and many others.

It is not hard to understand why the belief in a higher power is such a powerful force all over the world. Almost everyone feels a certain connectivity to the Universal Spirit, Creator, God, or whatever one's term is for this Creative Power. We see little miracles in our lives. Someone has a miraculous recovery. Money turns up just when we need it desperately. Or we experience a number of synchronicities (meaningful coincidences). We read something, perhaps a book, a phrase of scripture, or a quotation at just the time when it has great meaning to us. We meet someone, either known to us from an earlier time or not, who unexpectedly plays an important role in our lives for just a moment or longer. The purely mathematical probability of these things happening makes their occurrence unlikely. But such things do happen.

We also have moments when we transcend the mundane happenings of this life and, with a rush of blissful joy, we connect with something far higher than wealth and power. We begin to realize the presence of an unseen, but powerful, force that touches all of mankind. We begin to wonder if understanding this Unseen Presence could help us explain where we came from, what our purpose here is and what, if anything, happens after this earthly existence. We begin to try to make these moments of ecstasy occur more often because they seem to lift us up, help us heal our physical and spiritual wounds, and they take us to a place where we feel unconditional love.

What form this Creator Spirit takes, what our relationship to It/Him/Her/Them is, and what expectations we believe It/He/She/They have of us are most often determined by our family of origin's religious beliefs (I'm still trying to avoid assigning a gender or number to God). When people grow up with a certain *God format*, as I call it, their only way to view the Divine and this earthly existence is based on what they have been taught. Everything must be manipulated within this framework. For instance, most religions have strict Sabbath laws that limit a person's activities on that day. People have learned how to make almost any activity a Sabbath activity with a little bit of rationalizing; e.g., "You can't get much closer to God than when you're on the ski slopes." If we cannot create these rationalizations within our God format framework, we believe we risk losing our God connection. We often believe that either our God format is true as we have been taught it – *or there is no God at all!* Many see atheism or agnosticism as the only alternative.

People who believe they have been badly treated by the God they believe in usually try to manipulate their beliefs within that format to make it possible to be loved by the God with which they are familiar. And yet, even when they think their God hates them, they still believe that they are stuck with this God format and they often begin to hate themselves. People generally do not understand that they have an option to choose another God format than the one they grew up with. It is not even fathomable that what they have learned about God is at all challengeable or subject to modification. After all, that would be blasphemy, heresy or some other horrible thing, wouldn't it? In fact, writing this paragraph would have been punishable by death not that long ago. Even Jesus was persecuted and eventually killed because he had enraged the leaders of the prevailing God format of his time.

What is it then that keeps a person so strongly attached to his current God format? One of the most powerful forces that keep people attached to their current religious organization is that it may provide one of the only sources of being connected in many societies. You bring funeral potatoes to Uncle Larry's funeral, and I'll make green been casserole when Suzy gets married. You care about me and I'll care about you – I call this the *love connection*. We humans crave and seek this love connection, and it is easy to understand why we will do almost anything to find it and keep it. We can easily be kept tied to a religious organization if we think that it is inseparably connected to this love connection. We lose the ability to factor out this feeling of mutual caring from the rest of the dogma, rituals and faith-based beliefs that are a part of that religion. Very often this love connection includes our entire family and our close friends – our tribe. To alienate ourselves from our religion feels risky and often means immediate, and sometimes very severe, alienation from all the people that are so important to us; it's strange to think that this hateful alienation would be a part of so many God formats. So we would rather continue in a practice that, except for the love connection, is minimally useful to us and is often extremely detrimental in our evolutionary process.

Fear is another extremely powerful force in the God conundrum. We fear first and foremost losing our connection to our God. If our religious teachings have convinced us that God will withdraw from us if we leave a particular religious tradition, we may indeed lose that God connection when we leave – but only because *we* have disconnected ourselves from God, and NOT because God has cut the connection. No religious organization or belief tradition can connect us to God or cause us to be distanced from the Divine. We may feel distanced if we leave because our warm and fuzzy moments have been associated with these religious beliefs.

Most of the things we enjoy with our families and friends (holiday celebrations, family activities, weddings, etc.) are, in many cases, enjoyed within the religious framework. So we come to believe that the continuance of these love connection moments is completely dependent on a particular religious organization. It is unfortunately true that societal beliefs often value the prevailing God format more than **love** – the only thing God can *ever* be about. ***In truth, only we ourselves have complete control over our connection to God.***

Most of us have been taught that there are many things that our Supreme Being requires of us – anything from a long list of commandments we must keep to accepting Jesus into our hearts. While the concept of heaven and hell does not belong uniquely to the Abrahamic religions, it is certainly highly emphasized in them. The fear of being cast into an eternity of fire and brimstone, or whatever we envision as hell, can be horrifying if pounded into one's psyche from the early days of one's childhood. It broke my heart to see some of my beloved HIV patients, who were in the process of dying, hang on so intensely to life despite their great misery because they were terrified of the eternal punishment that was awaiting them.

Even if hell is not presented as such a miserable place, but just so much less than the highest degree of heaven, it can be a powerful force in keeping us from looking outside our particular religious box for other beautiful and helpful concepts. If you ask someone to describe heaven and hell in some detail, most people have not gotten past fire and brimstone vs. playing harps on clouds. They just believe that being in heaven means being with God, and being in hell means being with Satan. Religion gives people bad reasons for doing good things when there are actually better reasons for doing so.

Religion has yet another powerful force working for it. Some call it *testimony*. If a person is involved in a particular religion or spiritual movement and finds that he/she resonates with certain aspects of it, it is very easy to extrapolate that anything else from the same source must be just as true and perfect. If people have an unusually strong spiritual experience while belonging to or looking into a particular religious tradition, they may be led to believe that God has "testified" to them of the truthfulness of that particular religion or belief. In seeking spiritual guidance, one usually tries to bring oneself closer to Source Spirit. One may believe that the warm and fuzzy feelings he experiences during this time of connection are validating a revelation he seeks when, in reality, these feelings emanate from this momentary connection with the Divine. Especially when one has not had previous connections with the Divine, wherever one feels those first ecstatic moments is the place that person will associate with God. Very often it may be because the people who belong to that religion seem happy that the seeker is there and seem to accept and welcome him. Again, it's the love connection.

We all interpret things from within our own sealed premises. Charismatic personalities with the ability to emotionally move crowds can create great waves of ecstasy for those who become caught up in the experience. Some may take the experience to mean they have found the "one true religion or spiritual path." But these intense moments happen all over the world to people of every spiritual or religious tradition, and to those affiliated with none. They are almost always associated with moments of love, gratitude and acceptance – as mentioned above. Every human being has the ability and right to connect with the Divine on his own or in a group setting. To take these intense feelings when we connect with our Source to mean anything more than communication with God can be misleading.

Early in man's existence certain men figured out that they could use the belief in Deity to their advantage. It was not hard to convince their fellow humans that these warm connected feelings came from God. These influential leaders then convinced the people that God and man were very separate entities and that man was unable to fully understand or communicate with this Higher Power on his own. Of course this meant that these influential people that were eventually accepted as religious leaders would need to be the teachers and the go-betweens, placing them in a very powerful position. They could threaten the people that these intensely warm feelings would go away if worshippers did not adhere absolutely to a certain set of rules, rituals and donation requirements. No one wanted to lose this connection with their Higher Source, so people became blindly obedient to what was taught to them by such influential men. In many cases, the religious law became the law of the land, and the religious leaders became the highest governing powers in the land. This remains the case in many parts of the world today, and many people would like to see it become even more prevalent.

Now you may be asking what harm exists in having strong beliefs that conform to a particular religious doctrine set. How does that hurt anyone? The answer is very emphatically that BELIEFS

HAVE CONSEQUENCES! Every belief we hold has consequences, some beneficial and some detrimental, some large and some insignificant, and some that simply hinder us from acquiring other more personally relevant and beneficial beliefs. Some beliefs have nothing to do with religious traditions and are simply given to us by our society, our peers and our experiences. Some beliefs are based on what would be considered sound evidence – science, observation and deduction. Other beliefs are based on little, if any, evidence. Strange as it may seem, some of the most difficult beliefs to shake are those with no rational basis. Often these are referred to as superstitions – except in the unusual case of religion. We tend not to evaluate these unfounded beliefs logically because doing so would require that we question why we hang onto them so desperately. But one thing is certain: *Throughout history beliefs have had gigantic impacts on individuals and civilizations, so we cannot say that they do not matter.*

Superstition, whether religious or otherwise, is always based in fear. No matter how miserable or beautiful our current life situations are, superstition says that they can always get worse if we don't do something to maintain the status quo. Even if the sun has come up every day that anyone has recollection of, it just might decide not to show up if we don't sacrifice a few virgins. However well or poorly our lives are going, we have fears about what happens when we die. We believe we can improve our status in the afterlife by "pleasing" God in this life by keeping religious commandments, or we fear that we could be put in a more terrible place if we do things that don't "please" the God we now imagine. No matter how miserable or mundane our current existence is, the superstitious fear that things could get worse keeps us from discovering how much better they can be. *God has no ego and does not need to be pleased. God is only pure ecstatic love, and there is no judgment in love. You cannot discover the full potential of your life if you stay dedicated to the rules and rituals of superstitious beliefs – whether religious, cultural or self-created (like watching a football game wearing a lucky shirt).*

If we look at the Abrahamic religions, we see how powerful beliefs can be. In the Old Testament of the Bible the people were given the Law of Moses. It contained chapter after chapter of laws you must simply obey. Such practices as eating pork and seafood were considered an abomination (beetles and grasshoppers were OK), and eating these abominable foods would result in being cut off from society. Many things such as sexual improprieties, working on the Sabbath, and a child swearing at or hitting his parents were punishable by death (seems a little severe). But if you were a part of this society, you were bound by the beliefs of the society, whether you personally held every belief or not.

Then came Jesus. He tried to teach his fellow Jews that the Old Testament teachings needed to be updated with principles of love, compassion, tolerance, service and being nonjudgmental. This was not well accepted by people who believed and accepted the idea that, since the Law of Moses was the word of God, how could anything be wrong with it? And was it not heresy to say that their prophets of old had given them principles that were no longer relevant or could be greatly improved upon? This is exactly the same rationale used by many of today's Christians when they state that the Bible contains all that man could ever need and that every verse is the absolute word of God.

Even though Jesus was killed and his followers dispersed, his teachings would eventually attract enough believers that a religion would evolve and fill much of the Earth. Unfortunately, Jesus' teachings soon lost the spirit in which they were given and a reign of terror was unleashed by a religious organization that was supposedly founded on the principles of peace, tolerance and love. Pillage and plunder occurred all over the globe. The Spanish Inquisition claimed millions of lives, many of them being Native Americans who were doing perfectly well with their own traditions. The Crusades, the Thirty Years War and numerous other events of savagery, cruelty and bloodshed were committed in the name of mankind's greatest teacher of non-judgmental love. Somehow men of power were able to twist the teachings of Jesus into a calling to slaughter, steal and rape. Mark Twain said:

"Man is a Religious Animal. He is the only animal that has the True Religion – several of them. He is the only animal that loves his neighbor as himself and cuts his (neighbor's) throat if his theology isn't straight. He has made a graveyard of the globe in trying his honest best to smooth his brother's path to happiness and heaven."

As with everything else, religion cannot be looked at as all good or all bad. Many people have been lifted up and helped by belonging to a religious organization. Others whose lives have been out of control have embarked on more functional and productive lives after "finding God." But when religion causes fanatical and dogmatic behavior, it can be very destructive. Many families have been torn apart because one or more of their members have not adhered to the rituals, dogma or traditions of the religion practiced in their homes and communities. Marrying outside the family religion can lead to a child being disowned in some traditions. Being gay and out has very severe consequences all over the world. In some Islamic countries "honor killings" still occur where parents kill a gay child to honor their god. But the reality is that they do it to save face in their community and avoid persecution from fellow religious fanatics. Gay adolescents in the U.S. are often coerced into heterosexual marriages or into ex-gay ministries for "reparative therapy" because they have been made to feel that their God format cannot love them as they are.

In recent times people in the West are beginning to understand that there are other God formats available. Many people around the world believe in a God that does not have all the petty emotions that humans have. This God creates and loves but is not jealous, angry, vengeful, judgmental or anxious to send non-believers to eternal damnation in hell. In this format, each person is an eternal soul entity and opts to do as many incarnated lives (lives with physical bodies) as it takes to attain the level of spiritual evolution he desires. Certainly one lifetime is not enough to achieve the level of God-like attributes most souls seek. Earth life is a learning experience – University Earth. We may even have asked our soul friends to come with us to help us learn compassion, patience or tolerance just as we may have helped them learn their lessons in other lifetimes. Our struggles in this life may benefit our families and friends at least as much as they help us in our own evolution.

* * * * *

Joe was a successful lawyer working in a prestigious law firm in a large city. Everyday, on his way to and from the office, he would encounter the same alcoholic homeless man looking for a handout. Most days he would just look at the man in disgust and think to himself, "Why did he let himself get to this awful state? Why doesn't he get a life?" But something about this man haunted him and he was sure he knew him from somewhere. He could not figure out where, but the man would look at Joe as though they were old friends. Once in awhile Joe would throw the man a few coins and say, "Don't spend it on booze, spend it on food." But most of the time he would just walk on by and try not to make eye contact with him.

One day, as Joe came out of the office to head home, it was particularly cold and windy. As he passed the homeless man lying on the sidewalk he could tell that he was weak and shivering, and Joe thought he looked like he might even die there that night. Joe could not just walk by this time. He stopped and knelt down beside the man and said, "You look like you need to be inside tonight. I want to pay for a room at a hotel for you tonight. And let's get you some food too." Joe could hardly believe his own words.

The man looked humbly up at Joe and said, "You would do that for me? I could never repay your kindness, my friend."

"Don't worry about it," Joe said quietly. "Let me help you up."

The man looked into Joe's eyes as he got up, and Joe shivered with the recognition of something very familiar in the man's eyes. They stopped at a small grocery store and got some food and then Joe paid for two nights at an inexpensive hotel a block away. The man held the key in his hand and Joe was about to walk away when the man turned to him and said, "You didn't look like the kind of person that would do something like this for me. I cannot tell you how much joy this brings me that we finally got to meet."

Joe didn't know how to feel about the man's comments and, although he felt touched by them, he had to admit that they somehow bothered him. But he had to acknowledge that he had never felt the warm glow of compassion that he was feeling at that moment. His smile came from deep inside and tears welled up in his eyes as he continued on his way home.

He arrived home, ate supper and got ready for bed. He couldn't get it out of his mind that this man seemed to know him and vice versa. He eventually slipped into sleep and had an amazing dream – more like a vision. He saw this man to be a highly evolved personage of great light and understanding. And then it came to him who this man was. Joe and the homeless man had been great friends in previous existences. Joe had asked the man to accompany him in this earthly existence to help him learn compassion and not to judge. These were things that Joe needed and wanted to learn in this lifetime since he had not learned them well in previous incarnations. Joe's friend did not need to do another lifetime for his own spiritual evolution, but he had agreed to help Joe in this one and he had just been waiting for Joe to open his heart. He smiled at Joe and faded gradually away.

"How inconceivable," thought Joe the next morning, "that someone would live such a miserable existence in order to teach me such a powerful lesson." On his way to work he passed the hotel where the man was finally warm and satiated. He looked up and wiped the tears from his eyes as he realized that he had just embarked on one of the most important learning paths of his life.

* * * * *

We can incorporate whatever beliefs we find beautiful and uplifting into our own God formats. We are not required to hold beliefs that do not resonate with our view of the Divine Creator. Neither the Bible nor any other collection of writings should be the sole source of influence over how we develop our God formats. We can certainly use all words of light from these volumes, but there may be a lot of verses that simply don't belong in our God format. If one believes, as I do, that egoless love is the energy of God, then there will not be a place in one's God format for judgment day or the need to please God. The sun will come up whether or not we sacrifice virgins. Sin will only be anything that inhibits our joyful upward spiritual evolution. The loss of spiritual growth and the accumulation of dark energy is what we pay for our sins. My God does not require any further payment for them – either from us or from a proxy atonement figure. When we return to our spirit state and the veil of forgetting is lifted, we may see how we have wasted an embodied lifetime or even used it to create great darkness and suffering, and this could certainly cause hellish remorse as we realize what will be required to dissipate the dark energy we have accumulated. But God certainly takes no joy in our anguish. How can we possibly imagine that the Great Creator could have such dark feelings?

In my own experience, recreating my God format has been so liberating that I feel I have been given a new understanding of my place in the Universe. When God is remade to have no expectations or judgment of me, it is much easier to connect and be one with this Being of Pure Love. Realizing that I *am* allowed to imagine my Creator as this entity of pure love with no expectations and, therefore, no judgment of me has not in any way taken away my incentive to live a good life. Guilt and shame and the fear of punishment no longer come from *my* God, and they are not my motivation for doing or not doing anything. I am inspired to do good things by my desire to improve myself and make a better life for those living here with me. My Supreme Being does not support war or aggression of any kind and doesn't care who wins a football game. It is not my God's job to prevent tragedy or suffering. We, as embodied spirits, are here to learn to help alleviate the suffering of others whenever we can. If God were to use Divine Power to micromanage all lives so that all creations would live in heavenly bliss all the time, we would have no free agency and therefore have little opportunity to grow. In my God format suffering does not get you any extra Brownie points. My Source Spirit is just as happy when we learn our lessons in joy.

I have realized that God has given me this great opportunity to live another embodied existence so that I may learn to suppress my ego, gain control over addictions and become a person of love and compassion. How could I possibly waste this opportunity? I have learned to love myself again as a gay man, and I have gained tremendous insights from this challenge. I have no desire to judge any person and do not take joy in believing that anyone will burn in hell for the wrongs they have done – even wrongs against me. My God format is open to further evolution. I continuously seek new experiences and information because I have thrown open the door of my confining room and jetted out, never to return to it again. My relationship with my Creator has changed from endless futile attempts to please to one in which the same Divine Energy runs through both of us. How strongly my Creator and I resonate depends on how high the frequency of *my* energy is. That is why I always strive to live in love and beauty so that I may feel the incredible joy of living in the Light.

I certainly understand that leaving one's religious environment is not possible for all people. One's family and the rest of one's tribe are very important and, if someone feels strongly that he may completely lose this connection to these important people by leaving his religious tradition, this may not be the right time to do it. We each have our own path to travel. Many people are very happy in their religious organizations and enjoy being a part of them. But, whether we stay with our current religion or eventually leave it, one thing we can all do is create our *own* God formats to carry with us in our hearts. Regardless of the prevailing God format in our lives, we can understand that our Creator is pure love energy and loves us just as we are. We can stop trying to live lives of obedience and start living lives of compassion and acceptance. We can quit believing that suffering is a necessary part of life and start looking at challenges as opportunities for growth. As my sister says, "Love trumps everything."

How one imagines God to be is unique for each person – even those who belong to the most rigid religious traditions. Most people relinquish the entirety of the very important privilege of delineating their beliefs about God to people who tell us they know more about God than we could ever discover for ourselves. They tell us that the reality of God can only be found in ancient writings, venerable traditions and organized religion, and they have the audacity to try to make us believe that we need them to intercede and be our connection with God. How arrogant and absurd. ***Since a person's God format impacts so much of what a person thinks, feels and does, it is imperative that we all exercise our right and responsibility to create a God format that we resonate with and can live with. It should embody all the traits of the Most Spiritually Evolved Being in the Universe, and it should allow us to connect with this Source of All Light whenever we desire. No one else should ever be allowed to create our vision of God for us!***

We can consider any ideas we can uncover to help us create our beliefs about God, and we can freely discard any that don't lift us up. We do not have to understand every tiny detail right now – a little mystery is fine. When we finally understand that it is not useful to spend our lives trying to keep thousands of commandments, when we quit judging our fellow human beings and realize that each person is just where they are on their paths, and when love becomes the most important thing in our lives, we may want to shout the words of Martin Luther King, Jr.: "Free at last, free at last, Lord God Almighty – free at last!"

Chapter Nineteen

THE ENERGY EQUATION – 10%

*It is wonderful how much time people spend fighting
the devil. If they would only expend the same
amount of energy loving their fellow men, the devil
would die in his own tracks of ennui (boredom).*

Helen Keller

Barrels of oil, cubic feet of natural gas, kilowatts of electricity, BTU's of heat – there are many ways of talking about energy. Many societies around the world have become prosperous and high-tech because of their ability to put energy to work for them. The industrial age began as the steam engine started to provide energy for factories, transportation and agriculture.

Energy is the source of all life. The sun creates large amounts of energy from nuclear fusion. Plants absorb energy from the sun and use this energy to turn carbon dioxide and water into the substances that animals use to nourish themselves and build their homes. Energy is The Creator and all that is created. It is knowledge, and it is the wisdom to put that knowledge to use. It is the organization and beauty of nature, the power of the Earth's climate and the power to preserve or destroy our planet. Every thought, feeling and act creates

215

its own energy, and it is how every person's vector sum is stored. The energy we produce through our emotions and deeds will determine what our lives will be tomorrow and onward into the future.

The entire universe is about one thing and one thing only – ENERGY. Quantum physics and unified field string theory tell us that even matter is really just energy. Relatively recently scientists have begun to understand that approximately 95% of our universe is not directly observable or measurable. 72% of the universe is believed to be something called dark energy and 23% is called dark matter (*dark* meaning invisible to our current instruments). We know that electromagnetic waves surround us only because we have instruments to make them observable (radios, televisions and cell phones). At present we have no devices that allow us to directly observe dark matter or dark energy. We can only see their effects on the 5% of the universe our instruments can observe and measure.

Similarly, we know that there is a type of energy that is difficult to measure with existing instruments, although we can see and feel its effects. I'll call it high-vibration and low-vibration energy – or the light side and the dark side of The Force. The dark energy (not related to the dark energy spoken of above) is based in fear, greed, lust for power, anger, hate and violence. The light energy is found in love, gratitude, compassion and joy. There is, of course, no dividing line between the two, but shades of gray from darkest to lightest. Our bodies and spirits can feel and measure this energy if we pay attention to it. We are touched by beauty and high-vibration energy when we see acts of forgiveness, compassion, service or sacrifice. We feel the dark disturbance of cruelty, violence, anger and fear – unless we have numbed ourselves to it.

I will use the term dark energy interchangeably with negativity or low-vibration energy, and will use the term light energy, positivity or high-vibration energy. As a scientist I try to be careful to keep the metaphors as close to real science as possible, but here I ask you to look at the metaphor instead of the exact science. Since we have no instruments capable of measuring these subtler light and dark energies, we do not know if they are exactly additive. In other words, is the dark energy simply an absence of light as it is in classical physics, or does dark energy have a force of its own? I truly believe we will someday be able to see and measure this subtler, but most powerful of energies; but for now it is simply a metaphor.

Many believe that dark energy is stronger than light energy because this is what we have been taught by media news and what we see around us as well as in our video games, movies and other entertainment. This is not true. Think of a room of people where the power suddenly goes out and it becomes very dark. Humans have come to equate total darkness with fear. There is no need for darkness to create fear. The people in the room are the same, but we begin to imagine the fearful things we see in the movies. As soon as one person brings out a lighter, pocket LED flashlight or cell phone, just that much light dispels a huge amount of fear. For every additional small light, the darkness is dissipated even more. In reality, a power outage could be, and often is, a time of great trust and connectivity. "Does anyone have a light?" "I'll see if I can find some candles." "Since the TV and the computer are down, maybe we can talk to each other (Oooh no, communicating face to face?)."

Most societies have been programmed for fear. We see it in most of our entertainment and politics. Even the so-called family programs have a lot of darkness running through them. I was watching a Disney movie called "Tangled" with my nephews and was amazed at the number of fearful sinister images in this movie ostensibly made for children. We grow up with fear and it follows us into our adult lives. We believe that the only effective response to fear is anger and violence. Only a rare few reach out their hands to others and try to diffuse the angry energy.

Fear is one of the most infectious of all memes. It is easy to dive into fear at the smallest rumor, but it is very difficult to escape the dark goo once we're immersed in it. Clever men know that they can use fear to win elections, rally the troops, allow our governments to take away our freedoms or keep people in dead-end jobs. We seem to come into the world fearless, ready to try anything. But we allow that fearlessness to be pounded out of us, and then we think we must pound it out of others. We tell each other that those things we dream of are not possible. We propagate stories of evil people who want to harm us who live in another neighborhood or another country. But how many of us really understand the power of high-vibration energy? Have we let the darkness take over to the point that we don't even realize the power of love, forgiveness, peace and joy?

Yes, there will always be light and dark energy in the universe, and we will encounter both as we live our lives. To truly evolve and grow, we must experience the yin and the yang, the good and the evil, the heaven and hell. But it seems we have come to believe almost entirely in the power and necessity of dark energy. Aggressiveness must always be met with aggressiveness. We talk about wars on everything – the war on terror, the war on drugs, the war on illegal immigration and even the war on poverty. We think we have to fight fire with fire, but all we get are a lot of really hot destructive fires. We respond to fearful things with even more fearful things. We have relied on power, aggression, vengeance and violence so much that we have no concept of reality, which is this: ***You cannot fight dark energy with dark energy. You can only counteract dark energy by blessing it with the light energy of love and compassion. If you react to dark energy with more dark*** *energy, you will only multiply the amount of hate, anger, violence and fear that is present.*

The idea that the light energy of love and compassion could stop aggressiveness more effectively than vengeance and violence just does not seem to compute with most people, especially those we select to lead our countries, states and municipalities. We see the police becoming more brutal and using more violent weapons against our own citizens. We have more people per capita incarcerated than any country in the world. We spend trillions of dollars developing more clever and destructive weapons, and now, due to the remote operation of these weapons, we don't even have to feel the impact of their carnage. We have become convinced that this is the only way to deal with people we have labeled as bad.

In addition to the energy our actions have, our thoughts, beliefs and feelings also carry strong energies. Low-vibration energy can adversely affect our immune systems, cognitive functioning, moods and spiritual well-being. High-vibration energy can have a positive effect on all of these things. The energy we create not only affects us on a personal level, but also radiates to the area around us and to the planet in general. We may not even realize that our attitudes and behaviors are associated with energy. When we recycle, we often wonder if the tiny part we are contributing to the Earth's health is really helpful. But the very act of recycling puts out an energy that is felt fairly strongly close by and is perceptible even at a distance. We have seen how whole communities change their habits and thinking when a few people make an effort to improve the world in their own small area. Eventually the whole community has recycling bins and people are making a conscious effort to save water and use less toxic chemicals. Our thoughts, words and emotions not only create our behavior, but they also contribute to the positivity or negativity of our communities and our planet.

In societies where the Abrahamic religions are dominant, most people have no concept of another extremely important role our thoughts, words, beliefs and emotions play. In recent years, however, many people have come to understand that our thoughts and, more importantly, the emotional energy created by those thoughts, attract to us what we eventually experience. What this means is that the Universe reflects and amplifies the energy that is radiated from the center of each person. This principle is often called either The *Law of Attraction* or *The Power of Intention*. If someone wants abundance in his life but feels the emotions of scarcity deep inside, it is scarcity and wanting that will be reflected back into his life. If that person can begin to feel like he is already wealthy and start sharing his abundance with others in even the smallest ways, he will broadcast abundance to the Universe and will begin to discover ways to bring greater abundance into his life. If a woman thinks of herself as unattractive and undesirable, she will create that belief in others by the energy she radiates. If she can begin to see herself as attractive and desirable, others will be attracted to her by her self-confidence and inner beauty regardless of her external appearance.

Many books and movies describe the Law of Attraction in greater detail than can be gone into here. Napoleon Hill's *Think and Grow Rich* was one of the first books to become popular. More recently *The Law of Attraction* by Esther and Jerry Hicks as well as Louise Hay's movie *You Can Heal Your Life* are wonderful descriptions of this principle. Some people discount the energetic part of this concept, saying that thinking like a rich man simply leads to behavior more like that of a wealthier person. However, it is *feeling* like the person you want to become that has the most power to take you there. In twelve step programs, this is termed "faking it until you make it." There is no doubt that our thoughts and feelings are the precursors to what we do. However, until we truly *feel* wealthy (or attractive or healthy or lovable), it will be much more difficult to bring these things into our lives. This is the exact opposite of what we have been taught, i.e. – when a person is attractive, he will feel attractive. But countless "beautiful people" have had endless plastic surgery or have developed eating disorders because they never truly *felt* attractive inside.

Learning to control our thoughts, words and emotions will help us emit an energy that will bring us what we need. This powerful concept may be new to many people. As we begin to understand this concept, we become purposeful creators of what happens in our lives instead of letting random winds blow us in chaotic directions. The Law of Attraction is amazingly simple and works remarkably well. But how do we change the thoughts and the feelings deep inside us when they have been reinforced so powerfully throughout our lives? Affirmations are a good place to start. Affirmations are positive statements in the present tense about what we would like to see in our lives. We say them in the present tense, as though we already had them, to create a stronger attractive energy. Saying "I would like a relationship where both of us can live in love and joy," puts your desires into the future. As discussed before, the future never gets here. A more powerful affirmation would be stated like this, "I am so grateful for the kind and loving person who has been sent into my life to interact with me in a harmonious way." Yes, it will seem strange at first to say that you're grateful for things that have not shown up yet, but soon you will be able to feel your desires coming your way. Louise Hay has a lot of beautiful affirmations on her website at www.louisehay.com/affirmations/.

Most importantly, you cannot create what you desire if you do not feel worthy of it, because the Universe senses that unworthiness as not being quite ready for your blessing. This means you must learn to love yourself and understand that you truly are worthy of all good things. Learning to really love oneself is harder than it should be. I find it best to look in the mirror and say out loud, "I am perfect and beautiful just as I am. I love myself unconditionally so that I may share that unconditional love with others. I release the past with love, and I am open and receptive to all the goodness and abundance of the Universe. I love you, David. You are a positive energy for the planet." We may have to say these affirmations many times a day, especially if we are trying to bring healing into our lives. It was very difficult to convince my AIDS patients that they did not have to die when others had told them that no one survives this disease. Fortunately, many of my HIV patients rejected the "no one survives" concept and are healthy and happy thirty years later. The most difficult thing an overweight person has to learn is to look in the mirror and love what he or she sees. Only then can the Universe help that person conquer the obstacles to creating a healthier and happier body.

When we become filled with love, gratitude and compassion, we will be able to bring into our lives the good things that are in tune with Source Energy. However, we will have a more difficult time fulfilling our desires if we hold unkind feelings toward others. Most Christians will tell you that they believe the Bible verses that say, "Turn the other cheek," and "Love your enemies." They will also tell you that they live by them, but most do not. Most people spend too much of their time worrying about how to get even with someone who has offended them, done something they felt was wrong or caused them some sort of emotional or psychological pain. They often hold judgment and animosity toward all the "sinners" in the world. *These feelings hurt the ones who harbor them the most.* You will help yourself tremendously by letting go of these negative feelings and you will bring up the vibrational energy of the planet every time you forgive someone or make peace with your adversary.

You may say, "But I just can't let go of it. What she said hurt me so much." That is your bruised ego talking, telling you that you are justified in holding dark feelings against someone because of the pain they caused you. Tell your ego to TAKE A HIKE; stop emitting the dark energy of resentment and start radiating the positive light energy of forgiveness and unconditional love. The energy to heal yourself and make spiritual progress cannot exist in the same soul that harbors animosity, hate or vengefulness. *Changing the total energy of the planet depends on individual people changing the energy that they radiate to a more positive and loving vibration.*

It is surprising how few people radiating high vibration energy it takes to change the energy of the space around them. It becomes less surprising when we look at the transformative energies of Jesus, the Buddha, Gandhi, Mother Teresa, Nelson Mandela and others who have radiated love through their words and actions. The power of the Light Side of the Force is much stronger than we comprehend. War could be avoided altogether if we could really understand and use the power of the Light Side of the Force. By not giving in to the energy of fear, anger and hatred, the megalomaniacs who keep giving wars for their ego and profit would have no support. I am totally convinced that weapons could be inactivated by enough light/love energy (sounds crazy, I know). Even more importantly, light energy can change the hearts of men to stop them from using the weapons in the first place.

High-vibration energy, even when radiated in small amounts, has the power to change hearts. What one thinks about and concentrates his emotional energy on is what is radiated into the Universe. Fear is the strongest dark emotion and therefore has the power to create the most destruction when it becomes the strongest collective emotion among the Earth's people. Fear feeds dark energy and helps it create more fear until it becomes a vicious cyclone that can be stopped only by mountains of solid light. The only way to stop the power that fear has is to stop fearing. How? We have to melt that fear with the warmth of love. The Light energy of love and joy can burn through even the darkest gooiest concentrations of fear and anger.

Why is it that fear, greed and darkness are so often chosen over the light of love and service? For many people ego plays a large role. They think good looks, material goods or being thought of as cool or powerful is what we are here for, and they think these will make them happy. They will do whatever it takes to have more cool stuff or gain perceived power over others – this is usually called crime (or politics). For many, the dark side is just part of the Tribal Rules. When young men are taught the rules for manhood, being a "bad boy" is one of the first things they learn. "No one likes a goodie-goodie boy," they're told. For many men, being respected really means being feared. To disrespect someone shows that you don't have the right level of fear for that person. Our tribal rules also tell us that there is always someone out there to be afraid of. We must always have a larger military than anyone else if we are to survive. We are told that we are completely separate from other people and that we are superior to them. Many societies teach that women are less important than men and ought to be controlled by men. A society might also teach that you have every right to take away the abundance and well-being of other people and hoard it for yourself as long as you play by the economic rules of that society, however corrupt and ego-serving they might be. One of the most destructive tribal rules is the idea that *might makes right*. This is why men and women can so easily be gathered together into gangs, militias, secret societies and banking cartels. But might will never make right no matter how good one is at rationalizing.

Once people have chosen the bad boy path, their consciences become dulled to the point of being non-existent. To feel guilt or remorse is seen as a sign of weakness. To have compassion or empathy for someone makes you a wimp. These people learn to rationalize to the point of being able to do great harm to people with delight rather than remorse. Well-documented stories tell about men and women of great wealth and power who meet on a regular basis to decide the fate of nations. At the end of their meeting they burn someone in effigy and cheer to remind themselves of their lack of concern about their fellow human beings whom they see as inferior. At some point after becoming entangled in dark thoughts and behavior, a person seems to lose his free will and becomes absorbed into the field of dark energy. This does not mean he cannot emerge from the darkness, but it will take great determination. The power of evil is in the unity of purpose that those who choose it have – there is solidarity in achieving their ego-filled purposes. Greed and the lust for power are intoxicating and addictive.

Individual Light souls certainly have great power by themselves, but we seem hesitant to reach out to other like-minded individuals to become a synergistic unified force for good. If we fear being ridiculed, we do not recognize the real respect that most people will have for us when we participate in acts of kindness and compassion. When we really think about it, kind and loving people are usually seen as the strong ones. Many humans have the deep-seated desire to become beings of light and love, but their perceived tribal rules make it difficult to go there. If we are mocked for taking a different path, we should just send the mockers good healing energy. There is no need to judge them – just wish them the best possible outcome on whatever path they are on. And most of all, when we see people perform acts of kindness, we should be supportive of them and let them know that we stand with them in their love and compassion. Our *only* possibility for neutralizing negative energy is to replace it with love.

If we decide we want a planet of peace and shared abundance, we must raise the frequency of our own spiritual energy by taking careful control over what we observe, think and feel. I saw a cartoon of two women walking, one saying to the other, "I am terribly torn between the need to stay informed and the need to stay sane." For much of my life I have been a staunch activist. I have sent letters, I have marched and I have told others of the great evils that were occurring all around us with the hope that they would join with me to agitate for change. But recently I have realized that, despite my good intentions, I may have unwittingly created more negativity than positivity in some people. Not all people can hear of these great evils without becoming fearful, angry and hopeless. They are not inspired to increase the healing power they send to the country and the planet. They are not compelled to carefully ponder their choices and vote in the next election. They only become more fearful or want to kick some butt. They often don't even know whose butt would best be kicked, but they want to get kickin'. I apologize to those for whom I have created this negative energy and hope that you can join me in the healing process. That being said, in no way do I want to infer that there shouldn't be intense peaceful activism. Make your thoughts known to those who represent you, find and become a part of local grassroots organizations that work for what you feel passionate about, and march for positive change – but always do it with love, not anger.

The media news is probably the most powerful source of negative energy for most people. Although I have seen a slight trend toward presenting an occasional uplifting story, most of the news stories are about murders, tragedies and the less powerful people getting stomped on. Information has only the energy we give it, just as all the events in our lives have only the meaning and value we assign to them. Nevertheless, a constant diet of this kind of negative energy cannot help but harm our health, our minds and our spirits. If we must watch the news, we need to ask ourselves often, "Am I allowing myself to be manipulated into negative behavior to serve my own ego needs or possibly to build the ego-based empires of others?" If you watch the news and come away angry or depressed, you'd be better off being less informed. I only turn the news on at fifteen minutes after the hour to get the local weather report. In Arizona I hardly need to do that – the weather is usually sunny and hellish in the summer and sunny and gorgeous in the winter. If you just have to watch that big screen high-def TV you spent so much money on, switch from Fox News to PBS or some other uplifting programming. And just a word about PBS – it cannot survive without our help.

Instead of looking at things in an absolutist way, maybe we ought to look at them in the amount and kind of energy they create. We could tell Grandma that the pie she baked especially for us was pretty bad because we believe in absolute truth telling. Or we could create higher-vibration energy by telling her it was good and how much we appreciate her effort. Which of these creates the most healing energy? We can continue to judge people as bad or less-than, but we will not be able to send our love to them as easily if we do. We can continue to beat ourselves up over our past failures thereby letting that low-vibration energy keep us from enjoying the present moment, or we can learn all that is possible from our past and release all painful and unhappy moments in love so that we may enjoy what is happening right now. We can scoff at the person standing at the freeway exit who is holding a sign that says, "Please help. Lost job. Hungry. God Bless." Or we can hand him a dollar bill and wish him peace and joy. The money we give is for our good – not just his. We spend a huge amount of money incarcerating people for committing victimless crimes that harm no one. What creates the most high-vibration energy – to lock people away to punish them for drug addiction or to try to help them become useful and happy members of their society?

When we perform acts of kindness and service, we begin to radiate a higher-vibration energy, and people feel this energy around us. Even more importantly, we feel the energy change within us. When people do kind or positive things for us, we can pay it forward by smiling at people we encounter and by looking for opportunities to be of service. We all have cores of light energy, but those cores may have become coated with hard-to-crack layers of fear and cynicism. Our inner light can bore through all of those layers and begin to illuminate our own lives as well as the lives of others. We can become fearless by refusing to be fearful – fearless in our hopes and dreams, fearless in choosing the right things to do regardless of the derision of others, and fearless in sending our love to all living things. Imagine how this planet will transform when we do.

* * * * *

In 1959 Mahareshi Mahesh Yogi began teaching what he called Transcendental Meditation (TM) during a world tour, which included the United States. Millions have learned this meditative technique – including the Beatles and David Lynch – and a number of people have learned an advanced version of TM called TM-Sidhi. TM, and meditation in general, helps the meditator achieve a state of decreased anxiety, stress and depression while simultaneously increasing focus, peacefulness and creativity. It was postulated that a certain number of trained meditators focusing their energies together could reduce the communal stress in the Lebanon/Israel war zone, thereby decreasing the number of violent acts and increasing quality of life. In August and September, 1983, a group of TM-Sidhi meditators began practicing TM twice a day in Jerusalem.

The initial study showed a significant decrease in the violence, so seven subsequent experiments were done over a two-year period during the peak of the war. The results of these interventions included: war-related fatalities decreased by 71%, war-related injuries fell by 68%, the level of conflict dropped by 48%, and cooperation among antagonists increased by 66%. The number of meditators in the group fluctuated during these times, and a strong correlation was seen between increasing number of meditators and decreasing violence. Besides their meditations, the TM-Sidhas did not have any other interactions with the people. It was also noted that during the times of decreased violence there was also an increase in quality of life as measured by the Tel Aviv stock market index, automobile accident rate in Jerusalem, number of fires in Jerusalem and the national mood.[1]

Today there are almost 50 studies confirming this initial research. There are some startling statistics that arose from these studies. The first is how fast the so-called Mahareshi effect occurs. Within hours of the group meditations, the violence began to wane. As noted above, the more meditators in the area, the stronger the effect was. It has also been demonstrated that the energy was felt and the effect was achieved long distances from the meditators. But most striking to me was the small number of people dedicated to the energy of peace that was needed to achieve this soothing effect. In the case of TM-Sidhi trained people, it took only the square root of 1% of the area's population, e.g. – 100 meditators in a city of one million. In Baskinta (a small Lebanese war-torn village of 10,000), two teachers began teaching TM to the villagers. As soon as 100 residents had been taught to meditate – only 1% of the village's population – the village reached what is called the *Super Radiance threshold*. This term refers to the required number of people whose vibrational energies synchronize to create the Mahareshi effect. For intensely trained meditators, only the square root of 1% of the population is required to reach Super Radiance. For everyday meditators, the number is just 1% of the population.[2]

* * * * *

Whether it is TM, binaural beat training, yoga or some other practice, meditation is a way of getting the chatter out of one's mind and focusing on feeling connectivity with God, the Universe and our fellow human beings. It is beneficial in many areas – decreasing fear and depression, treating addictions and post-traumatic stress disorder, focusing one's mind for studying or being creative, helping people with attention deficit disorder, and helping one turn one's mind off from the worries and anger of the day. One of its most useful effects is in helping one tune in to the kind of energy one would like to have in one's core. I see my core as a sphere of energy in the region of my solar plexus that is completely in tune with what is going on in my body and spirit. It is the source of what I radiate from my being, and it is my power for bringing hostility or peace into the world. The more I can generate love, peace and joy in my core, the more it will heal my body, soothe my mind, bring peace to those around me and radiate out to affect positive change. Our core energy reflects our emotional state, i.e. – how we feel, and it is the strongest force contributing to what we create.

Well-practiced meditators have the ability to clear their minds of the meaningless minutia that wants to be there, and they can permeate their cores with an energy that is beyond that of the mundane thoughts and emotions associated with everyday living. Gunfire and bombs can be going off around these meditators, and they can continue to generate and radiate the beautiful Light of Peace. It's clear that we do not all have the opportunity to spend large amounts of time practicing meditation, but it is not an absolute thing – we are not either meditators or non-meditators. Whatever energy we produce at any given moment will be added in to the energy sum of our nearby surroundings and the planet. If we can quiet our fears, anger, greed, intolerance and resentment even for a part of our day, we will be more able to add peace and love to our surroundings. When we show our compassion with acts of kindness, acceptance and forgiveness, we raise the intensity of high-vibration energy that we send to the Universal energy grid. Each person's contribution is incredibly important. Do not discount the force for good you can be.

The combined force of all the individuals who radiate dark energy causes the dark behavior we see around us. Many of these people would love to live in peace and joy, but they are convinced that this is not possible because of all the "enemies" out there. Each person that makes a conscious effort to squelch that fear and bring in healing love will radiate a peaceful power that will help other people change their programming to let go of their fear and anger.

I sincerely believe that it would only take about **10%** of the world's population to create the Super Radiance effect and change the direction of the world. If you can take 15-20 minutes once or twice a day to concentrate on your intention to be a part of that joyful 10%, you will influence many in your vicinity. Of these, many of them will pass on this energy and it will not take a long time to reach the Super Radiance threshold. I am very certain that there is already more than 10% of the Earth's population that would love to become a part of this process of transformation. They are simply kept from joining us by their tribal rules, societal memes and fear programming. For most people, it could take awhile to dump all their fears, but each of us can work on maintaining a peaceful energy a little longer every day. *As more people allow themselves to be filled with love, we will see the changes occurring around* *us. This I promise you, for it is how the Universe works!* There will always be a number of dark ego-filled beings that will try to thwart the transformation process, but they will have less and less influence as more people put their high-vibration energy into the grid. Dark beings cannot survive in a pool of love – they will lose their control and they will drown.

Will you join us in creating this amazing transformation? There is nothing to do but become a kinder, less angry and more peaceful soul. It's very simple. Whatever degree of high-vibration energy you can contribute *will* make a difference. This love energy will spread and transfigure the planet. We are all meant to love and be loved, and now is the time for us to give that love to each other. The conflict is unnecessary and stupid, and it must end! Jesus said it simply, "Peace, be still."

Chapter Twenty

GENERATING LOVE

And the time came when the risk it took to
remain in a tightly closed bud became infinitely
more painful than the risk it took to blossom.

Anais Nin

The challenge of generating enough high-vibration love energy to displace the dark fear-based energy that so abundantly surrounds us may seem daunting to some and totally impossible to others. Fortunately, there are a large number of highly evolved souls that know how easily doable this is. It just takes a different mindset in which we realize that light energy has the power to displace the insanity that causes so much suffering. Generating love for all beings should be one of the easiest and most prevalent behaviors in humans, but many people don't even know how to get started since we have so few examples available to us. Everything is competition and separation instead of cooperation and unity in purpose. The following paragraphs contain ideas that I hope will be helpful in getting the creation of high-vibration love energy going. Some of these may seem a bit unusual, but the positive results will amaze you.

Walls – Many of us go through life as if we were surrounded by round brick walls resembling turrets on the corner of a castle, with vertical slits we can see through while staying reasonably safe from those who might fire angry arrows our way. The walls that surround us serve the purpose of any walls, to protect us and separate us from those we don't trust. Anyone who has been hurt often will likely have put up a protective wall to keep from being hurt again. Thus the walls give us the illusion of safety and protection, but they also serve to make us prisoners. We only let people into our lives that we trust, hoping they will not hurt us. When we share our love with these trusted people, we create light energy within our immediate sphere of influence. If we want to enlarge our positive influence even broader, however, we must take down our walls, learn to live with our vulnerability and seek friendship with a much larger group of people in our community of love promoters. If we are to work with others to generate more high-vibration energy, we have to dismantle the barriers that keep us from joining with them.

Vulnerability is an ego issue, since our egos tell us that it is important what others think of us and how they treat us. When we seek the acceptance and admiration of others, we attempt to do what we think they expect from us. If your friends and peers require that you be an uncaring and mean badass, you need to find other people to hang out with, or you could just quit feeling the need to live up to their expectations. Our fear of being vulnerable to the ridicule and bullying of unevolved souls keeps us afraid of taking down our walls. In some cultures, formality is well engrained and people are taught that too much familiarity breeds contempt. This occurs only when people of such cultures tend to be judgmental. Opening our lives to those around us can be a long frightening process, but as more people begin to dismantle their walls, the easier this process will be for others to do. The effect of wall dismantling is additive and synergistic. As you see me taking down my wall, you feel safer in starting to tear down your own. We begin to feel the reality of "I'm okay, you're okay." Living outside our walls of imagined protection may be uncomfortable at first, but gradually we will find those who will support us in love without judgment just as we support them.

Some people may decide to take a wrecking ball to their walls, while others may be more wary and take their walls down one brick at a time. Each time we say "hello" to someone in the checkout line, we take a brick off the top. Each random act of kindness takes another brick or two from the structure. Smiling, even when forced, takes bricks off the wall and helps you feel better at the same time. When someone behaves unkindly, if we return wishes of peace and love, we will not only disarm the unkind person, but we will knock a whole row of bricks from our walls.

Deconstructing our walls depends primarily on a secure knowing that the light of peace and love is the coolest, the most awesome and excellent energy we can radiate. It is *not* something to be ridiculed or scorned. It is the only way we will be able to save our planet and those who live here so there will still be a home for future generations. Do not be misled by those who preach fear and retaliation. Feeling a connection with other people, even with strangers, helps us gain confidence and lose fear. When we engage ourselves with other people without fear, we bring to our surroundings an energy of cooperativeness and sameness, and we displace the energy of competition and ego. When we surround ourselves with loving people and when we love others and ourselves unconditionally, we don't need walls of protection anymore.

We have seen that living our lives in the audience, rather than in the emotionally charged drama on the screen, can help us see things in a much different way. Martha Beck, in her book *The Joy Diet* [1], recommends interacting with other people in a meditative way. In other words, back away from the drama and detach yourself from any past or present emotional charges. See the person you're looking at as someone who is here dealing in the best way that he or she can with ego, addictions, fears, insecurities or personality problems. If we can smile and think, "Bless your heart, I wish you all the best," we will see them in a whole new light, and it will be much easier to send our love to them.

Random Acts of Kindness – I keep a few dollar bills clipped to my visor in my car. I give them to people who are asking for help on freeway exits or elsewhere. A friend was riding with me one day when I grabbed a couple of bucks and gave it to a man standing at a freeway exit with the usual cardboard sign. My friend immediately criticized me and told me that he was probably going to spend the money on alcohol or drugs. I told my friend that what that person did with the money was his issue and perhaps part of his challenge in life, but it is not up to me to decide what he might use it for. When I give money to someone, it is not as much for the person receiving the money as it is for me. It helps me to be less judgmental and increases the amount of loving energy I feel and radiate.

Acts of kindness may be random and spontaneous or planned and well thought out. Sometimes our gestures are misinterpreted and/or unappreciated, but usually they create a great deal of love energy. When we become less focused on our own desires and more on kind things to do for others, our own desires become less pressing. Cleaning up a mess someone else made, buying food for a homeless person, running an errand for an incapacitated person, phoning someone who would like to hear from us, holding doors open, and giving hugs to people who need them (and who doesn't?) are examples of gestures that can spread love energy. The ability to accept acts of kindness with appreciation is just as important as giving them. Without the receiver, the giver cannot exist. It is always an exchange of energy.

Spiritual Hugs – At times when we are alone and have no opportunity to do something loving for someone else, we can practice creating high-vibration energy by giving spiritual hugs to those we care about. I hope that we can eventually give those hugs to almost everyone. I often extend my arms to hug someone I want to send love to, even though they are not there. I bring them close to me in my mind and say, "I'm sending you my love. Everything will be all right."

People will very often feel the love we send to them, but more importantly, we are practicing staying in a loving state. Sometimes I give a spiritual hug to some random person on the television that looks like he needs some light energy in his life – even if the person has been accused of something terrible. This helps me get rid of my judgmental tendencies and realize more sincerely that we are all souls traveling on a learning path that is sometimes rocky, and many of us stumble and cause pain to ourselves and others. If someone interrupts my day by doing something rude or mean, I will often give that person a spiritual hug and wishes for a better day. This requires that I put my ego aside, and it neutralizes some of the negative energy the rude person has given off. Spiritual hugging is a powerful way to increase the vibrational energy we radiate, and it has great potential to change the course of our own lives.

Propagating Light – *Entrainment* is a scientific term used to describe the tendency of things that vary rhythmically to gradually fall into the same rhythm with each other. Dutch physicist, Christiaan Huygens, discovered that pendulum clocks mounted on a common board and set into motion out of sync with each other would gradually synchronize with the pendulums moving left and right at the same time. *Binaural beat therapy* is a type of brainwave entrainment that brings the left and right brains into synchronicity with each other. Entrainment is basically the synchronizing of energetic vibrations. You will notice that this kind of thing happens with light and dark energy, and it can happen fast.

Mob mentality, whether in the streets or at a sporting event, is a good example of synchronizing vibrational energy. The greed of Wall Street spreads from one person to another and one institution to another. There are numerous times when brutality in areas like Rwanda and Nazi Germany has caused a frenzy of violence and barbarism to spread like wildfire. A bully usually gains allies until someone steps in to provide protection to the bullied – and, most often, people with love energy will join these protectors. There are many examples along the light/dark spectrum of strong spirits being able to affect others for good causes or bad. We need to understand the power that each of us has and use it to create the greatest amount of healing and peaceful energy possible. We can be casual absorbers of energy or intentional radiators of it. In other words, we can be swept along by the prevalent energy in our environment, or we can create a bright energy that will carry others with it.

When we walk into a room, what kind of energy do we propagate? If we imagine that we are balls of bright white light radiating in all directions and that everyone in a room that we enter absolutely adores us as we adore them, the love energy we radiate will be felt, and the vibrational energy of the room will be brought up. If the room is filled with dark grumpy energy, we have the option of entraining with that energy or keeping our own happy mood going. People are often surprised at how easily the disposition of a group of people can be improved by one person refusing to join the fearful cantankerous mood of the crowd. It often seems much easier to go with the adversarial mood and get our barbs and arguments ready for the conversation, but we only add unpleasantness to the situation. When conversations on dark fearful topics begin (which seems to be all the rage), we can politely change the conversation to something more uplifting. A confident smile and an upbeat banter is infectious, "Come on guys, don't take the world news so seriously. Life is good."

Propagating love energy is dependent on our staying in a cheerful loving state. That energy will automatically warm others and they will pass it on. People want to be happy and hopeful, although they may not know it yet. We have allowed ourselves to be programmed for gloom and doom, but these are no more real than optimism and joy. It all depends on the perspective. When we make a conscious effort to be in a loving and hopeful state, we not only entrain that energy into those around us, but we will also find that our own lives change for the better.

Find Things to Love – Keeping our love energy strong requires a conscious and aware effort. Many of us are fortunate enough to have numerous people and things in our lives to love – family members, pets, friends, special relationships and even the beauty found in nature. To keep ourselves radiating the energy of love, it is easiest if we have things to focus our love on. Many people feel they have little to be thankful for and even less to love. Even people with families will often find it hard to love their family members significantly. The same goes for pets and spouses. Again, this is a matter of perspective – and we can change our perspectives. When we abandon our expectations of others and look for ways of appreciating what we can, when we train our eyes to see less ugliness and take in more of the beauty, and if we soften our hearts instead of thinking, "Every man for himself," our perspectives will begin to change and we will feel more love.

The things that bring warm feelings are unique to each person. They include, but are not limited to, organizations, gardening, pets, reading, sports and physical activity, cooking, aspects of one's job, music, movement such as dancing and yoga, techy stuff and certainly chocolate chip cookies. We should keep a mental list of those things that, when we bring them to mind, have the power to help us dispel fear, anger and depression.

Love has a higher healing energy than anything else. Love does not have to be returned to be powerful for both the giver and the receiver, and what we love does not have to be right next to us. When we hear of natural disasters or human-inflicted misery, we can feel compassion and empathy, and we can send love and healing to those places. When we see an accident, we can hope for good outcomes for all involved. When we are about to eat a meal, we can be grateful and send out the energy of abundance to the homeless and hungry. When we have a particularly good day, we can send wishes for happiness to those who did not have such a great day. As we observe the beauties of nature around us, we can send love to the planet and its inhabitants along with a desire to heal the planet and keep it safe from greed and plunder. When we stay in a loving state, we bring physical health and spiritual happiness to ourselves, and we supplant a large amount of fear. I highly recommend the writings of Martha Beck, who says that for every copy we send out, we keep two for ourselves. This is true for anger, resentment, fear and loathing; but it is equally true for empathy, kindness, peace, love and joy. Find something to love – find *many* things to love – and watch your fears disappear.

Gratitude, Love's Greatest Generator – When we're trying to generate love energy, going to a place of gratitude is one of the most effective ways of summoning high-vibration energy. We are surrounded by so many things to be grateful for that we often don't notice them until they're gone. People who go camping to enjoy the beauties of nature usually come home grateful for hot running water, flushing toilets and toilet paper, a comfortable bed, food without ashes in it, and electricity to run all the things that make our lives so easy. Many people are able to conjure up warm feelings of gratitude quite easily while others need to find ways to develop the habit of gratitude. Oprah recommends keeping a gratitude journal to which we add ten new items a day. If you find it difficult to find ten new things a day to appreciate, just look at the dire circumstances in which many people live.

Gratitude, like so many things, depends on perspective. Young people are often filled with expectations and entitlements. As we mature, we learn to set aside many of our expectations and entitlements and develop more gratitude for what we have. One person can see a particular event as dismal and depressing while another could find the challenge of the situation exhilarating. Florence Littauer describes a time when she couldn't remember where she had left her car in a large parking garage and couldn't even remember which car she had driven. Most of us would panic, but Florence got a number of good-natured people involved in finding either a blue or yellow car – make and model unknown. By the time her car was found, she had made new friends and turned a potentially scary situation into a party. Perspective turns the circumstances in our lives into fear and depression or gratitude and joy.

Gratitude has the power to help keep us in a state of love and joy. Whether or not we are aware of it, every person is radiating energy at all times, be it light or dark or somewhere in between. The more we can keep ourselves in a state of gratitude and joy and love, the more powerfully we will dissipate the dark energy of fear and depression and anger. The force of the love we can generate will be felt most intensely close to us, but we mustn't underestimate its influence on the entirety of the Earth's vibrational energy.

* * * * *

A Sufi story tells of a wealthy merchant who came upon a Sufi praying. Being inspired by the devotion of the Sufi, the merchant waited until the man was finished praying and went over to him and gave him a bag of gold coins. "Here," said the merchant, "please take this money and use it to help others. I'm sure you will do more good with it than I would."

"I am not sure I can take your money and deprive you and your family of it. Do you have more money at home?" asked the Sufi.

"I have a thousand more pieces of gold at home," came the reply.

"Do you pray to God for even more gold," the Sufi asked.

"Yes, of course. Every day I pray that God might increase my wealth."

The Sufi handed the bag of gold back to the merchant and said, "I cannot take your money. A wealthy man cannot take money from a beggar."

The merchant was shocked. After all, he was the wealthy man and the Sufi was the beggar. Then the Sufi explained, "I am wealthy because I am content with whatever God sends me, and you are the beggar because, in spite of all you have, you are constantly begging God for more." [2]

* * * * *

Praise Freely – There is little that will generate feelings of love and gratitude more than a sincere compliment or an expression of deep appreciation. I worked as an emergency room physician for several years at the beginning of my practice. I figured out early the value of praise and appreciation when dealing with the amazing nurses who worked there. While other doctors barked orders and complained about things not getting done fast enough, I would ask politely for things my patients needed and express real gratitude when they got done well. I would also occasionally bring in flowers or my sister's famous candied popcorn to share with the nurses. Guess whose patients got treated first and best.

Each of us knows – and it has been shown in study after study – that people will perform better when kindness and gratitude are shown in the workplace and the home. Fear can motivate people to do what you want them to do, but it does nothing for the long-term goals of peace and unity. Yet fear is the number one tactic in the American corporatocracy, in any military unit and in the way we deal with each other in general. Kindness and praise promote unity, encourage peace and raise the love energy of the planet. The bad boys who use fear to motivate have wreaked havoc on all countries of the world, and their time is coming to an end.

It is easy to give praise at the checkout counter, to our children, to our co-workers and pretty much anyone we meet when they have done something praiseworthy. So why not do it? Simply giving praise creates a lot of love energy and can help to change the direction of civilization.

Personal Responsibility – It is becoming more common to leave certain aspects of our lives to other people. Our doctors are responsible for our health, our clergy must ensure we get into heaven, our schools are responsible for educating our children, lawyers take care of our legal needs, accountants file our taxes, and plumbers and other fix-it people take care of problems that require special skills. We are busy people, and it is good to have specialists to help us in certain areas of our lives. However, when we give away our personal responsibility, there are always consequences. Our children fail to learn what they should, our health becomes a series of crisis interventions, and the things that should get fixed don't. The more we take personal responsibility for what happens in our lives, the more likely we will generate what we need and want.

Many do not realize they have abdicated the responsibility for their own happiness and given that power to others. These souls become the victims of their circumstances and spend their lives wishing that all those people out there would do what is needed to make them happy and fulfilled.

When we understand that it is our personal responsibility to raise the vibrational energy we radiate, the planet will change. When something needs fixing in our society – corruption, inequality, government by those with money, destruction of our environment – we may all agree that it needs fixing, but most believe they don't have the time or energy or know-how to be the kind of activist that will bring needed change. We therefore hope that others will do our part for us while, at the same time, they are hoping we will be the ones to activate the machinery of change. Most often we think that the tiny part we can do to relieve suffering in another part of the world or to clean up corruption here at home will do nothing to fix the problem, but the collective energy of such small efforts creates change. Small numbers of people have been able to initiate great change (women's suffrage, the civil rights movement, gay rights), so we know that the people who benefit from the status quo can eventually be prodded to do the right thing. There are great changes that need to occur in every land, and many enlightened people throughout these lands are working toward these needed changes.

Each person has a unique and powerful energy to add to the vector sum of the planet. Every human that chooses to add love to the vector sum increases the power for changing the earth's vibration. Simply radiating the energy of love will do a great deal to soften the hearts of the greedy and the power mongers. Every act of kindness will brighten a dark corner, and every peaceful gesture will rid the planet of some of its war energy. Other active ways to create change include writing letters or e-mails to legislators, boycotting businesses that harm the planet, voting for leaders with integrity or marching peacefully in protest. As mentioned over and over, the most powerful thing each of us can do to lift the planet's vibrational energy is radiating the energy of love as often and as intensely as we can. This is not something that someone else can do for you; it is entirely your own personal responsibility to put your unique energy signature out there – and it *will* make a difference! Don't worry about what everyone else seems to be doing; you are only responsible for the energy you give off.

Practicing Life – Fear is the greatest source of all human problems. It keeps us stuck, feeds our addictions, keeps our egos raging and creates the mistaken mindset that we are in some way different from other souls. Getting rid of fear and learning to generate love, like dealing with most other issues, does not happen instantaneously. It is a gradual learning process. For that reason I like to think of my life as a continuous practice session rather than a series of disappointments because I haven't reached a particular goal yet. When we attempt to break a bad habit, get rid of an undesirable emotion, create something better in our lives or change our personality traits for the better, there are things to be learned from every major step forward and every hop backward. The thing that hinders progression the most is attachment to the outcomes of the things we attempt. Joy at a good outcome is fine, but if we become discouraged or depressed every time we don't reach a goal in the timeframe we had hoped for, we will become stuck, and further effective efforts will be less likely.

When we try to create things like abundance, love, a good job or healing, we get discouraged if it begins to seem like it will never occur. Sometimes the Universe gives us what we need rather than what we desire. Perhaps one of the lessons we came to learn in this embodied lifetime is patience. It might also be to learn to be grateful for what we have rather than always needing more in order to be happy. If we can learn to avoid putting the emotional charge of disappointment or depression on things that don't work out as we hoped, it will be easier to keep joy and optimism in our daily experiences.

It would be better to say, "This isn't quite what I'd hoped for, but I'm sure there is something to learn here, and I am excited about giving it another try – possibly from a different vantage point." We cannot limit any possible sources of new information and support if we want to avoid continuously trying the same unsuccessful things. We all would like to have instant and easy cures for all our ills, but that rarely happens. Doing research, asking others what has worked for them and trying solutions that seem reasonable are usually required when approaching problems. We can seek the help of books, counselors, conferences, healers and friends to gain wonderful insights into becoming happier and freer. No single factor will completely change our lives for the better, but every one adds in to our vector sum. Things we learned earlier with no apparent value may suddenly become useful. We can use as many "aha" moments as we can discover, but we can also learn from mundane or challenging occasions in a way that will lift us up. Whether someone is happy or not depends more on how he views his circumstances than the circumstances themselves.

When we are hiking up a mountain and have only the butt of the person in front of us to look at, it is easy to get tired and discouraged. It is helpful to occasionally pause and turn around and see how far we've come and look at the panorama of what we have already learned. If we can enjoy practicing our lives and learning from each moment without being devastated by less-than-optimal outcomes, we will begin to look forward to each new day's learning experiences.

What Do You Have to Lose? – Believing that the course we humans are on can be changed by keeping ourselves in a state of love and fearlessness may seem far-fetched and out of touch with reality. It may seem unthinkable that such a simple thing could smash greed and corruption, stop the continuous adversarial confrontations we engage in, and create an equality-based society where *all* lives have worth and there are no enemies. But what do we have to lose in giving it a try? We don't have to disband all the world's military forces on the first day, nor can we expect that all animosity and fear will disappear after a week. As each of us makes an effort to stay in an energy of peace and love, we will feel the fear and anger melt away and the frightening world events will have far less effect on us. As we heal ourselves, we will be amazed at how those around us will be drawn into that energy. As others join us over time, the anger and hate that surrounds us will melt like ice in the Arizona sun.

Being in a state of inner peace and love has beneficial effects on our immune systems to help keep us healthy. This state replaces the anger and hostility that cause increased blood pressure, heart attacks and strokes, and it unties our gastrointestinal tracts for better processing of nutrients. It creates better bonds in our families, our jobs and our circles of friends. Why would we want to hang on to dark energy when all these benefits are available?

Feelings of vengeance or animosity cancel a lot of light energy. We cannot hold grudges if we want to maximize the effect of the high-vibration energy we try to radiate. We need to make up with our family members, coworkers and any others with whom we have hard feelings. We must love those who have been defined as our enemies and make them our brothers for these things to work. It's not hard to do and you will be amazed at the healing that it brings. If your offer to heal old wounds is rejected, that is okay. You are clear to heal the planet, and the other person will just have to work on getting rid of useless grudges.

In the movie *Cloud Atlas*, a young man tells his father-in-law that he no longer has interest in being a part of a slave trading business, but that he and his wife are going to go east to join the abolitionists. His angry father-in-law tells him that his puny efforts would amount to nothing more than a drop in an endless ocean. To this the young man serenely replies, "What is an ocean but a multitude of drops?" This is a beautiful metaphor for each person's contribution to the planet's energy sum. A few drops that have been transformed by light energy become a trickle, and a few trickles become a rivulet. These join to form beautiful streams, and these streams combine to create mighty rivers that eventually become part of the ocean again. The more droplets that transform into brilliant points of light as they fall to earth, the more their energy will spread to permeate the waters of the entire planet.

If your friends try to convince you that one person's love, compassion and peace energy can do nothing to deter the megalomaniacs, invite them to join you in a collective effort. It will cost them nothing to give up their fear and will give them all the benefits of light energy. When your government tries to convince you that yet another war is just what's needed to fix the bad things that are going on in the world, refuse to give this nonsense your support. Tell them you have a much more powerful way to counteract those dark deeds. When news shows try to fill you with fear and darkness, turn them off and read an inspiring book. Even though many would try to convince you that Armageddon is at the door, do not buy in to this ridiculous concept. You should understand that many enlightened beings are laboring diligently to elevate Earth's level of consciousness to a place where all its inhabitants can have meaningful lives. You can be one of the first to help with this transition by realizing how powerful your love light is. The more we can stay in love energy, the faster the transition will occur. *The energy of love and compassion is the ONLY hope for the survival of our planet.*

Chapter Twenty-one

IMAGINE

You may say I'm a dreamer,
But I'm not the only one.
I hope someday you'll join us,
And the world will live as one.

From the song *Imagine*
by John Lennon

Because of copyright restrictions, I cannot use the entirety of John Lennon's beautiful song *Imagine*. I hope you will take the time to look up the lyrics for it though. In my younger days, the song was something your parents might warn you about. What?! No hell, no heaven, no countries, nothing to kill or die for; and no religion or possessions? Absurd! That could never work! But what John Lennon is saying is that many people are already imagining it. He understood what many seem unable to understand, the simple fact that **you cannot create something that you cannot imagine**. Why is it we have such great ability to imagine dark fearful things but have little ability to imagine love, peace, sharing and unity?

Toward the end of World War II, a large group of brilliant scientists were brought together in The Manhattan Project for the purpose of creating the world's most destructive weapon – the atomic bomb. The bomb was feasible to theoretical physicists, but no one was certain that it could be turned into a reality. However, many imagined that it could be created. 100,000 people worked feverishly night and day to make it a reality. Scientists freely cooperated with each other to combine their knowledge and skills to birth this horrific device. Entire communities were relocated to make way for manufacturing and testing facilities. With their concerted efforts, the first evidence of what their horrific creation could do was seen at Hiroshima, Japan on August 6, 1945. Now there are enough of these terrible instruments of death to lay waste to the entire surface of the planet.

Man has always excelled at assembling large numbers of warriors and increasingly lethal weapons to inflict misery and death on other human beings. It is the history of our species. He has also been competently able to imagine ways of accumulating wealth and power by manipulating monetary systems and governance structures. Royalty has married royalty to keep their wealth sequestered. Bankers and wealthy merchants have controlled governments, and religions have been the hub of the wealth/war/control structures of our societies. The culture of fear has dominated the history of mankind to such an extent that most humans cannot even imagine another way of doing things. We have no frame of reference for countries without huge militaries and great suspicion of each other. Our hierarchies demand the existence of people who are superior to others and countries that deserve to rule over other countries. Occasional small pockets of society have embraced, even if temporarily, a paradigm of egoless compassionate caring for each other. It is time for more people to embrace this new paradigm in which it *is* possible to imagine a different Earth based on the high vibration energy of compassion, gratitude, love, being nonjudgmental, and the unity of all people. We are now at a point where many people around the world are beginning to understand that we create what we imagine and now we must imagine a more beautifully transformed world.

* * * * *

There are many "Not in Our Town" stories to be told. One of the best known occurred in Billings, Montana. In 1993, Billings was experiencing a wave of hate crimes. White supremacist skinheads had claimed Montana and four other states for their "Aryan homeland." The Ku Klux Klan had made itself highly visible too by throwing Klan newspapers in people's driveways. But the people of Billings decided to band together to tell the racists, "Not in our town!"

When a Native American's home was hit by racist graffiti and swastikas, 30 members of the painters' union showed up to paint over it. When skinheads disrupted an African-American church's services, members of other religious denominations came to protect the services from disruption. In September, four days before Rosh Hashanah (Jewish New Year), vandals overturned headstones in the Jewish cemetery, a bumper sticker reading "Nuke Israel" was plastered over a stop sign near the synagogue, and on the holiday itself, a bomb threat was made to the temple just before the children's service. Then, in early December, a brick was thrown through the bedroom window of a five-year-old Jewish boy named Isaac because he had a menorah and Star of David decals in his window. The policeman who was dispatched to the home told the family to take down the Hanukkah decorations to avoid further problems. Members of the synagogue were asked to speak out, but feared the dangers of doing so. The whole town seemed to have the idea that the less they said about the racist groups, the better it would be for everyone.

After these events appeared in a Billings Gazette article, a courageous parishioner from one of the Christian churches asked her pastor if it would be possible to print menorahs for the children to color in Sunday School and put up in their windows if their parents allowed it. Not only did the pastor agree, but he called other churches to request they do the same. The police chief took an active stance, saying that silence would be seen as acceptance of the racist behavior. The Billings Gazette printed a full-page menorah that could be cut out and put in windows. The haters lashed out again and broke church windows and kicked in car windows in front of houses with menorahs. These people got anonymous phone calls in which they were told, "Go look at your car, Jew lover."

By late December, local businesses had started distributing copies of the menorah and a billboard read, "Not in our town! No Hate. No Violence. Peace on Earth." A few hundred menorahs turned into nearly 10,000 throughout the city. The acts of violence stopped and the hate literature disappeared. An environment of fear had turned into a resolute community action to offer love and support to those who might have been seen as "not like us." Perhaps Jesus said it best, "...inasmuch as you have done it unto the least of these, my brothers, you have done it unto me." (Matt. 25:40)[1]

* * * * *

To imagine a gentler, more peaceful place to live, we must first adopt a gentler, more loving attitude toward ourselves. Trying to live up to others' expectations, depending on others to validate us, looking for approval from outside sources and trying to keep the commandments of a judgmental god can only cause us pain and frustration. It is difficult to be free from fear and be at peace with ourselves so long as our self-esteem depends on our perceptions of what others think of us. How can we love and trust others if we cannot love ourselves?

When we allow ourselves to gain new and uplifting insights from all possible sources, we begin to expand the experience of living enough to crack the hard confining shells that we have allowed others to layer onto us. One who is no longer concerned about the esteem of others cannot be easily hurt or angered. Only in this state can a person reach out to fellow travelers and offer friendship and trust without fear of rejection. Only in this state can one begin to imagine a world of peace and love.

Imagine the wonders that would emerge from a planetary society where all information and technology could be exchanged and shared for the benefit of all Earth's people. Scientists around the globe would collaborate with other scientists to develop inventions that would improve lives through medicine, transportation, energy production, communications, entertainment and many other aspects of our lives. It is almost unimaginable (can't believe I used that word) to think what would evolve if even a modest percentage of the planet's most brilliant minds could work together freely to solve the world's toughest – and also its simplest – problems. Technology could progress at an unthinkable rate, especially if no one cared who got the credit for new ideas. Ego would not be the driving force on the planet and all people involved in a new development would be glad to share the kudos for it. No one would be hurt, monetarily or emotionally, if they did not receive credit for their part, because all technological advances would belong to the planetary society and there would be no incredible personal wealth to be derived from any invention or advancement. The investment to bring the technology to fruition would come from the pooled resources and labor of the people, not from corporate investors expecting large returns on their investments. Engineers of all types would work together with the scientists who created the technology to design the most efficient and eco-friendly ways to put that technology to use.

City planners, sociologists, designers and numerous others would work together to be sure the workspaces were as comfortable and non-stressing as possible. Teachers would create new curricula designed to help students learn the necessary skills to heal the planet. Newly manufactured goods would be durable, long-lasting and easily upgradable with future improvements. Resources would be carefully considered when producing anything, and all materials produced would be as recyclable as possible. There would no longer be a need for a disposable society in order to have economic growth. Neither technology nor resources would be available for the purpose of creating weapons for use in war machines – for there would be no war machines.

Imagine living a life free of expectations from your society or any individual parts of it. Tribal rules, family traditions and expectations, religious teachings and societal memes would all be evaluated for their ability to contribute beneficially to *everyone's* existence. Your expectations of other people would be turned into suggestions of things that have worked well for you. There would be no judgment or hurt feelings if a person chose to disregard any of the suggestions you offered him. There would only be wishes for a good journey and lots of learning and joy.

Once our egos play smaller roles in our lives, it is surprising how little we care about the concepts of popular, normal, attractive and cool. Peer pressure would feel less intense because we would feel that our own opinions of how we should look, act and think are the most important opinions of all. It should not mean, however, that we have no regard for the opinions and ideas of others, for there may well be some very good advice and experience in those recommendations. If the expectations of others were not a great influencing factor in our lives, would we stay in a religion that created conflict and separation? Would we sign up to fight in a war when we thought that there were much better ways to spend our resources and our passions than in violence and destruction? And how different would our lives be if we did not feel inclined to live up to our tribe's image of manhood or womanhood? What if everyone could offer the benefit of their learning and experience with no expectations that their advice would always be followed? And even if others made painful mistakes by not taking those suggestions, we should be supportive and caring instead of always saying, "I told you so!"

Imagine having realistic imperfect heroes. We could even be our *own* heroes. What if individuals, organizations, cultures, historic writings and ideas about such topics as health, politics, economic systems and God-formats did not need to be labeled as good or bad? Think of what would result if we could accept whatever is good and uplifting from any source without feeling compelled to accept everything from that source. And the same holds true for useless concepts – can we discard them without discarding all the good that came from that particular source? Imagine turning patriotism away from distrust and war and aiming it at improving the infrastructure, enabling people to work and support their families, and creating a people unified for good right here in our own country.

And what is gained by judging people? People come into this life with their own personalities, strengths and weaknesses. Nothing is gained from thinking of people as good or bad, saint or sinner, brilliant or idiotic. We're all just getting through life the best we can with the tools we currently have. Distancing ourselves from someone or something in order to avoid harmful consequences from their dysfunctional behavior does not mean we need to condemn them. Radiating a strong high-vibration energy will do more to counteract detrimental behavior than all the punishments we can impose. We *must* be able to accept what is good and uplifting from any source and reject all that divides, feeds intolerance, makes us fearful or angry and does not lead to peace and unity.

Imagine a life free from anxiety, distrust, anger, hate and fear. Extinguishing fear would be a tremendous thing for even a small society, much less a planet. Although it may seem like an insurmountable task at first, such a task always starts with a few courageous individuals. In his first inaugural address in 1933, at the depth of the Great Depression, President Franklin Roosevelt said, "So, first of all, let me assert my firm belief that the only thing we have to fear is fear itself – nameless, unreasoning, unjustified terror which paralyzes needed effort to convert retreat into advance." He is saying that fear is infectious and that, when we see the fear in others, it deepens our own. Indeed, we cannot fight fear with fear or anger or violence – that just increases the dark frightening energy.

I have found it best to hug fear away. When I feel fearful – often not even knowing what it is I fear – I reach my arms out and gather all the fear I can find in close to my core from which love is emanating. I say something like this, "I don't know where you came from or why you're here, but it doesn't matter because I just need you to dissolve into the light. Even though I have been taught that fear is necessary for my survival, I know that's almost never true. In fact, you create hateful and violent circumstances that endanger my survival. So now I will smother you in the white light of love, peace and joy." Fear cannot persist in the presence of compassion and love, so I imagine intense high-vibration energy going out through my arms as if I were hugging and comforting a small child who had lost her mother. I hug ever more tightly and pour in more love until the fear has been completely absorbed into the light.

Can you imagine a society in which people understand that the only way to change that society for the better is to change its attitudes? Laws can be legislated, but nothing changes until people alter the way they think about themselves and their roles in the greater picture. Today in America cigarettes are still legal, but the percentage of smokers in the U.S. has dropped from 43% in the 1940's to around 20% in the last few years. We are no longer subjected to second hand smoke in our workplaces, restaurants and public buildings, and the morbidity and mortality from smoking has dropped too – all because a cigarette is no longer a sign of being cool and rebellious, just stupid. The way African-Americans are treated did not change significantly as a result of the legislation and court rulings that arose from the 1960's civil rights movement. That movement was the spark that lit the fire of change, but it took a much longer time before attitudes really began to move. Generations had to pass before the bigotry and prejudice toward racial minorities began to fade – and there is still a long way to go.

How do attitudes change? A few brave and enlightened souls move away from the dark to stand in the light, and others who see them there gain the courage to do what they have always felt is right and join them. Since people of low-vibration energy feel uncomfortable in the presence of love, eventually the control over our societies would no longer be in their hands. Their greedy, fearful, and angry energy would finally be seen for what it is – the energy of young, ego-controlled souls throwing tantrums.

Many white people gave their support to the civil rights movement, and many straight people have marched with their gay brothers and sisters for equality. Now it is time for all people to support their fellow Earthlings to change our adversarial attitudes to those of peace and love. In most earthly societies, it is important to be seen as the tough guy, the warrior, the one who wins the competition. If we are to survive on this planet, we must change our stance from competition to cooperation – and we must do it now.

Badass is over – no longer cool. Do you have the courage to stand in the light of peace and love with me?

Imagine that you could authentically live just one day as though it were your last. What would be important to you on that day – possessions, ego, power? Or would you bring close to you those with whom you can share love and joy? Would it be a day of counting your money, of wielding the sword of fear and violence toward others, of bulldozing down rainforests or otherwise raping Mother Earth for profit? Or would you spend your day enjoying the beauties of this planet and caring nothing for any accumulated wealth that is so meaningless in these final hours? The art of living in the moment is this ability to see each day as the only thing we have to work with. The past is just our history and the future *can only be* the sum total of all our present moments from now to that future day. If we stay stuck in our addictions, live our lives in fear, or spend our time playing with our toys rather than developing our relationships with others, our future (when it arrives and becomes the NOW) will be just as meaningless and unfulfilling as today is for many.

Imagine that this generation of Earthlings could collectively reject the deeply entrenched need to seek revenge for past offenses that occurred a few days ago or so long ago that no one can remember what the original offenses were. Most of the atrocities of any current day are based in the anger and hatred of past conflicts. These will continue to be passed on to devastate future generations if someone does not break the chain and refuse to perpetuate this constant seeking of revenge. This seething craving for retaliation can be on a personal or national level, it can be based in tribal or religious conflicts, it can be petty or horrific, but it will devour our lives if we allow it. Revenge is just another product of our egos and is one of the greatest blocks to developing planetary love energy. Many people have learned that the greatest counterattack for vicious actions against them is to show love and compassion in return. This will disarm and pierce perceived enemies more dramatically than anything else we can do.

Letting go of hate, anger and vengefulness has developed into a much more difficult thing than it needs to be. This is because fathers teach their sons to always fight back when threatened, a country's leaders remind their people of past conflicts to increase patriotism, and we are taught that we should never forget how our warriors have suffered in past wars. What we need to ask ourselves is this – if we continue to glorify and honor the warrior, can we ever be without war? If we continue to fear being attacked should we ever put our weapons down and sit quietly in peace, can we ever expect peace to rest upon the world? We have a large number of extraordinary souls living at this time who can choose to use their passion to wage angry wars or to bless the planet with healing and joy. Each person needs to take time for thoughtful introspection before choosing which energy he or she will support. Can we raise the vibration of the planet enough to give this generation the courage and power to be the end link of this very toxic chain of revenge?

Many people around the globe long to love boundlessly with no tribal rules, no societal memes, no expectations or any other walls that hinder them from reaching out to their fellow Earth travelers. There is great goodness in the world, but we seem to need permission to let this goodness emerge. Many of us would love to reach out to people in places that are far away and who have been painted as our enemies by our heads of state. We wish we had an easier way to find the poor and hungry to nourish them with some of the abundance we have been blessed with. How wonderful it would be to be able to open our arms to those who are lonely and frightened. What a liberating day it would be if our egos no longer required that we feel superior to anyone else or less than anyone else. Many

Jews and Palestinians would love to live in peace and compassion with each other. More and more people are understanding that skin color, hair texture and facial features are only genetically determined parameters of how one appears to others and that people of all races and ethnicities have the same hopes and dreams that we do. The tide is rapidly turning in the way many societies regard gay people and their families – it's just love after all. But it seems we all need some sort of permission slip to think, feel or do what we know in our core to be right. It always takes a courageous few to give that permission to others.

Imagine a world in which people understood the incredible power of high-vibration energy. I sincerely believe that enough love, compassion and thoughts of peace could keep bombs from exploding and bullets from penetrating. More importantly though, the love energy we radiate could keep those bombs from being sent and those bullets from being fired in the first place. The Light Side of the Force can touch the hearts of the wealthy and powerful to transform them into compassionate people who want to feed and heal the poor and the hungry as well as support and nourish Mother Earth. ***Changing people's hearts is the great power of the Light Side of the Force.***

We have very little history of this on any kind of scale in man's existence so far, but that doesn't mean it can't happen now. Our legislators are stuck in adversarial competition and are almost completely controlled by the puppet masters who are concerned only with wealth and power. We must create change without them, at least for a time. All around me I see people compassionately giving to food banks – even when they themselves have little. Even big produce and grocery businesses as well as restaurants are pitching in to donate their leftovers to the hungry instead of taking them to the landfill. Large businesses of all kinds are changing their behavior to help save the planet and its people. These difficult times have brought out the worst and the best in our planetary society. We must support each other with substance and caring, and we must champion and patronize those businesses that are supporting us.

In the last few years, many people have seen, as I have, a rapid shift in people's hearts to be more accepting of all, to be less judgmental, to see less benefit from war, to be happier with less so that others do not go hungry, and to be kind and loving to Mother Earth. Some people believe that a great planetary shift to higher-vibration energy has begun. This simply means that the dark fear energy that now saturates the planet will be abandoned for that of love, cooperation and people living in peace. This shift in energy will be the largest transformation of energy and matter ever to occur on this planet. Greater energy will be released during this time than was released when the Chicxulub asteroid wiped out the dinosaurs and created an environment in which man could flourish. Participation in this great transformation will be our most significant opportunity for soul growth and spiritual progression.

Imagine being among the first courageous individuals to abandon fear and stand up quietly, but firmly, for peace. Think of this peaceful energy spreading to your immediate neighbors and then to your neighborhood. As others across the globe begin this same process, men will become enlightened and women will become empowered, resources will be treasured and be distributed cautiously and equitably, and "might makes right" will no longer be the planetary motto. At first there will be the expected backlash from greedy fear-based souls, but they will gradually learn that they are no longer supported and that the needed warriors to do their bidding will not be there. The great empires of wealth will collapse as humans learn alternative ways of trading goods and services for the benefit of all. We will learn new ways of maximizing each person's contribution to society. Women will bring their children to play with children of people who were once considered their enemies. Men and women will get great exhilaration from working together to invent and put into place great things for the benefit of mankind. Imagine yourself being a part of this great transformation.

There exists in every soul the seed of Source Spirit, Creator, The Universe – GOD. This seed longs to seek the light and emerge above the darkness to blossom with all other souls into a giant field of ecstatic beings of all colors of the spectrum resembling a vast expanse of gorgeous wildflowers. Each soul-flower knows that its well-being is nourished by the flourishing of every other blossom. Here, above the opaque layers of low-vibration energy, is ecstatic joy just for the magnificent pleasure of being, of existing as an eternal entity that makes its own progress along its path in the midst of all other entities who are finding their way at their own pace and according to their own style. Some ground is harder and more difficult to push through because of early life trauma, cultural environment, and how absolutely one's tribal rules have been enforced, but the nurturing rain of nonjudgmental love and compassion can soften the tough soil and help each soul-flower break through.

Each seed that expands to escape its shell breaks up the dirt and helps the seeds next to it to emerge. As more seeds crack free from their limiting beliefs and emerge into the daylight, the number of low-vibration beings decreases and it is harder for them to support each other in the creation of fear, greed and suffering. The process of creating this beautiful field of wildflower souls begins with a few courageous beings coming together to push through the fear and nourish the ground to make it easier for others to emerge. This courage develops when our self-esteem increases and we no longer fear being ridiculed should we choose to set aside some detrimental tribal rules. The shells that keep us bound with sealed premises, tribal rules and societal memes must fall away to enable us to emerge and become one with all other awakening seeds.

Come on now. Just let yourself sprout. Break through! The incredible warmth of the light that awaits you will make the struggle to overcome fear worthwhile. As we emerge, we may still have residual walls around us that were erected to protect us from those who once ridiculed us and those who did not give us the love we longed for. These walls of vulnerability and insecurity must be torn down brick by brick (or a wrecking ball would be even better) so that we may make meaningful contact with our fellow planetary citizens. Each of us is just trying to get through this embodied existence with as little damage and as many learned lessons as possible. We all long to be loved and cared about. We need our occasional moments in the limelight to help us feel connected to others and accepted by them. Why can't we give each other the kudos and spiritual hugs that we all need? Why do we cling to the incorrect notion that we elevate ourselves by beating each other down? Why are we often required to look to an invisible god for our only source of unconditional love, acceptance and support? It should not be that difficult for us to provide these things for each other. What kind of walls have we built – and for what purpose?

In most societies it is difficult to say, "I love you," to a stranger or acquaintance without feeling awkward because of possible mistaken romantic overtones, but there are many other ways of connecting positively with others. Saying, "Thanks so much, I really appreciate that," to someone who has served you, mending animosities with family members or work colleagues, or greeting people in public places will take a brick out of your wall. I've always thought that a good expression of our recognition of other people's existence as eternal souls would be that famous phrase from James Cameron's movie *Avatar* – "I see you." It could imply that we recognize that each soul is learning his/her lessons as we are, and we wish them well. If other people do not respond, it matters not. Every person's wall is deconstructed at a different rate. It is *your* wall that is most important for you to work on. Just keep removing the bricks layer by layer as you reach out to connect with those around you. By radiating nonjudgmental love, you may provide just the wrecking ball someone else needs to start bringing down his/her wall.

You are the only person you need permission from to think and explore whatever you want. The concepts presented in this book may sound unusual and difficult to grasp at first. Contrary to what you may have been taught, you **do** have the right to consider and implement any of them you find compelling. You **are** allowed to feel any way you want to about the events and circumstances in your life. You have the power to feel joy and radiate love under the most difficult of circumstances. If you want to understand and believe that the high-vibration energies of love, compassion, joy and peace are stronger than the dark energies of fear, anger, hate and intolerance, you now have that understanding – **love *is* the most powerful energy there is and *can* conquer fear.** If you're afraid to try living in a world of peaceful energy because there might be dark angry souls who will attack you there, don't be. Fear and evil can be drowned in the light of love – but only enough of us giving it a try can ever prove that. It is time for you to give yourself permission to join all others who long to increase the vibrational energy of this planet, but never knew it was actually a possibility. Let us believe in our hearts that it is. Now is the time to give it a try.

You have the permission. You know what's possible. You know how important your part is. There is nothing more to fear. You have exited the room and torn down any walls between you and your fellow Earthlings. Take a deep breath and feel the warmth of the Light...

You are now free to imagine.

APPENDIX

Health Related Resources – Complimentary/Alternative

www.naturaldatabaseconsumer.therapeuticresearch.com/home – A very comprehensive data base for nutritional, herbal and other alternative therapies with drug interactions and disease/medical condition searches.

www.mercola.com - Dr. Mercola is one of my favorite sites for alternative medical viewpoints that are backed up by research and have a brief summary of each topic without having to read the entire article.

www.herbs.org - Herb Research Foundation. Provides links to articles and research on plant-based therapies.

The Complete German Commission E Monographs: Therapeutic Guide to Herbal Medicines, Blumenthal, et al (Integrative Medicine Communications, 1998). A compilation of 380 papers of medicinal herbs evaluated and used in Germany. The English language translation is available in print or can be viewed online at the American Botanical Council's website at www.abc.herbalgram.org/.

Standard Medical Resources

www.webmd.com - A consumer-oriented website with basic information on a large number of medical topics.

www.drugs.com - Useful information on thousands of medications, their side effects and uses. Also includes a pill identifier for medications you don't recognize.

INDEX PHRASE LIST

ENDNOTES

Chapter 1

1   *A View on Buddhism: Buddhist Stories*. Retrieved from http://viewonbuddhism.org/resources/buddhist_stories.html#s

Chapter 2

1   This term is found in the book: Ron Schow, Wayne Schow, Marybeth Raynes, eds., *Peculiar People* (Salt Lake City: Signature Books, 1991)

2   Richard Brody, *Virus of the Mind* (New York: Hay House, 2009)

Chapter 4

1   Story adapted from the film *Trembling Before G-d*, a film by Sandi Dubowski (2001)

Chapter 5

1   Eli Roth (Writer and Director). (2011) *Curiosity: How Evil Are You?* Simon Andreae (Sr. Exec. Producer) Left/Right Productions for the Discovery Channel.

2   Deepak Chopra, *The Path to Love* (New York: Random House, 1997).

Chapter 7

1   Suzannah Scully: The Live Well Space (web page) *The Story of the Taoist Farmer*. Retrieved from http://www.livewellspace.com/2012/12/19/the-story-of-the-taoist-farmer/

Chapter 8

[1] Art Markham, *Psychology Today*, "Ulterior Motives": June 27,2009.

[2] Newton Frazer, *The Effects of Punishment to Deter Crime.*

[3] Kristen Mitchell: Beyond the Orange Wall (web page) *Rehab or Prison?* Retrieved from http://www.beyondorange.wordpress.com/2010/05/02/rehab-or-prison/

[4] William J. Duffy, Jr., *Warden Clinton Truman Duffy* (web page). Retrieved from http://freepages.history.rootsweb.ancestry.com/~sanquentin/sqsp/wardens/ctduffy.htm#ctduffy

Chapter 9

[1] Brody, *Virus of the Mind*, chapter 8. Much of the material in this chapter comes, at least in part, from this very important book.

Chapter 10

[1] Joseph Goebbels, Hitler's Minister of Propaganda. Retrieved from http://www.searchquotes.com/quotes/author/Joseph_Goebbels/

Chapter 11

[1] John Ortberg, courtesy of Trudi Barnes in the movie *Zeitgeist: Moving Forward* (Peter Joseph – writer, director, producer, editor, and narrator), 2010, Gentle Machine Productions.

[2] Ricardo Fuentes-Nieva and Nick Galasso, *Working for the Few*; Oxfam International (2014) as calculated from: Credit Suisse (2013) *Global Wealth Report 2013*, Zurich: Credit Suisse. https://publications.creditsuisse.com/tasks/render/file/?fileID=BCDB1364-A105-0560-1332EC9100FF5C83 And Forbes' *The World's Billionaires* (accessed on December 16, 2013) http://www.forbes.com/billionaires/list/

[3] John Heminway (Producer/Writer), John Bredar (Senior Executive Producer), Randy Bean (Executive Producer – Stanford University). (2008), *Stress: Portrait of a Killer.* Co-production of National Geographic Television and Stanford University as seen on Public Broadcasting System.

Chapter 12

1   C. Adams, V. Brantner (2006): *Estimating the cost of new drug development: Is it really 802 million dollars?* Health Affairs (Millwood) 25 (2): 420-8.
2   Candace Pert. *Your Body is Your Subconscious Mind*. Sounds True (2004) compact discs.
3   Christopher J.L. Murray, M.D., et al.; *Ranking 37th – Measuring the Performance of the U.S. Health Care System*. New England Journal of Medicine (2010); 362:98-99.

Chapter 13

1   Jean Twenge, *Yes, Violent Video Games Do Cause Aggression*. (Dec. 21, 2012) Psychology Today; originally in Our Changing Culture.

Chapter 15

1   Taylor Hartman, *The Color Code* (1987). A Taylor Don Hartman Publication, P.O. Box 87, Trabuco Canyon CA 92678.
2   Florence Littauer, *Personality Plus for Parents: Understanding What Makes Your Child Tick*. (2000), Fleming H. Revell, Grand Rapids, MI.

Chapter 16

1   Tria Thalman (Writer and Producer), Beth Hoppe (Executive Producer), Dan Riskin (Host). (2011). *Human Nature: Born to Kill*, Alan Eyres (For Discovery Channel: Executive Producer), Discovery Communication, LLC.

Chapter 17

1   Kenneth Davis, *Don't Know Much About the Bible* (New York: HarperCollins, 1998).
2   G. Y. Craig and E. J. Jones, *A Geological Miscellany*. (Princeton University Press, 1982) retrieved from Donald Simanek's webpage www.lhup.edu/~dsimanek/ussher.htm.
3   Bart Ehrman, *Misquoting Jesus: The Story Behind Who Changed the Bible and Why* (New York: HarperCollins, 2005), p. 52.
4   Bart Ehrman, *Misquoting Jesus*, pp. 83-90.

Chapter 19

[1]   *Global Peace Initiative*, retrieved at http://www.globalpeaceproject. net/. At this site you will find a bibliography of papers from which this information was gleaned as well as the information itself.

[2]   *Baskinta Peace Project Gives Hope to Syria*, retrieved from http://www.worldpeacegroup.org/baskinta_peace_project.html

Chapter 20

[1]   Martha Beck, *The Joy Diet: 10 Daily Practices for a Happier Life* (New York: Crown, 2003)

[2]   Robert Frager, *Sharing Sacred Stories: Current Approaches to Spiritual Direction and Guidance* (New York: Crossroad, 2007)

Chapter 21

[1]   Patrice O'Neill (Executive Producer), Rhian Miller (Senior Producer), *Not In Our Town, The Billings, Montana Story* (1995), The Working Group, Oakland, CA for PBS.

Made in the USA
Las Vegas, NV
09 December 2021

36931529R00173